10/98

Cultural Diversity
In
ORGANIZATIONS

Cultural Diversity In ORGANIZATIONS
Theory, Research & Practice

TAYLOR COX, JR.

Berrett-Koehler Publishers
San Francisco

Berrett-Koehler Publishers, Inc.
155 Montgomery St.
San Francisco, CA 94104-4109
Tel: 415-288-0260   Fax: 415-362-2512

Ordering Information
Individual sales. Berrett-Koehler publications are available through most bookstores. They can also be ordered direct from Berrett-Koehler at the address above.

Quantity sales. Special discounts are available on quantity purchases by corporations, associations, and others. For details, contact the "Special Sales Department" at the Berrett-Koehler address above.

Orders for college textbook/course adoption use. Please contact Berrett-Koehler Publishers at the address above.

Orders by U.S. trade bookstores and wholesalers. Please contact Publishers Group West, P.O. Box 8843, Emeryville, CA 94662; 510-658-3453; 1-800-788-3123.

Printed in the United States of America

Printed on acid-free and recycled paper that meets the strictest state and U.S. guidelines for recycled paper (50 percent recycled waste, including 10 percent postconsumer waste).

Library of Congress Cataloging-in-Publication Data

Cox, Taylor, 1949–
    Cultural diversity in organizations : theory, research and
practice / Taylor Cox.
        p.   cm.
    Includes bibliographical references and index.
    ISBN 1-881052-19-2 (alk. paper) : $29.95
    1. Pluralism (Social sciences)   2. Organizational behavior.
I. Title.
HM131.C749   1993   93-17920
302.3'5—dc20   CIP

First Edition.
First Printing August 1993

Cover Design: Pawlak Design
Book Production: Pleasant Run Publishing Services
Composition: WESType Publishing Services, Inc.
Cover Graphic: Original quilt designed and
pieced by Marilyn Merkt Felber, Berkeley,
California; original mask quilting design
by Laura Lee Fritz, Napa, California.

To my wife, Cynthia, with much love

Contents

Preface

In this book I have assembled learnings from ten years of teaching, research, and consulting related to the topic of cultural diversity in organizations.

My objective in creating the book was to provide a comprehensive text that would be useful as an aid for teaching, organization development, and scholarship. My primary targets are teachers and students of diversity, whether they are on university campuses or in the classrooms of business and community organizations. I also hope that *Cultural Diversity in Organizations* will be found useful by organizational scholars seeking to build a foundation for—or to extend—their own ideas and research directions on topics related to diversity in organizations.

Useful Features of This Book

There are several features of the book that I believe will make it especially useful to readers. One is that the book is developed around a specific conceptual model that frames the issues in a systematic way. The model represents my attempt to communicate dimensions and dynamics of diversity, which are generic issues across many types of group identities. Hence I do not have separate chapters on gender, race, age, and so on. Instead, I have attempted to integrate examples using these group identities throughout the book as various aspects of the model are discussed.

A second feature is that the book addresses the topic on three levels of analysis: the individual, the group, and the organization. I believe this multidimensional approach comes closer to capturing the enormous complexity of the topic than would be true if only one perspective were emphasized. This complexity exacts a price: it was not feasible to present a thorough discussion of all the relevant literature on each aspect of the model. Thus the book is intended to give examples of pertinent theory and research on the points raised rather than provide definitive coverage of individual topics.

Third, the book provides what I hope is a substantive and fairly comprehensive treatment of the topic, applying knowledge collected from several fields of inquiry to the organizational context. A considerable amount of relevant theory and empirical research is reviewed, which I believe makes clear that there is a base of knowledge that we can use to inform teaching, organizational interventions, and future research related to diversity in the workforce. The liberal use of references in the book is intended to aid further study of specific issues.

Overview of the Contents

Part One opens with a chapter that explains what I mean by cultural diversity and presents my conceptual model of diversity (the Interactional Model of Cultural Diversity), on which much of the book is based. Chapters Two and Three make the case for why managing diversity is among the most important management challenges of this decade. These chapters should increase the reader's motivation to study the material presented in Parts Two through Four.

Parts Two, Three, and Four explain how gender, race, nationality, and other cultural diversity dimensions influence organizational behaviors and outcomes. I have attempted to write these segments in such a way that readers will gain important insights into the complex social and psychological phenomena that underlie diversity, as well as how they are manifested in the work setting. This dual purpose reflects my strong belief that personal and organizational excellence in working with and leading diverse groups of workers will only be achieved if we are educated about the phenomena themselves as well as their practical implications. For example, I think it is important to help people understand not just that stereotyping hinders people from working together, but also such things as what stereotyping is, why people do it, and why it is different from acknowledging and valuing differences.

A distinctive feature throughout the book (except in Part Five) is that major learning points are summarized in proposition statements at the end of each chapter. These statements might be used by teachers and workshop facilitators to frame discussion questions, class exercises, exam questions, or for other learning objectives. Also, scholars interested in research on diversity may find them useful to stimulate ideas for future research agendas.

Finally, in Part Five, two full chapters are devoted to a discussion of organization development for managing diversity. Suggestions are given for the design and implementation of organization change processes for enhancing the capability to manage diversity.

At the time of this writing, teaching, research, and organization change initiatives on cultural diversity are still in an early stage of development. More and more organization leaders are coming to realize that the potential creativity and problem-solving advantages of a culturally diverse workforce is a resource that remains grossly underutilized in most of the world. I hope that readers will share some of the excitement that I experienced in writing the book as I reflected on a future so ripe with opportunity.

Ann Arbor, Michigan   Taylor Cox, Jr.
May 1993

Acknowledgments

Many people have contributed to the development of the ideas presented in this book, and I will no doubt leave someone out who should be mentioned. My sincere apologies. I would like to thank my research assistants: Paul Bacdayan, Joycelyn Nickelson, Karen Nowak, Cheryl Middleton, Anthony Forbes, and Noel Willis. I would also like to thank Susan Jackson, Angelo DeNisi, and Ann Morrison for their reviews. Many thanks are also due to publisher Steven Piersanti and all the staff at Berrett-Koehler Publishers. I also want to acknowledge and express my appreciation to colleagues Jane Dutton, Lance Sandelands, Karl Weick, and Bob Quinn for their helpful comments on drafts of earlier manuscripts on which parts of this book are based.

Finally, my greatest appreciation is reserved for my wife, Cynthia; my children, Stephanie, Aaron, and Ty; my father, Taylor Cox, Sr.; my mother, Betty Cox; my stepmother, Edith Cox; and other members of my family who have loved and supported me over the years.

PART ONE

DIVERSITY AND ORGANIZATIONAL PERFORMANCE

Part One presents the Interactional Model of Cultural Diversity. This model explains why the presence of cultural diversity—and its management—are logically linked to organizational performance. In addition to describing the conceptual logic on which the book is based, this part reviews research that supports the linkage of diversity to individual and organizational work outcomes.

1

1

A Conceptual Model of the Impact of Diversity

Several major workforce-related trends highlight the magnitude of cultural diversity that characterizes the workforces of organizations in the 1990s. First, the workforce in many nations of the world is becoming increasingly more diverse along such dimensions as gender, race, and nationality (Fullerton, 1987; Johnston, 1991). For example, in the United States roughly 45 percent of all net additions to the labor force in the 1990s will be non-White (half of them first-generation immigrants, mostly from Asian and Latin countries), and almost two-thirds will be female. These trends go beyond the United States. For example, 5 percent of the population of the Netherlands (de Vries, 1992) and 8–10 percent of the population in France are ethnic minorities (Horwitz & Forman, 1990). There are also substantial and growing non-Caucasian segments of the workforce in many parts of Italy and Germany. Moreover, the increases in representation of women in the workforce in the next decade will be greater in much of Europe—and in many of the developing nations of the world—than it will in the United States (Johnston, 1991).

Behind these workforce facts are some rather startling world population demographics. For example, it is estimated that by approximately the year 2000 a majority of public school-age children in the United States will be non-White. Further, virtually none of the traditional industrial powers of the world have a fertility rate that is great enough to replace their existing population. This means that growth of the labor forces in these nations, including that of the United States, must come from immigration or from increasing labor-force participation by groups that are presently underrepresented. In nations such as Japan, which are strongly averse to immigration, the pressure to increase work opportunities

3

Table 1.1. Fertility and Age Data.

	Average Age of Women	Fertility Rates
Whites	33.6	1.7
Blacks	27.7	2.4
Hispanics	26.0	2.9

Source: Adapted from Wall Street Journal, 1990.

for women will be especially intense. In the United States, greater realization of the potential of racioethnic minorities and White women will be more crucial in the next decade than it has ever been before. This is especially true with regard to racioethnic minorities, because they have much higher growth rates than the White sector of the population.[1] A look at age and fertility data tells why (see Table 1.1).

Regarding the Asian American population, recent data indicate that it is growing at a rate that is ten times that of the population overall, and 70 percent of all Asians in the United States today are either first- or second-generation immigrants.

In addition to these demographic trends, organizations in the 1990s are emphasizing the importance of cross-functional teams in creating a basis for competitive advantage (Bassin, 1988; Levine, 1987; Raudsepp, 1988). Since different work functions and departments in organizations can have different cultures, this trend adds a strong element of cultural diversity to today's workgroups in many organizations.

A third major factor emphasizing the relevance of diversity to organizations is the increasing emphasis on global marketing and multinational business operations. It is well known that understanding the effects of culture on human behavior is crucial to the business success of multinational companies. What is perhaps less well known is the extent to which business success in the 1990s is dependent on foreign markets. In the United States, many busi-

---

[1] Common practice is to capitalize Hispanic and Asian, while leaving Black and White lowercased. In my view, this is not only illogical but conveys the erroneous message that there is no cultural significance to the identities of Blacks and Whites. Therefore I have chosen to capitalize the names of all racioethnic groups in this book.

nesses, including familiar names like IBM, Exxon, Coca-Cola, Dow-Chemical, and Digital Equipment, now derive more than half their revenues from overseas markets. This trend is even beginning to extend to predominately service operations like Citicorp, which obtained 52 percent of its revenues from foreign markets in 1991 ("U.S. Corporations," 1992).

Still another recent workforce diversity development that will impact organizations in the 1990s is the recent passage of the Americans with Disabilities Act. This legislation is expected to increase pressure to accelerate employment opportunities for the six million unemployed Americans with disabilities.

The amount of change indicated by this combination of trends and events for the cultural milieu and intergroup relations of organizations is mind-boggling. It is therefore imperative for employers, and for educational institutions seeking to prepare people for leadership in the twenty-first century, to understand the effects of this diversity on human behavior in the workplace. In view of the magnitude and importance of the challenge that cultural diversity poses to organizations in the 1990s, several reviewers have noted that pertinent teaching and research literature on the topic seems inadequate (Nkomo, 1992; Cox & Nkomo, 1990; Alderfer & Thomas, 1988; Ilgen & Youtz, 1986).

The primary goal of this book is to address this need by providing a comprehensive text for educators, organization development specialists, and practicing managers charged with learning and teaching about cultural diversity in the workplace. A secondary goal is to stimulate thinking among faculty and doctoral students seeking to build research agendas on the effects of diversity in workgroups. As research increases, additional help will be available to practitioners seeking to meet the challenges of increasing diversity in workgroups.

In pursuing these goals, the book presents a comprehensive conceptual model that ties together learnings from theory, research, and anecdotal information on gender, racioethnicity, nationality, age, and other dimensions of diversity to create a generic model of the impact of cultural heterogeneity on work behavior and outcomes.

Throughout the book *culture group* or *cultural group* will refer to an affiliation of people who collectively share certain norms, values, or traditions that are different from those of other groups. Therefore *cultural diversity* means the representation, in one social system, of people with distinctly different group affiliations of cultural significance. Also, throughout the book I will be addressing diversity in the context of social systems that are characterized by a majority group and a number of minority groups. *Majority group* here means the largest group, while *minority group* means a group with fewer members represented in the social system compared to the majority group. For our purposes, majority group also signifies that members have historically held advantages in power and economic resources compared to minority group members. In most social systems one group may be identified both as larger in size and as possessing greater power and economic advantages. For example, in most large corporations in the United States, White American men of full physical capacity represent the largest, most powerful, and most economically successful group. In some cases, however, the control of power and resources is split between two or more groups rather than being identified with the largest group. An example is South Africa, in which Whites control the government and economic resources despite the fact that Blacks outnumber Whites by four to one. In the United States, organizational examples are found in industries such as insurance and banking, in which the workforce is typically 60–70 percent female but the management ranks typically have more men than women.

A Model of the Impact of Diversity

Figure 1.1 presents the Interactional Model of Cultural Diversity (IMCD), which I developed on the basis of learnings from my study of the relevant literature and my own research, consulting, and teaching experience over the past decade. There are several features of the model that I view as somewhat distinctive. First, this is a general model designed to explicate effects of diversity for many cultural configurations. Thus I believe much of what is said here is applicable to all kinds of cultural identities, including job function, religion, age, and physical ability. The book will, however, emphasize diversity that is based on racioethnicity (racially and/or ethnically distinctive within the same nationality group), gender, and nationality.

Figure 1.1. An Interactional Model of the Impact of Diversity on Individual Career Outcomes and Organizational Effectiveness.

DIVERSITY CLIMATE

Individual-Level Factors

- Identity Structures
- Prejudice
- Stereotyping
- Personality

Group/Intergroup Factors

- Cultural Differences
- Ethnocentrism
- Intergroup Conflict

Organizational-Level Factors

- Culture and Acculturation Process
- Structural Integration
- Informal Integration
- Institutional Bias in Human Resource Systems

INDIVIDUAL CAREER OUTCOMES

Affective Outcomes

- Job/Career Satisfaction
- Organizational Identification
- Job Involvement

Achievement Outcomes

- Job Performance Ratings
- Compensation
- Promotion/Horizontal Mobility Rates

ORGANIZATIONAL EFFECTIVENESS

First Level

- Attendance
- Turnover
- Productivity
- Work Quality
- Recruiting Success
- Creativity/Innovation
- Problem Solving
- Workgroup Cohesiveness and Communication

Second Level

- Market Share
- Profitability
- Achievement of Formal Organizational Goals

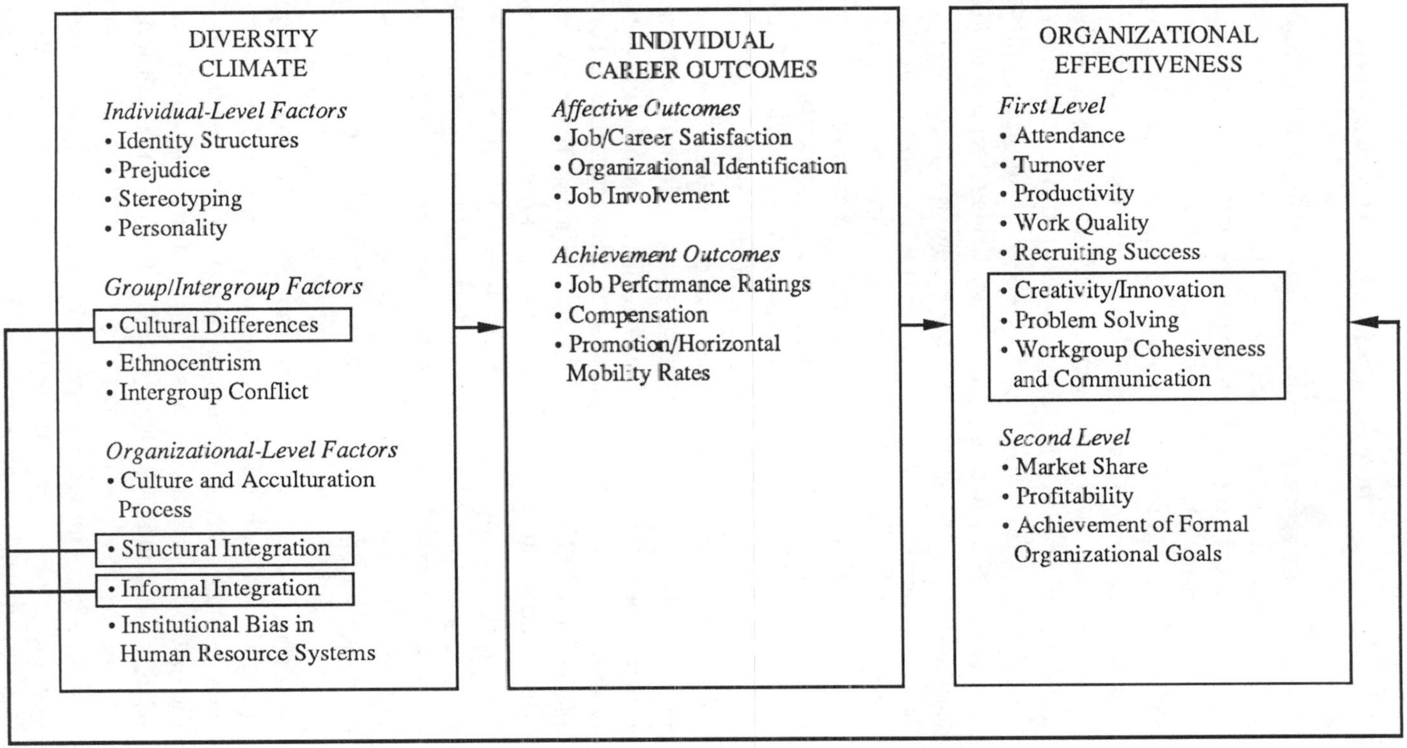

There are several reasons for these points of emphasis. Previous research and organization development work have shown that these bases of diversity are extremely important in understanding human transactions. Also, they are group identities that are not changeable, as compared to many others (such as age, work function, and religion) that can, and often do, change over the course of a lifetime. In addition, and most important, the base of knowledge in the social sciences is more fully developed for these identities than for others that may be relevant. Thus we are in a better position to apply knowledge from social psychology and other fields to organizations if we focus initially on these identities rather than others.

A second point of distinction about this model is that it treats group identity in a more sophisticated way than past writings in the organizational literature. Whereas the traditional treatment of group identities such as racioethnicity and gender in the management literature has been to assign people to categories solely on the basis of physical identification, this model views certain effects of cultural diversity on individual and organizational outcomes as being due to both the physical and the culture identities of organization members. It also recognizes that there is variability along both of these dimensions within, as well as between, groups. For example, employees have typically been classified as Black, White, Hispanic, and so on in accordance with equal opportunity categories. This categorical treatment of racioethnicity, in placing emphasis on the physical dimension of race, largely ignores the crucial issue of the extent to which the individual identifies with the cultural traditions of the group. The importance of this distinction has been illustrated by empirical research (see Chapter Four).

Third, it should be noted that the IMCD model proposes that the impact of diversity on organizational outcomes is a complex interaction of individuals and their environment. The environment includes both intergroup and organizational forces. In this regard, the model builds on previous work on interactional research (Mischel, 1977; Chatman, 1989; O'Reilly, Chapman & Caldwell, 1991) and on the concept of embedded groups (Rice, 1969; Alderfer & Smith, 1982). This work assumes that behavior in organizations is best understood by examining the interplay between the individual and the environmental situation. Much of the previous work has emphasized the relationship between an employee and the employee's job or occupation, while the person-organization relationship has received less attention (Chatman, 1989; Schneider, 1987; House, 1988).

In applying this previous work to effects of cultural diversity on work outcomes, I am suggesting that the environmental situation includes not only organizational factors but also a set of intergroup factors focusing on relations between the majority group and the various minority groups represented. Thus, the effects of a person's group affiliations such as gender, race, and nationality can be analyzed on three levels: (1) individual, (2) group/intergroup, and (3) organizational. These roughly correspond to the interpersonal, group, and systemic levels of analysis advocated by embedded group theory (Alderfer & Smith, 1982; Rice, 1969). A full understanding of the impact of cultural diversity on organizations must therefore give attention to all three levels of analysis. It is also true that relations among employees of organizations occur in a broader societal context. Throughout the book, the societal context will be developed in the course of explaining the intraorganizational dynamics of diversity. For example, phenomena such as prejudice, stereotyping, and conflict between women and men in organizations will be partly explained by facts from the sociocultural history of male-female relationships in the society at large.

Logic of the Model

The model in Figure 1.1 posits that four individual-level factors (personal identity structures, prejudice, stereotyping, and personality type), three intergroup factors (cultural differences, ethnocentrism, and intergroup conflict), and four organizational context factors (organizational culture and acculturation processes, structural integration, informal integration, and institutional bias) collectively define the *diversity climate* of an organization.[2]

The diversity climate may influence individual career expe-

---

[2]This term has been used previously by Kossek & Zonia, 1993. It is used differently here and is defined specifically to include the items specified in Figure 1.1.

riences and outcomes in organizations in two ways. Affective outcomes refer to how people feel about their work and their employer.
Thus in many organizations employee morale and satisfaction are
related to identity groups such as gender, racioethnicity, and so on.
Second, the actual career achievement of individuals as measured by
such things as job performance ratings may be related to group
identities in some organizations. These individual outcomes, in
turn, are expected to impact a series of first-order organizational
effectiveness measures such as work quality, productivity, absenteeism, and turnover. For profit-making organizations, these first-
order measures ultimately translate to second-order results such as
profitability and market share. In nonprofit organizations, individual contribution is still crucial in determining the extent to which
organizational goals will be achieved.

In addition to these indirect effects of group identity, certain
aspects of the diversity climate are thought to impact directly on
organizational performance. Specifically, the amount of diversity in
both formal and informal structures of organizations will impact
factors such as creativity, problem solving, and intraorganizational
communications.

The terms and relationships of the model will be defined and
discussed in detail in subsequent chapters of the book. First, however, Chapters Two and Three will develop further the major premise of the book, namely, that managing diversity is a critical
competency for leaders in the 1990s, and that organizational capacity to manage diversity well has major implications for organizational performance.

2

Why Managing Diversity Is at the Core of Leadership Today

In Chapter One, I suggested that a series of environmental forces have combined to make managing diversity a high priority issue for contemporary organizations. By *managing diversity* I mean planning and implementing organizational systems and practices to manage people so that the potential advantages of diversity are maximized while its potential disadvantages are minimized. Further, I view the goal of managing diversity as maximizing the ability of all employees to contribute to organizational goals and to achieve their full potential unhindered by group identities such as gender, race, nationality, age, and departmental affiliation.

In this chapter, I wish to develop more thoroughly the idea that managing diversity is crucial to the accomplishment of organizational goals and therefore should be of paramount concern to managers. Three types of organizational goals facilitated by managing diversity are (1) moral, ethical, and social responsibility goals; (2) legal obligations; and (3) economic performance goals.

Managing Diversity as a Moral Imperative

In most organizations, the representation of culture groups in the overall work population, and especially in the most powerful positions, is highly skewed. For example, in the Netherlands, Dutch men are dominant; in New Zealand, Pakeha men are dominant; in the United States, White men are dominant. This fact and the pervasive tendency for in-group members to be favored over out-group members in human transactions combine to make dominance-subordination and other equal opportunity issues prominent aspects of diversity

11

work in organizations. Thus for nations and organizations that subscribe to a creed of equal opportunity, a major motive for investing in managing-diversity initiatives is that it is morally and ethically the right thing to do. Moreover, it is certainly prudent to include, among the many goals of organizations, social responsibility objectives such as promoting fairness and improving economic opportunities for underachieving members of society. It also seems fair to say that achievement of social responsibility goals enhances economic performance goals in the long term. For example, in the United States it seems clear that improving educational achievement among non-Cuban Hispanics, Blacks, and poor people of all racioethnic groups has major implications for national economic competitiveness.

Since the moral and social justice objectives of managing diversity have been addressed in the management literature for many years (mostly under the heading of equal opportunity), I will not dwell on them here except to reemphasize that the ethical, moral, and social responsibility motives for managing diversity work remain highly relevant in today's organizations.

Legal Requirements

Certain aspects of managing diversity are necessary, or at least strongly advised, as a matter of law. In the United States, the Civil Rights Act of 1964 (as amended in 1972), the Pregnancy Discrimination Act of 1978, the Age Discrimination Act of 1967, and the Americans with Disabilities Act of 1990 (ADA) collectively outlaw discrimination on the basis of sex, color, race, religion, pregnancy, national origin, age, or physical ability. With regard to the ADA, the act provides that a physical disability cannot be an issue in an employment decision if the individual is qualified or could be made qualified to do the job by a "reasonable accommodation" on the employer's part. In addition to the above legislation, the Equal Pay Act of 1963 specifically outlaws pay discrimination on the basis of gender, and the Vietnam Veterans Readjustment Act of 1974 expressly outlaws employment discrimination against veterans of the Vietnam War. The vast number of workers covered by these laws suggests that employers are well advised to invest in such managing-diversity activities as worker training and organizational research to uncover evidence of unfair treatment of workers related to the various group memberships addressed in the legislation. Moreover, history has shown that the failure of organizations to manage diversity in this respect can lead to costly lawsuits. To mention just a few examples, in 1991 a jury awarded $20.3 million to a single person in a sex discrimination suit involving denial of promotion ("Jury Awarded," 1991); in 1988, Honda Motor Company made a $6 million settlement of a suit involving charges of discrimination by Blacks and women in its U.S. operations (Cole & Deskins, 1988); and in 1992, Shoney's agreed to set aside $105 million to compensate victims of racial discrimination after a lawsuit was filed against the company (Pulley, 1992). Although the above examples deal with race and gender, age has been the subject of more litigation under Title VII of the Civil Rights Act than either gender or race in recent years. Thus it is clear that there are economic as well as good-citizenship implications of the legal obligations in this area of management.

In addition to the laws protecting members of workplace minority groups against discrimination, Executive Order 11246 requires that U.S. businesses wishing to serve as government contractors take steps to ensure that past discrimination is remedied and that discrimination does not occur in the future. Ostensibly, this requirement means that a large percentage of U.S. firms must maintain active affirmative action programs in order to ensure the right to bid on government contracts; however, in practice the penalties for not doing so are rarely enforced (Werther & Davis, 1993). Thus organizations have considerable latitude in defining how aggressively they will pursue affirmative action efforts. Despite this fact, many organizations have sustained active affirmative action initiatives since the late 1960s.

The previous discussion makes clear that in addition to the ethical and social conscience goals of managing-diversity initiatives, there are legal reasons for managers of organizations to give attention to diversity issues. However, I believe that a third, equally important but often overlooked motive is that managing diversity affects organizational performance in ways that have little to do with the social and legal rationales.

Diversity as a Factor in Organizational Performance

In my contacts with practicing managers of organizations, the question managers ask more than any other is how does diversity and its management affect the bottom-line performance of organizations. Moreover, they ask whether there is any tangible evidence that there is a relationship between them. These difficult but important questions will be addressed next. The remainder of this chapter will be devoted to explaining the philosophical foundations for connecting diversity and organizational performance, while Chapter Three will discuss relevant research supporting this linkage.

As suggested in Figure 1.1, two types of diversity effects on organizational effectiveness can be identified. One type addresses effects that derive from the impact of group identity on the experiences and work outcomes of individual members. I will refer to this type as equal opportunity and motivation to contribute (EOMC) effects. The other type of effects relates to the impact of cultural diversity in itself. These effects of diversity on organizational outcomes address the question of how the performance of homogeneous workgroups compare to that of heterogeneous workgroups. Both types of effects are explained in more depth below.

EOMC Effects

The IMCD model of Figure 1.1 suggests that EOMC effects of diversity occur because a set of individual, group, and organizational factors interact to influence a set of individual outcomes that in turn influence organizational outcomes. The set of individual, group, and organizational factors in the model were defined previously as the *diversity climate*. Also, the individual and organizational outcomes may each be thought of as occurring in two forms. At the individual level, the diversity climate impacts affective outcomes and achievement outcomes. As noted previously, *affective outcomes* refers to how people feel and think about their jobs and their employers. In Figure 1.1, these outcomes include job/career satisfaction, job involvement, and organizational identification. In emphasizing affective outcomes, the importance of employee perceptions about the workplace is duly recognized. It is well known that behavior is driven by perceptions of reality. Therefore, what people believe about their opportunities in the work environment is of vital importance regardless of whether or not these beliefs are consistent with the facts. In a recent study illustrating the relevance of individuals' perceptions to work outcomes, Eisenberger, Fasolo, and Davis-LaMastro (1990) examined the impact of attitudes on various individual work outcomes with samples of police officers, brokerage clerks, and public school teachers. The authors found that employees' perceptions of being valued by an organization had a significant effect on their conscientiousness, job involvement, and innovativeness. A sense of being valued, in turn, may well be influenced by cultural differences. Because of such things as stereotyping, ethnocentrism, and prejudice, members of minority groups often feel less valued, and hence the dynamics of diversity as explained in this book have implications for organizational innovation.

In support of the premise that perceptions in the workplace are influenced by diversity dimensions such as gender and racioethnicity, both Jones (1986) and Fernandez (1981) report survey data indicating that many non-Whites perceive that their race has hindered their advancement. Likewise, Beehr, Tabor, & Walsh (1980) found that Blacks were more likely than Whites to say race is a factor in promotion decisions. In my own recent work diagnosing organizational climate for diverse workgroups, I have found consistent differences of perception that are predictably related to group identities. In general, non-majority-group members are more likely to be aware of the effects of group membership than majority group members. For example, in one recent analysis of three-hundred managerial/professional employees in a research and development company, White women were nearly three times as likely as White men to say that being a man was an important factor in being promoted to senior positions, and non-Whites (both men and women) were three times as likely to say that race was an important factor.

The fact that perceptions are so vital is a major factor behind my recommendation (presented in Part Five of this book) for extensive use of employee opinion data in organization development work on managing diversity.

Returning to the logic of the IMCD model, *achievement outcomes* refers to tangible measures that are, at least theoretically, indexes of the employee's contribution to the organization. These include performance ratings, promotion rates, and compensation.

Affective and achievement outcomes of individuals are thought to influence organizational effectiveness measures such as product/service quality, productivity/efficiency, and labor turnover. These first-level organizational outcomes, in turn, directly impact the profitability of profit-making firms and instrumental goal attainment of nonprofit firms.

Thus, according to the logic of the model, by understanding the diversity climate we can predict effects on individual outcomes and ultimately effects of diversity on organizational effectiveness. The specific relationships between diversity-climate factors and individual outcomes is addressed in subsequent chapters of the book. For example, in Chapter Five, which deals with stereotyping, it is pointed out that stereotyping behavior tends to adversely affect the individual outcomes of persons in the stereotyped groups. Carrying this a step further, stereotyping is predicted to indirectly lower organizational performance.

In summary of the EOMC effects, a major theme of this book is that in many organizations diversity dynamics such as ethnocentrism, stereotyping, and cultural differences interact with a highly imbalanced power structure (on a culture group basis) to produce work outcome disadvantages for members of out-groups. As suggested previously, the poorer work outcomes include affective and achievement outcomes, and these in turn are thought to adversely affect first-level organizational measures such as productivity, absenteeism, and turnover. In such circumstances, it is necessary for organizations to improve the diversity climate in order to fully tap the potential of all workers to contribute to organizational performance. EOMC-related effects of diversity follow the line of thought suggested by Roosevelt Thomas's (1990) definition of managing diversity: "Managing in such a way as to get from a heterogeneous work force the same productivity, commitment, quality and profit that we got from the old homogeneous work force" (p. 109).

The research reviewed in this book suggests that these EOMC effects of diversity can be of great magnitude, and hence a major reason for organizations to manage diversity is to minimize barriers to performance that may occur due to diversity-related dynamics.

Direct Effects of Diversity

The previous discussion clarifies how group-identity diversity in organizations may indirectly determine levels of organizational performance. There is evidence, however, that the existence of diversity, in itself, may affect certain organizational processes such as communications, creativity, and problem solving, which are closely related to performance. One prominent perspective on diversity that follows this line of thought is the "value-in-diversity" philosophy (Cox, Lobel, & McLeod, 1991; Mandell & Kohler-Gray, 1990; Marmer-Solomon, 1989; Esty, 1988; Copeland, 1988). These writers are among those who argue that, when properly managed, diverse groups and organizations have performance advantages over homogeneous ones. I will refer to this possible impact of diversity in workgroups as the VID effect. Standing somewhat in contrast to the VID perspective is the argument that increasing diversity in workgroups may lead to certain dysfunctional outcomes such as miscommunications and lower team cohesiveness (Cox, 1991).

The potential for these direct effects of diversity on organizational performance are indicated in Figure 1.1 by the arrow extending from the diversity climate items of cultural difference, structural integration, and informal integration to the organizational outcomes of creativity, problem solving, and communications.

These potential direct effects of diversity on key organizational processes related to performance hold considerable importance for organizations. Enhancing creativity and problem-solving quality are prime concerns of organizational leaders. To the extent that the existence of group-identity diversity facilitates these, it adds an important motivation for actively seeking to maintain a diverse workforce rather than merely to manage one if it happens to present itself. Likewise, if increased diversity can hamper communication and reduce member attraction to workgroups, managers must find ways to minimize these effects. This need is made even more critical by the trend toward the increased use of self-managed workteams in organizations.

Summary

This chapter has provided a conceptual logic for the relationships between cultural diversity in workgroups and various aspects of organizational performance. Both direct and indirect (EOMC) effects were discussed. In the next chapter, some of the available empirical research relevant to these effects is reviewed.

Review of Research on Diversity and Organizational Performance

Chapter Two discussed the moral, legal, and economic performance factors that make working and managing diverse workgroups a core competency issue for leaders in the 1990s. With regard to the economic performance of organizations, the logic of the EOMC and VID perspectives was explained. Although the logic itself should provide substantial motivation for investment in organization change to create a positive diversity climate, I have found that individuals often ask for empirical evidence of the relationships discussed in Chapter Two. This chapter will provide some assistance by responding to this concern.

EOMC Effects of Diversity on Organizational Effectiveness

There is research evidence to support the idea that affective and achievement outcomes of individuals are influenced by dimensions of diversity such as gender, racioethnicity, and age. For example, in a recent study of compensation among 503 MBAs of various industries, Cox and Harquail (1991) found that female MBAs earned less than male MBAs from the same business school even after controlling for seniority, industry, job performance, and other factors that determine salaries. Other researchers have found similar results (Reder, 1978; Strober, 1982; Devanna, 1984; Olson & Frieze, 1987).

A second example is research on the early career experiences of 729 Black and White MBAs in which both gender and racioethnicity affected job involvement levels of the employees. Black MBAs had significantly lower job involvement than Whites, and women had significantly lower job involvement than men (Cox & Nkomo, 1991). Job involvement is defined as the extent of psychological identification with one's work (Jans, 1985). It is closely associated with job motivation and has specifically been shown to predict expected or actual turnover (Lee & Mowday, 1987; Siegel & Ruh, 1973). Thus this research directly links the career outcomes of non-majority-group members to the organizational outcome of employee turnover.

A third example is the often-cited "glass-ceiling" effect, which refers to barriers causing the underrepresentation of women and of non-Whites in organizations with predominantly White-male power structures (Morrison, White, & VanVelsor, 1987; Jones, 1986; Nkomo & Cox, 1989). The evidence of underrepresentation is ubiquitous. Although women constitute around 46 percent of the U.S. workforce and around 30 percent of management jobs, only 519 of the largest 1,000 companies have a female on the board of directors, and of the 4,000 highest-paid officers and directors of these companies in 1990 only 19 (less than .5 percent) were women ("Women on Boards," 1992; Fierman, 1990). Banking is one of several large industries that employs more women than men. Nevertheless, of the 72 directors of regional Federal Reserve Banks in 1990, there were only 3 women and 2 non-Whites (Crutsinger, 1990). In a similar vein, although non-Whites make up more than 20 percent of the U.S. workforce, they hold less than 3 percent of senior management jobs (Cox & Nkomo, in press).

It should be noted that underrepresentation in itself does not necessarily signify less opportunity for advancement, since a variety of other factors could account for it. However, there is some further evidence which suggests that promotion probabilities are indeed influenced by group identities. For example, data from the Quality of Employment Panel on career measures of men and women revealed that women were held to higher promotion standards than men and received fewer promotions than men with equal measured abilities (Olson & Becker, 1983). Likewise, in a survey study of 692 managers in a large Canadian company, gender had a significant effect on chances for promotion even after career-relevant factors such as formal education and childhood socialization were controlled (Cannings, 1988).

On racioethnic identity, Greenhaus, Parasuraman, and Wormely (1990) studied managerial personnel in three large U.S. companies and found that Blacks had lower promotability ratings and were more likely to be plateaued (to spend more than seven years at the same job) than their white counterparts. Such results have not been universally observed, however. For example, in a study of 125 lower-level managers in a public sector firm, Cox and Nkomo (1986) found no significant effects of race on promotability ratings, and Juster (1986) found no gender effects on promotion chances in a study of federal government workers.

When evaluating glass-ceiling effects, managers and researchers must also give attention to the possibility of group-identity effects on entry level. For example, some studies have found that women entered their organizations at significantly lower levels than men despite the fact that they had essentially identical education and years of experience. Moreover, the importance of entry level is underscored by the fact that entry level has been found to have a significant effect on later career success (Cox & Harquail, 1991).

As a final example of research demonstrating the link between diversity climate and individual work outcomes, let us consider a possible implication of cultural differences among the different cultural groups represented in an organization. Organizations may be thought of as having their own distinctive cultures (a point discussed extensively in Chapter Ten), and therefore the degree of congruence or fit between organization and individual culture is of potential importance to various career outcomes of individuals. In empirical tests of this proposition, O'Reilly, Chatman, & Caldwell (1991) and Chatman (1991) have shown that value congruence between employees and their firms has a significant effect on organizational commitment, employment satisfaction, likelihood to quit, and actual turnover.

In another relevant study, the degree of agreement in values between production workers and their supervisors was assessed. The data strongly supported the conclusion that organizational commitment and job satisfaction are enhanced by value congruence but produced mixed results on the achievement outcomes. For example, employees who had more congruent values were late less often but did not have significantly fewer absences (Meglino, Ravlin, & Adkins, 1989).

One additional example is a study of 2,300 Black and White enlisted U.S. Army personnel (Butler & Holmes, 1984). They found that likelihood to stay in the organization was partly determined by the degree of congruence between the employee's personal beliefs about racial separation and the army's policy of thorough integration. Of course, it is likely that values about racial separatism are closely aligned with attitudes, specifically racial prejudice. Nevertheless, the degree of fit between personal values and those of the organization was an important factor in continuation of employment.

Thus research has shown that individual outcomes, both affective and achievement outcomes, and organizational outcomes such as turnover rates and innovation are influenced by value congruence. The relevance of the value congruence research to cultural diversity is demonstrated in the material presented in Chapters Seven and Ten. To the extent that organizational cultures are defined by majority group members (because of their historical control of the power in the organization), we would expect, if everything else is equal, for their value congruence to be greater than that of members of minority groups. This again illustrates how the cultural diversity dynamics of the model operate indirectly to influence organizational outcomes.

The message of the foregoing discussion of value congruence may seem somewhat ambiguous. It may seem to suggest that diversity results in lower organizational performance. However, this is only true if we make certain assumptions about organizations such as that they should seek to assimilate all entrants into a monolithic culture, which tends to produce culture clash for entering members who are different from the traditional norm. Instead, my intended message is that the importance of value congruence illustrates the need for multicultural organizations, one feature of which is that the organization culture specifies alternatives that are equally appreciated rather than the one best way. Thus it is important to bear in mind that person-organization fit, in a cultural sense, is a function of the flexibility and inclusiveness of the organization as well as the individual.

EOMC and the Bottom Line

The above review of research data has shown that organizational experiences of out-group members tend to be less positive than those of majority group members. The implications of such EOMC effects for the economic well being of organizations are easily demonstrated. For example, data from the U.S. workforce indicate that turnover and absenteeism are often higher among women and non-White men than they are for White males. One study found that the overall turnover rate for Blacks in the U.S. workforce is 40 percent higher than the rate for Whites (Bergmann & Krause, 1968). Corning Glass recently reported that during the period 1980-1987 turnover among women in professional jobs was double that of men, and the rates for Blacks were 2.5 times those of Whites (Hymowitz, 1989). A two-to-one ratio in the turnover of women and men was also cited by Felice Schwartz in her much discussed article on multiple career tracks for women in management (Schwartz, 1989). Finally, a recent study of absence rates in the U.S. workforce shows that rates for women are 58 percent higher than for men (Meisenheimer, 1990).

Let us consider the implications of these differences in turnover and absence rates for the cost structure of a hypothetical firm of 10,000 employees. Assume that half of the workforce is composed of women and non-Whites, that the turnover rate for White men is 5 percent, and that the turnover rate for women and non-Whites is double the rate for White men. Based on this scenario, the differential turnover rates would produce an additional 250 losses annually. Formulas for calculating the costs of turnover suggest that a conservative figure for replacement costs for each loss would be $15,000 (Darmon, 1990; Mercer, 1988). Therefore, the annual cost of the turnover differential is estimated at $3.8 million.

As a second example, assume that the same hypothetical organization has $40,000 invested annually in salary and benefits per employee. If absence rates for men are 3 percent of scheduled hours and women average 58 percent higher, then absence rates for women would be 4.74 percent. If we assume further that 35 percent of the firm's workforce are women, the additional 1.74 percent in lost paid time represents a productivity loss of $2.4 million annually.

This analysis indicates that our hypothetical organization could potentially cut costs by over $3 million annually if even half of the turnover and absence differential could be eliminated by better management of diversity and its effects.

Can Managing Diversity Really Make a Difference?

The data reviewed above strongly suggest that the affective and achievement outcomes of individuals are influenced by group identities and that organizational outcomes like turnover rates and absenteeism are ultimately affected. The question remains, however, can focused attention on diversity issues in workgroups really impact these outcomes? In this regard, information from several sources on diversity in U.S. firms indicates that frustration over lack of career growth and cultural conflict with the dominant White-male culture are major factors behind the less favorable turnover, absenteeism, and satisfaction levels for women and non-White men. For example, two recent surveys of male and female managers of large American companies found that although women expressed a much higher probability of leaving their current employer than men, and had higher actual turnover rates than men, their major reason for quitting was lack of career growth opportunity or dissatisfaction with rates of progress. It is also instructive that one of the surveys found that women have higher actual turnover rates than men at all ages, and not just during the years when they are bearing children or raising young children (Trost, 1990).

Additional evidence supporting the conclusion that managing diversity has the potential to improve effectiveness measures like turnover can be found in reports of organizations that have changed benefits and work schedules as an adjustment to the greater career interests of women. In one study, companies were assigned an "accommodation score" on the basis of the adoption of four benefit-liberalization changes associated with pregnant workers. Analysis revealed that the higher a company's accommodation score, the lower the number of sick days taken by pregnant workers and the more willing they were to work overtime during pregnancy ("Helping Pregnant Workers," 1987).

In two other studies, the effect of company investment in day care on human resource costs was investigated. In one study, turnover and absenteeism rates of working mothers using a company-sponsored child development center were compared to those of women who either had no children or had no company assistance. Results indicated that the absenteeism rate for the day-care users was 38 percent lower than that of the other groups, and that they had a turnover rate of less than 2 percent compared to over 6 percent for the nonbenefit groups. In a second study, a company that initiated an in-house child-care facility found that worker attitudes improved on six measures, including organizational commitment and job satisfaction, and that turnover declined by 63 percent (Youngblood & Chambers-Cook, 1984). Similarly encouraging results are reported by the SAS Institute, a computer software firm that absorbs most of the costs of an on-site day-care facility. According to company spokespersons, the company's support of child care is a major reason for the company's employee turnover rate of just 7 percent, a figure which they say is less than a third of the industry average (Cusack, 1990).

It should be noted that organizational support for child care and not on-site child care per se seems to be the key factor in improving organizational outcomes. Not every company that has invested in on-site child care has witnessed drastic improvements in absence or turnover rates. Goff, Mount, & Jamison (1990) studied absenteeism effects of on-site child care at a large midwestern electronics and communications firm. They did not find that on-site child care per se reduced absence, but they did find that support from supervisors regarding work-family conflict issues and satisfaction with child-care arrangements were related to lower absence rates among employees who were parents.

Another management response to increasing diversity in the workforce is greater use of flextime work scheduling. A recent field experiment assessing the impact of flextime use on absenteeism and worker performance found that both short-term and long-term absences declined significantly and that three of four worker-efficiency measures increased significantly under flextime (Kim & Campagna, 1981).

There is also evidence that workteam productivity is improved by managing diversity. In a study of the productivity of culturally heterogeneous and culturally homogeneous workteams, findings indicated that some of the heterogeneous teams were more productive than the homogeneous teams and some were less productive than the homogeneous teams. This research was interpreted to show that if work teams manage the diversity well (for example, by ensuring that all members have ample opportunity to contribute and by dealing successfully with the potential communications, group cohesiveness, and interpersonal conflict issues presented by cultural diversity), they will be able to make diversity an asset to performance. Alternatively, if the diversity is ignored or mishandled, it may become a detractor from performance (Adler, 1986).

Although accurate dollar cost-savings figures from managing-diversity initiatives of specific companies are rarely published, a recent published report of the early savings of Ortho Pharmaceuticals stated savings of $500,000, mainly from lower turnover among members of minority groups (Bailey, 1989).

From an economic viewpoint, the potential cost savings of organizational initiatives to effectively manage diversity must be judged against the investment necessary to implement them. Nevertheless, the limited available data strongly suggest that managing-diversity efforts undertaken by some leading organizations have been somewhat successful in improving performance on absenteeism, turnover, and productivity.

The failure of organizations to manage non-majority-group members as successfully as White males translates into unnecessary costs. Since the diversity of workforces is growing throughout the world, the costs of *not* managing diversity well will escalate greatly in the coming years. Organizations that do not make appropriate changes to more successfully retain and utilize persons from different cultural backgrounds can expect to suffer a significant competitive disadvantage compared to those that do. Alternatively, organizations that are able to preempt competitors in creating a climate where all personnel have equal opportunity and motivation to contribute should gain a competitive cost advantage.

Direct Effects of Diversity

The discussion of the previous section makes it clear that organizations which already have diverse workforces need to become proficient at managing diversity in order to avoid EOMC-related performance barriers. However, as mentioned earlier, numerous authors have maintained that, when properly managed, cultural diversity is an asset to organizations that can be used to enhance organizational performance (the VID perspective). There is also evidence that heterogeneity in workgroups has certain disadvantages compared to homogeneous workgroups. Accordingly, the following segments will present theory and research on how the presence of diversity, in itself, may directly impact organizational performance.

Potential Performance Benefits of Diversity

The major arguments supporting the VID perspective on diversity and organizational performance revolve around five factors: (1) attracting and retaining the best available human talent, (2) enhanced marketing efforts, (3) higher creativity and innovation, (4) better problem solving, and (5) more organizational flexibility (Cox & Blake, 1991). Each of these will be addressed in the following sections.

Recruiting of Human Resources. A major competitive factor for organizations is attracting and retaining the best available human-resource talent in the context of the current workforce demographic trends. As women and non-White men increase in proportional representation in the available labor pools in the United States, Europe, and many other parts of the world, it becomes increasingly important for organizations to be successful in hiring and retaining workers from these culture groups. Furthermore, unless one believes that the most talented people all belong to one culture group, the ability to be equally successful in recruiting and retaining people from all culture groups should be viewed as a total quality issue.

The recruiting factor has gained significance from the recent flurry of published accounts of the best companies for women and for minorities (Zeitz & Dusky, 1988; "Twenty-five Best Places," 1992; Konrad, 1990; Staff, 1992). These publications have fostered the development of highly public reputations among organizations in terms of effective management of diversity. It is worth noting that, in addition to listing the best companies, the publications also discuss why certain companies were excluded from the list. Evidence of the impact of these developments on the recruitment of quality personnel has already begun to surface. In their recruiting efforts, companies such as Merck, Xerox, Syntex, and Hoffman-LaRoche have been aggressively using publicity they have received as good places for women and/or racioethnic minorities to work. According to company spokespersons, the recognition they have received is, in fact, boosting recruiting efforts. For example, Merck cites its identification as one of the ten best companies for working mothers as instrumental in recent increases in applications (Feinstein, 1989; Dreyfuss, 1990). As these reputations become increasingly visible, and as the supply of Anglo males in the labor market continues to shrink, the significance of the recruiting factor for organizational competitiveness will tend to be magnified.

As a final example of how the acquisition and utilization of human talent in organizations is influenced by managing diversity, multinational companies are often not adept at attracting and utilizing the best available talent of all nationalities. For example, it has been noted that U.S. citizens have had some difficulty in gaining acceptance in Japanese companies operating in the United States (Pucik, Hanada, & Fifield, 1989; Patterson, 1989). Clearly, access to the best available human talent requires that multinational firms be able to attract and retain managerial talent beyond their own host nationality.

Enhancing Marketing. Just as the workforces of organizations are becoming more culturally diverse, so are their markets. In the United States, for example, Asians, Blacks, and Hispanics now collectively represent nearly $500 billion annually in consumer spending.

The Asian segment of the population is growing at a rate that is ten times that of the overall population. Moreover, research on consumer behavior has consistently shown that sociocultural identities do affect buying behavior. For example, Redding (1982) outlines the following eight characteristics of how a Chinese manager approaches a business transaction:

1. Desire for wealth for security reasons
2. A strong consciousness of family obligations
3. A sense of being Chinese, which may manifest itself as anti-other feeling
4. Sensitivity to "face" that often manifests itself as a concern over the rank of the person sent to deal with him or her
5. A desire to avoid conflict
6. An emphasis on building friendships in business relationships
7. A tendency to see things as a set of alternatives rather than a universal set of guidelines
8. The assumption that interpersonal trust is of great importance, which manifests itself, for example, as a disdain for the "contract type of relationship"

Redding notes that this thinking diverges in many respects from the typical Western approach to business, and goes on to discuss implications for marketing practices in dealing with Southeast Asian customers.

As a second example, Tse, Lee, Vertinsky, and Wehrung (1988) studied characteristics relevant to buying behavior among 145 mainland Chinese, Hong Kong, and Canadian executives and found that culture had predictable effects on decision-making behavior. Among their specific conclusions was that culture affects problem identification and the objectives motivating choice in decision situations.

While much of the research on cross-cultural differences in consumer behavior has focused on cross-national comparisons, it should be acknowledged that continued high rates of immigration in much of the world make this research highly relevant to domestic marketing as well as exporting. In addition, the evidence on acculturation patterns among Asians and Latinos in the United States indicates that substantial identity with the root national cultures remains even after three or more generations of citizenship.

It should also be noted that these effects of culture identity on consumer behavior are not limited to nationality identity. For example, it has been shown that consumer behavior of Hispanic Americans is influenced by the strength of identification with their ethnic group (Deshpande, Hoyer, & Donthu, 1986).

In view of the effects of culture on consumer behavior, selling goods and services in the increasingly diverse marketplace should be facilitated by a well-utilized, diverse workforce in several ways. First, there is the public relations value alluded to earlier of being identified as managing diversity well. Just as people, especially those who identify with a nonmajority culture, may prefer to work for an employer recognized for valuing diversity, they may also prefer to buy from such organizations.

Second, firms may gain competitive advantage from the insights of employees from various cultural backgrounds who can assist organizations in understanding culture effects on buying decisions and in mapping strategies to respond to them. A case example of this type of competitive advantage is the experience of Gannett News Media. According to then-president Nancy Woodhull, the early marketing success of the USA TODAY newspaper was largely attributable to the presence of people from a wide variety of cultural backgrounds in daily news meetings. Diversity in group composition was deliberately planned and led to a natural representation of different points of view, because people of different cultural backgrounds have different experiences shaped by their group identities (Cox & Blake, 1991).

A second illustration of using cultural diversity to improve the marketing effort is the experience of Avon Corporation with low profitability in U.S. inner-city markets. After the company made personnel changes to give substantial authority over these markets to Black and Hispanic managers, results in these formerly unprofitable sectors improved to the point where they are now among the most productive of Avon's U.S. markets. Avon president Jim Preston has commented that members of a given cultural group are uniquely qualified to understand certain aspects of the world view of persons from that group (Cox & Blake, 1991).

A third, somewhat different example, is Maybelline's Shades of You line of cosmetics developed specifically for women with darker skin colors. Introduced in 1991, the product line did $15 million of sales, beating the industry standard for a major first-year success by 50 percent (Morgenson, 1991). This example illustrates the potential value of market segmentation based on culture identity groups.

There is also evidence that persons from a minority culture group are more likely to give patronage to a representative of their own culture group. For example, some American Indian tribes have been found to prefer to receive counseling services from Native American counselors. Thus, there are some circumstances under which the ability to match identities of salespersons and customers may facilitate sales.

The trend toward cultural diversification of markets is not limited to U.S. companies. Globalization is forcing major companies from many nations to give more attention to cultural-difference effects among consumers. Nations such as the United States that contain more culturally heterogeneous populations therefore possess a possible advantage in "national" competitiveness. However, as the discussion of EOMC made clear, just having diversity is not sufficient to produce benefits. Organizations must also manage it in such a way that this potential advantage is fully realized. The importance of this was brought out in two interviews recently conducted by my consulting team in the international division of a large U.S. company. One involved a male engineer from Colombia and the other a Japanese male. The South American stated that his ideas were often discounted in meetings, a result that he attributed partly to the fact that he had a strong foreign accent. The Japanese man stated that in cross-national contacts with Japanese business people he was often called upon to interpret for American executives. He complained that there was much more that he could contribute to the transactions but his role was invariably limited to language translation. The potential for lost opportunity to the organization in these instances seems obvious.

Creativity. Advocates of the VID perspective have also suggested that heterogeneity in workteams promotes creativity and innovation. There are several streams of research that tend to support this relationship. Kanter's study of innovation in organizations (1983) revealed that the most innovative companies deliberately establish heterogeneous teams in order to "create a marketplace of ideas, recognizing that a multiplicity of points of view need to be brought to bear on a problem" (p. 167). Kanter also specifically noted that companies high on innovation had done a better job than most in eradicating racism, sexism, and classism in the work environment and also tended to employ more women and non-White men than less innovative companies. Other innovation gurus have also cited diversity as a key ingredient in creativity. For example, in his book on innovation and change, Gareth Morgan (1989) propounds a "law" that states that, to adapt successfully to its external environment, a system must incorporate all of the variety found in that environment. He further states that "creativity thrives on diversity" (p. 76).

The conclusion that creativity is fostered by diversity is also supported by research on schools showing that the tolerance of diversity, defined as judging relatively few behaviors as deviant from norms, is a defining characteristic of innovative organizations (Siegel & Kaemmerer, 1978).

A second line of relevant research is that of Charlene Nemeth (1986), which shows that minority views can stimulate consideration of nonobvious alternatives in task groups. In a series of experiments, participants were asked to form as many words as possible from a string of ten letters. In each experiment, individual approaches to the task were determined and then two types of groups were formed. "Majority" groups were those where all members subscribed to the strategy for forming letters advocated by the majority of participants. "Minority" groups contained participants who subscribed to strategies that diverged from the majority perspective. Nemeth found that the minority groups adopted multiple strategies and identified more solutions than the majority groups. She concluded that the groups exposed to minority views were more creative than the more homogeneous, majority groups. She further concluded that persistent exposure to minority viewpoints stimulates creative thought processes.

In another series of experiments testing the effects of diversity on creativity, the creativity of teams that were homogeneous on a series of attitude measures was compared to teams with heterogeneity of attitudes. The creativity of problem solutions was judged on originality and practicality. Results indicated that as long as the team members had similar ability levels, the heterogeneous teams were more creative than the homogeneous ones (Triandis, Hall, & Ewen, 1965). This research suggests that if persons from different sociocultural identity groups tend to hold different attitudes and perspectives on issues, then cultural diversity should increase team creativity and innovation. In this connection, recent reviews of research evidence indicate that attitudes, cognitive functioning, and beliefs are not randomly distributed in the population but rather tend to vary systematically with demographic variables such as age, race, and gender (Jackson, 1991; Jackson et al., 1991).

The limited amount of research comparing diverse to homogeneous groups on creative performance has rarely defined group diversity along the specific dimensions of gender, nationality, and racioethnic identity, which are points of emphasis in this book. However, in a recent study of ethnic diversity and creativity, the quantity and quality of ideas generated during a brainstorming task by diverse groups of Asians, Blacks, Anglos, and Hispanics were compared to the ideas generated by homogeneous groups of Anglos. No significant differences were found in the quantity of ideas, but the ideas produced by the ethnically diverse groups were rated an average of 11 percent higher than those of the homogeneous groups on both feasibility and overall effectiveness (McLeod, Lobel, & Cox, 1993). Thus increased cultural diversity in organizations will often lead to higher levels of creativity and innovation.

Problem Solving. Managing diversity also has potential for competitive advantage through improved problem solving and decision making. The rationale for this statement is similar to that for increased creativity through diversity. The idea is that diverse groups have a broader and richer base of experience from which to approach a problem, and that critical analysis in decision groups is enhanced by member diversity. A series of research studies conducted in the 1960s at the University of Michigan found that heterogeneous groups produced better-quality solutions to problems than did homogeneous groups. The dimensions of group diversity included personality measures and gender. In one of the studies, 65 percent of heterogeneous groups produced high-quality solutions (defined as solutions that provided either new, modified, or integrative approaches to the problem) compared to only 21 percent of the homogeneous groups. This difference was statistically significant. In commenting on the results, the authors note that "mixing sexes and personalities appears to have freed these groups from the restraints of the solutions given in the problem" (Hoffman & Maier, 1961, p. 404).

These early findings have been confirmed in later studies on the effects of heterogeneity on group decision quality (Shaw, 1981; McGrath, 1984). In addition, the same conclusion is indirectly indicated by the research on the well-known "groupthink" phenomenon (Janis, 1982). This term refers to an absence of critical thinking in groups, caused partly by excessive preoccupation with maintaining cohesiveness. Most of the examples cited, such as the decision of the Kennedy administration to invade Cuba in 1961 and the *Challenger* space-shuttle disaster, portray decision processes that are affected by groupthink as producing disastrous results. Because group cohesiveness is directly related to degree of homogeneity, and because groupthink only occurs in highly cohesive groups, the presence of cultural diversity in groups should reduce the probability of groupthink.

Additional support for the argument that diverse workgroups are better problem solvers comes from the work of Nemeth (1985) and Nemeth and Wachter (1983). In a series of studies, they found that the level of critical analysis of decision issues and alternatives was higher in groups subjected to minority views than in those that were not. The presence of minority views improved the quality of the decision process regardless of whether the minority view ultimately prevailed. Among the specific differences in problem-solving processes they found were (1) a larger number of alternatives considered, and (2) a more thorough examination of assumptions and implications of alternative scenarios.

Some writers have noted that too much diversity in problem-solving groups can be dysfunctional (Shephard, 1964). When communication barriers, style conflict, and points of view lack even a core of commonality, decision making may become impossible. Thus another aspect of managing diversity is to balance the need for heterogeneity to promote problem solving and innovation with the need for organizational coherence and unity of action on some core dimensions of organizational culture.

In sum, culturally diverse workforces have the potential to solve problems better because of several factors: a greater variety of perspectives brought to bear on the issue, a higher level of critical analysis of alternatives, and a lower probability of groupthink. However, it is again important to emphasize that specific steps must be taken to realize these potential benefits of diversity in work-groups. This fact is reinforced by the research of Triandis et al. (1965) referenced above. They found that, in order to produce superior performance for the heterogeneous teams, it was necessary for members to have advance awareness of the attitudinal differences of other members. This finding indicates the importance of managing the diversity by informing workgroup members of the attitudinal differences of others. This type of information sharing is frequently a part of educational programs on diversity designed to increase awareness of cultural differences among organization members.

Organizational Flexibility. There are two primary bases for the assertion that managing diversity enhances organizational flexibility. First, there is some evidence that members of minority groups tend to have especially flexible cognitive structures. For example, research has shown that women tend to have a higher tolerance for ambiguity than men (Rotter & O'Connell, 1982). Tolerance for ambiguity, in turn, has been linked to a number of factors related to flexibility, such as cognitive complexity (Rotter & O'Connell, 1982) and the ability to excel in performing ambiguous tasks (Shaffer, Hendrick, Regula, & Freconna, 1973). In addition, a series of studies on bilingual and monolingual subpopulations from several different nations of the world have shown that bilinguals have higher levels of divergent thinking and cognitive flexibility than monolinguals (Lambert, 1977). Since the incidence of bilingualism is much greater among minority culture groups (especially racioethnic or non-native nationality groups such as Hispanics and Asians in the United States) than among majority group members, this research strongly supports the notion that cognitive flexibility is increased by the inclusion of minority groups in workforces.

In addition to these individual-level factors, the process of managing diversity itself may also enhance organizational flexibility. The changes to organizational culture and management systems needed for managing diversity will impact other areas of management. For example, as policies and procedures governing how business is done are broadened and operating methods are made less standardized, the system should become more accommodating of uncertainty and more adaptable. Also, the tolerance for alternative points of view that is fostered by managing diversity should lead to more openness to new ideas in general. Perhaps most important of all, if organizations are successful in overcoming resistance to change in the especially difficult area of accepting diversity, they should be well positioned to deal with resistance to other types of organization change.

As a final point on the flexibility argument, Chapter Ten of this book discusses "high-prescription and low-prescription cultures." It is suggested that narrowness of thinking and evaluation criteria characterize cultures that are antidiversity. Such cultures also tend to be rigid, not flexible. I have found in my consulting work that narrowness of thinking, rigidity, and a tendency to standardize definitions of "good" work styles are common obstacles to contribution for employees of all identity groups. In this respect, the cultural transformation needed to manage diversity and the changes needed to enhance organizational flexibility seem to be closely related.

Potential Problems of Diversity

Although diversity in workgroups holds strong potential performance advantages, it is also clear that cultural diversity in workgroups presents some potential problems for organizations. These problems largely revolve around the issues of group cohesiveness and communications. Each will be briefly discussed.

Diversity and Group Cohesiveness. The conclusion that group cohesiveness is reduced by cultural diversity is largely based on the idea that people are more highly attracted to, and feel more comfortable and satisfied with, group members who are like themselves. Thus, in general, cohesiveness is easier to achieve in homogeneous groups. Ziller (1973) outlines three theoretical explanations of the effects of diversity on groups that are related to cohesiveness. One theory holds that members of groups emphasize status congruence among members. When members differ on many characteristics, as often occurs in heterogeneous groups, opportunities for status incongruence increase. For example, a woman who is a team leader may present status incongruity for some persons who are accustomed to being supervised by men. Thus, diversity in groups may lead to lower cohesiveness due to status incongruence.

A second theory is that perceived similarity increases attraction, which in turn enhances cohesiveness. Therefore, homogeneity reinforces the closeness of groups. In this regard, it should be noted that demographic similarity along dimensions such as gender and nationality does not necessarily indicate attitudinal or behavioral similarity. Nevertheless, research has shown that both demographic and attitudinal similarity influence attraction (Jackson et al., 1991).

A third theoretical perspective on the effects of heterogeneity on cohesiveness in groups noted by Ziller is social comparison theory. This theory holds that people tend to seek homogeneity in groups or to create it through pressures for conformity, in order to facilitate social comparisons, which they rely on to conduct self-evaluations. Since such comparisons are more reliable when the comparison person is viewed as similar (that is, all other things are equal), diversity may be avoided because it makes valid social comparisons more difficult.

It should be noted that the importance of the relationship between diversity and cohesiveness rests on whether or not cohesiveness affects the performance of groups. In this regard, work on group dynamics has consistently indicated that highly cohesive groups have higher member morale and better communications than less cohesive groups (Lott & Lott, 1965; Randolph & Blackburn, 1989). Putting this together with the previous discussion of diversity and cohesiveness, we can conclude that diversity in workgroups potentially lowers member morale and makes communications more difficult. In addition, at least one empirical study has shown that heterogeneous groups experience higher member turn-over than homogeneous groups (Jackson et al., 1991).

It should be emphasized, however, that research has *not* shown that cohesiveness improves the work performance of groups. The largest-scale study of the relationship between the cohesiveness and productivity of groups revealed that highly cohesive groups are just as likely to have lower productivity as they are to be more produc-tive (Arnold & Feldman, 1986). There is also empirical evidence that tests the effects of diversity on group productivity more directly. The University of California, Los Angeles, study reported by Adler (1986) was mentioned earlier in this chapter. In addition, Fiedler (1966) studied the effects of cultural diversity on group performance using Dutch and Belgian participants. He found that heterogeneous groups performed equally well with the homogeneous groups on the assigned tasks. It should be noted, however, that Fiedler's data do not address the possibility of performance declines due to com-munications and morale-related problems that persist over an ex-tended period of time.

Finally, the well-known groupthink phenomenon referred to earlier in the chapter illustrates that excessive cohesiveness and preoccupation with preserving it can lead to highly ineffective task performance.

Diversity and Communications. Another potential obstacle to per-formance in diverse workgroups is less effective communications (Steiner, 1972). In the empirical study by Fiedler (1966) mentioned above, he found that culturally heterogeneous groups reported a less pleasant atmosphere and experienced greater communications dif-ficulties than the homogeneous groups. Although the possibility for communication-related barriers to performance is most obvious in multi-national workforces, it is also clear that other forms of diversity in workgroups can hamper communications. For exam-ple, Chapter Seven provides a discussion of numerous differences in communication styles based on gender and racioethnicity. More-over, in my consulting work on diversity, I have often been told that members of different departments of organizations "don't speak the same language." Indeed, in a recent organization devel-opment project, I found that only about half of the respondents to a questionnaire agreed that cross-functional communications in the firm were good. This compared to figures of 75–85 percent agreement for the same question concerning communications among people of different gender and racioethnic groups. Interestingly, the finding that interdepartmental communications were perceived as more problematic than communications across racioethnic and gender groups was consistent for respondents of all culture identities (that is, Asians, Hispanics, Blacks, and Whites of both genders). Although this finding should not be generalized to all organizations, it does make the point that communication difficulties in organizations may be related to many forms of diversity.

There can be little question that communication differences related to culture may become the source of misunderstandings and ultimately lower workgroup effectiveness. Once the existence of these differences is acknowledged, an obvious action step is to educate members on cross-cultural differences so as to minimize their detrimental effects.

In summary, there is reason to believe that the presence of cultural diversity does make certain aspects of group functioning more problematic. Misunderstandings may increase, conflict and anxiety may rise, and members may feel less comfortable with membership in the group. These effects may combine to make decision making more difficult and time-consuming. In certain respects, then, culturally diverse workgroups are more difficult to manage effectively than culturally homogeneous workgroups. In view of this, the challenge for organizations, as suggested in my definition of managing diversity, is to manage in such a way as to maximize the potential benefits of diversity while minimizing the potential disadvantages.

Summary

This chapter has reviewed a significant amount of relevant research demonstrating the importance of managing diversity for effective leadership in organizations. Additional research is clearly needed, especially on the direct effects of diversity. Nevertheless, the arguments, data, and suggestions presented here should be useful to organizations in building commitment among their members and in promoting action for managing diversity and organization change efforts.

Propositions for Discussion

Proposition 3.1:   To the extent that organizations can at-
                          tract, retain, and promote maximum
                          utilization of people from diverse cultur-
                          al backgrounds, they will gain compet-
                          itive advantages in cost structures and in
                          maintaining the highest-quality human
                          resources.

Proposition 3.2:   To the extent that organizations can
                          capitalize on the potential benefits of
                          cultural diversity in workgroups, they
                          will gain a competitive advantage in (a)
                          creativity, (b) problem solving, and (c)
                          flexible adaptation to change.

Proposition 3.3:   In the absence of effective management
                          of diversity, culturally diverse work-
                          groups will have more communication
                          problems, longer decision times, and
                          lower member morale than culturally
                          homogeneous workgroups.

· PART TWO

INDIVIDUAL-LEVEL FACTORS IN UNDERSTANDING DIVERSITY

In the IMCD framework there are three components of the diversity climate: individual factors, group/intergroup factors, and organizations factors. Part Two addresses the individual-level factors of group identity, prejudice, personality, and stereotyping.

4

Group Identities
in the Self-Concept

A group identity is a personal affiliation with other people with whom one shares certain things in common. Such identities are central to how cultural diversity impacts behavior in organizations. Nevertheless, one of the questions that frequently comes up in training sessions on workforce diversity is why people need to be understood as members of groups. Some ask, "Can't we simply treat people as individuals and not as members of groups?" Others feel that by paying attention to group affiliations, we simply reinforce the tendency to stereotype. While these views raise legitimate concerns, they are somewhat insensitive to several key facts about the role of group identities in human behavior. First, social identity theory informs us that individual identity—the self-concept in psychological terms—is partly *defined* by various group affiliations (Tajfel, 1978; Ashforth & Mael, 1989). For example, in responding to the question "Who am I?" an individual might say: (1) "I am an inquisitive person" (individual trait), and (2) "I am a Christian" (a group identity).

Brewer and Miller (1984) capture this aspect of the importance of group identities well in their description of social identity theory: "An individual's personal identity is highly differentiated and based in part on membership in significant social categories, along with the value and emotional significance attached to that membership" (p. 281).

I wish to emphasize the words "in part" in the above quotation. My message is not that the self is *solely* determined by group identities but rather that various group identities play a part in how we define ourselves as well as how others view us. The theory of cultural diversity presented in this book emphasizes the portion of

the self that is defined by group identities. Thus it does not purport
to fully explain individual experience but rather to contribute an
understanding of an important, and often overlooked, element of
that experience. Data from the fields of social and organizational
psychology show that group identities are indeed important components of the self-concept for most people (Alderfer, Tucker, Morgan, & Drasgow, 1983; Abrams & Hogg, 1990).

A second reason that group identities must be recognized is
that for some, the recognition and preservation of these identities
is a matter of personal pride and self-esteem. For example, many
American Indians turn down lucrative job opportunities elsewhere
in order to remain on reservations. Such decisions are made partly
out of a sense of responsibility for, and identification with, the
educational and economic challenges faced by other members of
their tribes. Thus to ignore these identities is to undermine something of great significance to the individuals themselves.

A third reason that group identities are important to our study
of behavior in organizations is that even if these identities are relatively unimportant in our self-definition, they will still often be
influential in how others interact with us. For example, despite the
fact that gender may not be a salient group identity for a particular
female executive, some colleagues will still interact with her as a
woman first and only secondarily as an executive. Thus there is a
certain inevitability to the influence of group identities. To ignore
them is to deny an important reality of human interaction in society
and in organizations.

Thus inherent in the concept of group identities advocated in
this book are the following: (1) every individual has group identities
that are salient in interpersonal relations, and (2) transactions
among individuals are, in part, intergroup events (Alderfer & Smith,
1982).

Types of Group Identities

Various types of group identities have been found to be important
to human behavior. In this segment we will first consider *phenotype identity groups,* which are based on physical, visually obser-
vable differences. We will then address *culture identity groups,*

which are based on shared norms, values, and common sociocultural heritage. In each case we will define the terms, give specific examples of them, and then discuss how identity groups influence human behavior in organizations.

It should be noted that several of the most important group identities have both physical and cultural significance. Among them are racioethnicity, gender, and, in many cases, nationality. However, I will first examine them separately for purposes of clarity. I will then consider the implications of combinations of phenotype identities and culture identities on behavior in organizations.

Phenotype Identity Groups

As previously suggested, members of phenotype groups are visually distinguishable from members of other groups. I will use phenotype and physical identity interchangably in this book. For example, women are physically distinguishable from men and thus gender represents a phenotype identity. Although there are instances in which physical attractiveness is a major factor underlying the treatment of people of a particular group identity (e.g., certain physical abilities [Stone, Stone, & Dipboye, in press]), attractiveness will be treated here as mainly an individual trait rather than as a basis for phenotype grouping.

With racioethnic groups, members are often distinguished by such things as hair texture, skin color, and facial features. Because phenotype identities are visible, our initial impressions of, and predispositions toward, people are greatly influenced by them. Reactions such as stereotyping and prejudice are typically activated on the basis of phenotype. For example, we use visible signals as a basis for categorizing people as men, women, Blacks, Asians, Caucasians, physically disabled, and so on. Once that visual identification has been made, our minds automatically call forth any stored data about other members of that group. A set of expectations or assumptions is therefore often attached to these phenotype identifications and may predispose us to interact with a person in a particular way.

Members of minority groups vary in the extent to which they are physically different from the typical majority-group member.

This fact is important because the magnitude of physical distinctiveness is often the source of differences in the life experience of minorities. This subject will be addressed next.

The effects of phenotype identity on life experience have received only limited attention in the social psychology literature and virtually none in the organizational literature. Most of the attention that has been given to them has focused on racioethnic differences. Davis (1985) observes that skin color has played an important role in majority-minority relations in America, and that it has profound effects on the dynamics of small groups. Similarly, Triandis (1976) argues that the tendency for unattended heterogeneity within a group to lead to conflict is accelerated when majority and minority group members are physically distinct. Lincoln (1967) goes further by arguing that "skin color is probably the most important single index for uncritical human evaluation" (p. 572).

Slavery played an important role in the use of skin color in intergroup relations in the United States. As Lincoln observed: "If the success of the White man lay in his color, it stood to reason that the closer to being White a Black man was, the more likely he was to have power and status. This reasoning was reinforced by the slave-era tradition of making household servants of the slave-master's mulatto offspring, thus securing them in positions of relative privilege vis a vis the unmixed field hands" (p. 531).

In more contemporary times, this tendency for the majority group to respond more favorably toward minorities that are physically closer to Caucasian in appearance can be seen in patterns of residential segregation. Based on extensive studies of residential patterns over a twenty-year period, Massey and Mullan (1984) and Massey and Denton (1988) have shown that independent of socioeconomic status, Anglos are significantly more likely to live near Hispanics than to Blacks, and that the presence of Hispanics does not render a residential area unattractive to Anglos to the same extent that the presence of Blacks does. They also note that the social status required of Blacks in order for them not to be viewed as threatening to Anglos is significantly higher than that required for Hispanics. Although the authors do not directly state that Anglos prefer Hispanics over Blacks because Hispanics are physically less different, they come very close by stating that Anglos avoid Blacks on the basis of race rather than class.

The importance of skin color differentiation, and the concept of a hierarchy of preference based on nearness to being physically White, is also strongly supported by research on Hispanics who are dark-skinned. Goldstein and White (1985) cite data from a study of Hispanics that they classified as Black Hispanics, White Hispanics, and other Hispanics on the basis of the degree to which they had Caucasian physical features. They found that the so-called Black Hispanics were the most residentially segregated from Anglos and concluded that "Whites not of Hispanic origin seem willing to live residentially integrated with Hispanics provided they are also White" (pp. 394–395). They note that their results reinforce those of Lincoln (1967) and call for attention to the effect of intragroup stratification on the basis on skin color. In a similar vein, Ghali (1977) writes regarding the experience of Puerto Ricans in the United States: "The issue of color is an enormous factor for Puerto Ricans to contend with upon arrival in the U.S. Cinnamon color is a desired shade to possess. While the higher classes are more snobbish about their whiteness, their attitudes toward their darker brothers never approximate the hostility toward blacks in American society. When Puerto Ricans arrive on the mainland they are judged either white or black for the first time, and if pronounced black, are attributed all of the racist stereotypes of the black people" (p. 466).

In a rare reference to phenotype identity in the literature on organizations, Fernandez (1981) states that "whiter" racioethnic minorities reported less racism than respondents whose appearance was less Euro-American.

The importance of physical distinctiveness and the presence of bias based on physical differences from the majority group are also illustrated by research on the dress of women in male majority settings. In one study, fifty-four campus recruiters representing thirty-three organizations completed a questionnaire designed to measure preferences in dress for male and female job applicants. Results indicated that conservative dress (defined as a tailored suit for women) was preferred for men and women but it was more important to hiring ratings for women candidates than for men (Jenkins & Atkins, 1990). In another study, 109 managers from banking and marketing viewed videotapes depicting different styles of dress of women applicants for management jobs. Results indicated that applicants wearing more masculine clothing were perceived as possessing more managerial characteristics and received more favorable hiring recommendations (Forsythe, 1990). The first study illustrates that gender, as a phenotype, influences work-relevant judgments of people. Both studies illustrate the importance often placed on the physical characteristics of people in the workplace, and highlight how perilous deviation in physical appearance from the majority norm can be to career success.

Culture Identity Groups

A culture identity group is based on sociocultural, as opposed to physical, distinctiveness. Members, in general, share a particular subjective culture. The term *subjective culture,* as coined by Triandis (1976), means a group's typical patterns of viewing the environment. Another way of expressing the term is that members of identity groups tend to share certain worldviews (Alderfer & Smith, 1982). For my purpose here, culture group will also mean individuals who share norms, values, and goal priorities that distinguish one culture group from another.

Because the culture group affiliations of individuals can be complex, I will use the term *culture identity structure* to refer to a particular culture group configuration. Culture identity structures have two components. The first, which I will call the culture identity profile, refers to the culture group or groups with which an individual personally identifies. The second component of culture identity structure is *identity strength* and refers to the relative importance or value that an individual places on a particular culture group identity. Both components of culture identity structure may be illustrated by the examples contained in Figure 4.1.

The examples of culture identity structure shown in Figure 4.1 were created by four graduate students in a recent session of my course on managing cultural diversity. The students created these pie charts during an exercise in which I asked them to respond to the question "Who am I?" by drawing slices of pie to indicate the

Figure 4.1. Examples of Culture Identity Structure.

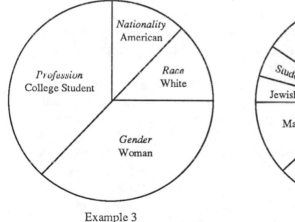

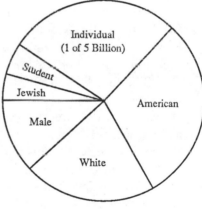

group affiliations that impacted on their self-concept, with the size of the slices reflecting the relative importance of each identity.

One of the interesting aspects of the first example is the inclusion of the employer. This is the only example that includes an employer and, further, the employer is one of the most important group affiliations in this person's self-concept. The fact that the respondent is Japanese helps us to understand this inclusion as a

likely manifestation of the well-known tendency for Japanese employees of large Japanese companies to have a high degree of
company loyalty and identification (Johnson, 1988). Examples 2
and 3 of Figure 4.1 show the identity structures of a Black man and
White woman respectively. It is perhaps noteworthy that race is
more salient than gender for the Black respondent and gender is
more salient than race for the lone female respondent. This points
up another conclusion I have reached based on information from
dozens of focus group discussions and hundreds of interviewees and
diversity workshop participants: most individuals have relatively
high awareness of the identity that most distinguishes them from
the majority group in a particular setting and considerably less
awareness of other identities. For example, in summarizing fifty
one-on-one interviews from a large international company, I found
that when discussing their observations about how culture identities had affected interactions at work, 89 percent of white women
focused exclusively on gender, 88 percent of expatriates focused on
nationality, and 78 percent of non-White men focused on racioethnicity. Interestingly, non-White women was the only group in
which a significant number of people (50 percent) addressed both
racioethnic and gender issues.

The fourth example shows a white male who acknowledges
five group identities, the most important of which is nationality
(U.S.). It is interesting that despite the instruction calling for group
affiliations, this person felt compelled to indicate that the major
determining factors of his self-concept were based on his individuality and not group identity. This response is especially revealing
in view of the fact that the respondent clearly understood that the
pie was only intended to reflect a part of his self-concept, that part
which is based on group affiliations. It in no way denied that other,
more individualistic factors would account for a large part of the
self-concept. In my consulting work on diversity, I have found that
among the larger cultural groups in the United States, White men
are much more likely to give this response than members of other
groups. I believe there are two reasons for this. First, as Hofstede
(1980) has shown, individuality is a strong cultural norm for Anglo
American men. Second, as the majority group in many organizational and higher-education settings, White men are often less

aware of group identities than members of minority groups. This point has been supported by the research of Alderfer (1982) among others.

Approaches to Measuring Culture Identity

The vast majority of work that has been done on culture identity structures has focused on racioethnic identity. Therefore, I will concentrate here on what has been learned from that body of knowledge. There are three primary approaches that have been employed in the theory and research on racioethnic identity structures. They are (1) stages of development models, (2) acculturation models, and (3) direct-questioning models. Each of these will be briefly discussed.

Stage Models of Culture Identity

According to stage models, culture identity evolves over time through a series of distinct stages of development, each representing a "higher" level of identity formation than the previous one. For example, Cross's (1971) widely quoted model of identity development among Blacks has five stages: (1) preencounter (Blacks reject Black heritage and define themselves in terms of White culture), (2) encounter (they seek identification with Black culture), (3) immersion/emersion (they have complete identification with Black culture and hostility toward Whites), (4) internalization (they become comfortable with Black identity; anger leaves and racism is transcended), (5) internationalization/commitment (they become behaviorally active in fighting racism). In a similar vein, Helms (1990) has developed a stage model of identity development in Whites. Her model proceeds through six stages ranging from contact (Whites have awareness of other groups but without conscious thought about their own racioethnic identity or how it relates to that of others) to autonomy (they have complete awareness and acceptance of their own identity as well that of others, along with an interest in learning from members of other groups and transcendence of racioethnic prejudice).

As a final example, Ponterotto (1988a) reports that graduate students in his counseling program progress through four stages of racial consciousness during the course, in which he teaches about the impact of diversity on their work. All of these writers observe that persons may become stuck at a particular stage, and thus the progression to the highest level of development is by no means assured.

A common thread in the stage models is a progression of the individual from a state of ignorance and total insensitivity through several stages of struggle with identity, the individual's own as well as that of others, and finally a state of transcending group identity. In the earliest stage, people often deny that racioethnic identity is relevant in interpersonal relations. In the middle stages, common reactions to the realization that they were wrong include anger, guilt, and confusion. In the final stage, the emotional turmoil and uncertainty of the middle stages have been worked through to a point where the individuals are fully aware of their identity, are comfortable with it, and will often seek opportunities to further examine the implications of group differences on human transactions as well as to actively combat prejudice and discrimination.

Acculturation Models of Culture Identity

Acculturation models of culture identity measure identity structures by the extent to which an individual identifies with the subjective culture of the majority group versus the subjective culture of minority groups. Most research of this type classifies individuals as monocultural majority, monocultural minority, or bicultural. Monocultural majority individuals subscribe totally to the norms and value system of the cultural majority group. In the United States this is an Anglo cultural system. Monocultural minority individuals enact behaviors based on their minority group and reflect a minimum of assimilation to majority group norms. Individuals who identify strongly with both the majority group culture and their minority group are characterized as bicultural (Bell, 1990).

The most common method of assigning people to these groups is on the basis of what might be termed life history data. For example, one approach is to ask a series of questions about levels of contact with majority group members and minority group members in settings such as work, education, and social functions.

Individuals who have had little or no contact with persons of other identity groups are assumed to be monocultural, whereas individuals who have regularly interacted with persons of other identities in a variety of settings are assumed to be bicultural (or multicultural). Questions about the use of language, knowledge of a group's history, and activity to teach these to subsequent generations are also frequently used. For example, a Chinese American who speaks Chinese at home, teaches Chinese culture to her children, and has a strong sense of pride in Chinese history and culture would be classified as having high identity with the Chinese American minority group, whereas a Chinese American who did none of these things would be classfied as having a monocultural majority identity (that is, as being fully assimilated). A considerable amount of research has been conducted in the United States using the acculturation model of identity. Some of this research is summarized in Table 4.1.

Several important observations can be made from the research data of Table 4.1. First, there is considerable evidence that significant numbers of Hispanic, African, Asian, and Native Americans identify strongly with their minority culture. The Table 4.1 data indicate that for all of these groups the percentage of group members with either mono-minority or bicultural identities ranges from 40 to almost 90 percent. Second, a significant amount of assimilation of these minority groups is indicated by the large percentage of individuals who display either bicultural or mono-majority identities. A third observation is that identification with the culture of minority racioethnic groups is often quite strong even after a minority group has existed in a particular society for several generations. For example, in the study by Matsumoto, Meredith, and Masuda (1970) referenced in Table 4.1, even third-generation Japanese Americans were found to have relatively high scores on ethnic identification with Japanese culture and the scores were virtually unchanged between second- and third-generation respondents.

It is somewhat difficult to predict how identity, as measured by the acculturation approach, will impact organizational experience. Based on the discussion that has been presented here, it can be predicted that members with monocultural minority identity structures will have significant problems in traditional assimilationist-oriented

Table 4.1. Research Data on Culture Identity Profiles.

Group(s)	Source	Summary of Findings
Hispanics (primary = Mexican Americans)	Deshpande, Hoyer, & Donthu (1986)	Forty-two percent identified strongly with the Hispanic ethnic group.
Mexican Americans and Anglos	Montgomery & Orozco (1984)	On a scale of 1 (extremely Mexican-oriented) to 5 (extremely Anglo-oriented), Mexican Americans scored a median of 3.35 versus 4.42 for Anglos.
Blackfeet Indians	McFee (1968)	Some 27 percent were monocultural minority; 27 percent bicultural; 47 percent monocultural majority.
Mexican Americans and Anglos	Hazuda, Stern, & Haffner (1988)	Some 44–45 percent of Hispanics were highly acculturated to Anglo values and attitudes compared to 12 percent of Anglos who showed significant acculturation to Hispanic values.
Hispanics (Latin American countries); Vietnamese; Anglos	Wong-Reider & Quintana (1987)	Hispanics identified strongly with both their Hispanic culture and the Anglo culture (3.02 and 3.75, respectively, on 1–5 scale).
Mexican Americans	Fernandez-Barrillas & Morrison (1984)	Some 56 percent were bicultural; 22 percent monocultural Anglo; 22 percent monocultural Hispanic.
Japanese Americans	Matsumoto, Meredith, & Masuda (1970)	Even third-generation Japanese Americans had scores of 140 (out of 250) on an ethnic identification scale, and scores were unchanged between second- and third-generation respondents.
Asians (Chinese, Japanese, Koreans, Philippinos); Hispanics (Mexican Americans); Black Americans; Anglos (high school age)	Phinney (1989)	Percentage of each group displaying either moderate or strong ethnic identification were: 11 percent for Anglos; 4 percent for Asians; 49 percent for Hispanics; 44 percent for Blacks.
Blacks, Hispanics, Anglos	McGuire et al. (1978)	When asked, "Tell us about yourself," only 1 in 100 Whites mentioned racioethnicity versus 1 in 6 Blacks and 1 in 7 Hispanics.

organizations. However, the relationship between biculturalism and career outcomes of minorities in assimilationist organizations is less clear. While biculturals would be expected to have some difficulty due to their strong identification with an alternative culture group, there is also evidence that when functioning in a system dominated by another group, biculturalism presents advantages to overall mental health (Szapocznik, Santisteban, Kurtines, Perez-Vidal, & Herdis, 1988; Szapocznik & Kurtines, 1980; Fernandez-Barillas & Morrison, 1984). As one example of the research evidence on this, Fernandez-Barillas and Morrison found that bicultural Mexican American students at a predominantly Anglo university experienced significantly less stress and displayed significantly better adjustment to the college environment than students with monocultural minority identities.

Also, research with Latinos and Southeast Asian immigrants has shown that biculturals have higher work satisfaction than persons with monominority identities (Wong-Rieger & Quintana, 1987).

Another interesting finding from the Table 4.1 data is that in the few studies which included them, the vast majority of White Americans (in the range of 85 to 90 percent) displayed a mono-majority identity structure. This conclusion was reinforced for me during a recent executive education program in which I collected social life history data from eighty utility industry managers (seventy-eight of whom where White men). I found that in general the White male respondents tended to have largely monocultural life histories with only limited involvement with members of other racioethnic groups. For example, the typical manager in the group had rarely or never participated in educational or social experiences in which non-Whites represented 15 percent or more of those present.

These findings about differences in identity structures between Whites and non-Whites, which I believe are generalizable to other majority-minority group situations, have important implications for cross-group understanding and career experiences in organizations. These implications will be discussed below in the section on relating cultural identity to career outcomes.

Direct-Questioning Models

Direct-questioning models of culture identity measure identity structures by asking people straightforward questions about the strength of their identity with a particular group. This method has been used in consumer behavior research reported in the marketing literature. For example, in one study of consumer behavior among Hispanics, subjects were first asked to indicate the racioethnic group(s) to which they belonged and then asked to indicate how strongly they identified with each group. Subjects were classified as strong identifiers with their racioethnic minority group if they answered either very strongly or strongly; otherwise they were classified as weak identifiers. The research demonstrated the usefulness of this approach to measuring culture identity by showing that marketing-related behaviors such as brand loyalty and prestige-product purchases differed predictably between strong and weak Hispanic identifiers (Deshpande, Hoyer, & Donthu, 1986).

Congruence of Phenotype and Culture Identities

It is important to recognize that members of racioethnic minority groups vary in both phenotype and cultural distinctiveness from the majority group. In the previous segments of the chapter, we dealt with phenotype and culture identity groups as separate classification systems. For group identities which have both physical and cultural manifestations (such as race and gender), however, it may also be important to consider how these two types of identifications operate in combination. Specifically, let us consider the possibility that expectations of culture identity structures are created by phenotype. For example, a Mexican American with Caucasian physical features and a monocultural majority-group culture identity structure may be perceived by others as having congruent (matching) identities. By contrast, a Mexican American with Caucasian physical features who identifies strongly with the Mexican American culture might be perceived by others as possessing incongruent identities. As another example, a person with a nonobvious physical disability will often be treated inappropriately because she is assumed to be fully physically able. People who are physically male are often assumed to identify with the cultural traditions of men, and so on. If we utilize a classification system in which each type of identity is labeled as either high or low, the four possible identity combinations would be as shown in Table 4.2.

Table 4.2. Congruent Versus Incongruent Identity Structures.

Culture	Phenotype Identity	
Identity	Low	High
Low	No dissonance	High dissonance
High	High dissonance	No dissonance

Incongruent Identities as a Source of Cognitive Dissonance

The term *cognitive dissonance* has been used to refer to situations in which perceptive cues about an object are inconsistent or contradictory. Theory and research on cognitive dissonance indicates that dissonance creates psychological discomfort (Festinger, 1957). The relationships specified in Table 4.2 suggest cognitive dissonance may occur when a person's phenotype and culture identity are perceived as incongruent. It is important to note that the states of dissonance shown in Table 4.2 refer more to the perceptions of others than to self-perceptions. Thus an African American with very Caucasian features who also has a monocultural majority-group identity would present no dissonance. Alternatively, an African American (let's call her Ann) with a Caucasian appearance who identifies strongly with African American culture might present dissonance for those with whom she interacts. In the latter situation, the physical cues suggesting a White identity would not match up with certain behaviors deriving more from Ann's culture identity. The resulting dissonance may cause persons who interact with Ann to experience some psychological discomfort or even to react negatively toward her as the source of dissonance. A similar reaction might result for an Anglo who for some reason identified strongly with a minority-group culture. The apparent lack of fit between the visual/physical cues and the behaviors could produce discomfort for other Anglos as well as for members of other culture groups who interacted with the person. One example of this reaction is the ostracism that some White men have suffered from other White males as a result of becoming actively involved in organizational change efforts concerning diversity. As one White male assigned to be diversity coordinator in a large corporation said to me: "Friends ask me questions like, 'Why are *you* getting involved in this—what's in it for us?' "

Empirical research is needed to determine the actual importance of the effects proposed in Table 4.2. However, there is some existing evidence of these dissonance effects in research on the interaction of phenotype and behavior. Since these effects represent a form of prejudice, this research is discussed in Chapter Five.

It seems logical that dissonance based on identity incongruence would be most pronounced in interactions involving relative strangers. Nevertheless, such situations occur frequently enough in organizations for them to have an influence on work experiences

Relationship of Identity Structures to Career Experiences of Minority Group Members

There are several ways in which this discussion of the culture identity concept helps us to better understand the work experiences of individuals, especially the generally less favorable career experiences of minority members of organizations. Among them are the following:

- The cost of acting unnaturally
- The added complexity in behavioral choices
- The psychological cost of a loss of identity

The Cost of Acting Unnaturally

One way in which having a culture identity that differs from the majority in an organization may impact career experience is that non-majority-group individuals are constantly under pressure to enact behaviors that may not be natural for them. This is captured well in the following quotations. The first, taken from the files of my consulting group, is from a 1991 interview with a White female professional employee in a large research and engineering company. "Many women conform to the male standard and use successful males as role models because there are no others. Sometimes this backfires because it requires the woman to behave differently than what may be her natural personality. This adds stress to her life and she literally becomes two different people (one at work; one at home). This can also negatively affect performance. People are at their best when they can be themselves. There is a strong desire to fit in and be one of the guys because this is the only way to get ahead."

This person addresses her own personal discomfort and stress due to repressing expression of a part of herself, and also explicitly acknowledges the drag on her performance created by the unnatural behavior.

Below is a second example, taken from a White female MBA student answering the question: "How, if at all, does the fact that you are _____ influence how you interact with other people in general or certain other people at the business school?" Her response: "I make a strong effort not to act too feminine, vulnerable, or less competent."

In this case, the concern about not appearing feminine clearly suggests a change that would not be comfortable or natural for many women. In addition, one might speculate that references to vulnerability and competence reflect concerns about not reinforcing stereotypes about women that may exist in a business school environment.

Complicated Behavioral Choices

A second way in which the culture identity concept helps to explain how majority group members and minority group members may have different experiences in organizations is that for the latter environmental cues often invoke responses from two or more distinctly different cultural backgrounds (biculturalism). For example, in many Asian, Hispanic, and American Indian cultures, great deference is given to older and more experienced members and to those holding formal authority, regardless of whether or not they have the best ideas. In a meeting calling for direct challenges to the ideas of an older manager, members from these cultures are more likely to experience some conflict over whether they should join in the lively critique or refrain out of respect to the managers. This conflict makes day-to-day decisions about how to act or react in a particular situation more complicated for bicultural members of organizations. The problem is compounded by the fact that because of cultural ignorance, majority-group members are often unaware of the conflict and therefore may misinterpret the behavior of other members. For example, silence may be wrongly interpreted as having nothing to say when it is actually a culture-based hesitancy to speak out or criticize under certain conditions. More is said about how specific cultural differences impact on work experiences in Chapter Seven.

Loss of Identity

A third consequence of identifying with a second culture that occurs in many organizations is that individuals feel a part of their identity is sacrificed in order to hold on to or succeed in their jobs. This is a high price for many minority group members. An example may be taken from U.S. West, a leading company in organization change toward multiculturalism during the past decade. According to a company spokesperson, the company employs more American Indians than any other large U.S. firm. One of the major obstacles to employment and retention of some of the most talented Indians is that they are torn between working on the reservation and leaving the reservation to live and work in the Euro-American–dominated society outside. A major concern for American Indians is that living and working outside the reservation inevitably means a loss of the cultural heritage of their tribes. This concern over loss of the Indian identity is a major cause of recruiting and retention problems for the company.

In my interviews during consulting projects on diversity, I often hear a similar concern voiced by White women and non-Whites of various cultural backgrounds in statements like "I have to check my culture at the gate when I come to work here." It is important for organizations that emphasize assimilation of new members to prevailing cultural norms to appreciate the price paid by bicultural members in loss, or repression, of identities they may hold as precious. It is also important for biculturals to understand that for many majority group members, the behavioral insensitivity that is often shown about the impact of culture identity on behavior is due to ignorance and not callous indifference.

Identity Strength

From the discussion of the three previous points, one can easily see that putting norms, values, or work styles that may derive from a minority culture identity aside in favor of those of the majority group is more difficult for high identifiers than for those who have weak identities with the minority group culture. Therefore an organization that socializes new entrants by seeking to assimilate them into the norms of the majority group will be an especially difficult environment for persons who identify strongly with their alternative culture. More is said about the topic of assimilation and other forms of acculturation in Chapter Ten.

Summary

This chapter has discussed group identity as an individual-level factor with important implications for organizational experiences. Types of identities and their relevance to behavior in work settings have been addressed. In learning from this chapter, it is important to acknowledge that all members of organizations, not just members of minority groups, have salient group identities. To the extent that gender affects organizational experience, it affects both men and women. To the extent that racioethnic identity has effects, it affects Whites and non-Whites. If accountants are disdained in favor of engineers, both engineers and accountants are affected. Appreciation of this simple fact, that we all have group identities which affect our own behavior and how others treat us, is a vital step toward building personal competence for working in diverse groups.

The IMCD framework introduced in Chapter One holds that the identity structures of employees are related to individual career outcomes such as organizational identification, career satisfaction, and promotion rates. In general, career outcomes are expected to be less favorable when the identity structure of an employee does not fit well with the organizational context. However, it should be noted that the extent to which identity differences will impact organizational experiences and outcomes will be influenced by intergroup and organizational context factors. If organizations are able to create a working environment that is distinctly more favorable than traditional settings for intergroup relations among people who are physically and culturally different, career effects of identity should be minimized.

Propositions for Discussion

In traditional, assimilationist-oriented organizations (organizations that are not multicultural):

Proposition 4.1: Persons of phenotype groups that are different from the majority group will tend to have less favorable work experiences and career outcomes (for example, satisfaction, compensation, and promotion) than persons from the same phenotype group as the majority group.

Proposition 4.2: Within phenotype groups, there will be an inverse relationship between the amount of physical distinctiveness from the majority group and career outcomes such as satisfaction and promotion rates (for example, when everything else is equal, women with long hair and ultra-feminine dress will fair less well than women with shorter hairstyles and more masculine dress; non-Whites of light skin color will fair better than non-Whites of darker skin color).

Proposition 4.3: Strong identification with the majority culture will enhance one's career outcomes.

Proposition 4.4: Persons with monocultural minority-group identity structures will experience more negative career outcomes than those with other identity structures.

Proposition 4.5: Biculturals will also experience some disadvantages compared to monomajority members but will have better career outcomes than monominority identifiers.

Proposition 4.6: The career outcomes of individuals will tend to be more favorable when their phenotype and culture identities are congruent than when they are incongruent (see high dissonance conditions of Table 4.2).

5

Prejudice and Discrimination

In this chapter we will consider bias in personal attitudes and behavior toward others based on differences in group identity. It should be noted that the personality factor in the IMCD framework will be addressed here as a source of prejudice. *Prejudice* refers to attitudinal bias and means to prejudge something or someone on the basis of some characteristic. In the abstract, prejudice may be manifested as either a positive or negative predisposition toward a person; however, most experts on the subject define it in terms of negative attitudes toward certain groups and their members (Pettigrew, 1982, p. 28). Prejudice may also entail negative emotions or feelings toward a person or group (Bobo, 1988). For our purposes here, we will focus on prejudice based on culture group identities such as gender, physical ability, racioethnicity, nationality, and work status/discipline.

Discrimination refers to behavioral bias toward a person based on the person's group identity. It should be emphasized that this chapter addresses bias at the individual level of analysis. The manifestation of bias at the organization level of analysis, sometimes called institutionalized bias, is addressed in Part Four. Although prejudice and discrimination are conceptually distinct, they are so closely interrelated that they will be considered together here.

Sources of Prejudice

Following Pamela Trottman Reid (1988), prejudice and discrimination will be discussed here as arising from three sources: (1) intrapersonal factors, (2) interpersonal factors, and (3) societal reinforcement factors. As we shall see, these sources are interconnected and overlap to some degree.

Intrapersonal Sources of Prejudice

One concept of the source of prejudice is that certain personality types are more prone to prejudice and discrimination than others. This is the primary basis for the inclusion of personality as a factor in the IMCD framework. Perhaps the most well researched example of this perspective is the authoritarian personality. The authoritarian personality involves a constellation of several traits such as aggressiveness, power orientation, political conservatism, cynicism, and a strong commitment to conform to the prevailing authority structure. The original work on this personality type was done by Adorno, Frenkel-Brunswik, Levinson, and Sanford (1950), and since then more than 1,200 studies have been done on the concept, mostly in Western countries. In one of the most relevant studies to our purpose here, the Dutch researcher Ijzendoorn (1989) has shown that persons with authoritarian personalities are less tolerant toward members of minority groups than other persons.

A closely related body of work on personality as it may influence responses to persons of other culture groups is *tolerance for ambiguity*, which refers to an individual's typical reaction to situations that are ambiguous or difficult to interpret. A person who is intolerant of ambiguity perceives ambiguous situations as threatening, whereas a person who is tolerant of ambiguity does not experience ambiguous situations as threatening and may even view them as desirable (Budner, 1962).

A considerable amount of research has been done on this personality variable, which tends to validate it as a measurable personality component that impacts on human behavior at least in certain situations (see Shaffer, Hendrick, Regula, & Freconna, 1973; Harlow, 1973; Comadena, 1984). For instance, it has been shown that persons who are high producers in brainstorming tasks are more tolerant of ambiguity than low producers (Comadena, 1984).

Although I was unable to locate any study that directly tested ambiguity tolerance and effectiveness in working with diverse workgroups, the logic of connecting these two traits seems straightforward. Cultural differences create uncertainty about human behavior. When the cultural systems driving behavior are unknown, the behavior of others becomes less predictable. According to the ambiguity tolerance concept, a person with high tolerance for ambiguity should not experience cultural difference as threatening and may even prefer it, while a low-tolerance person would feel threatened by the difference and therefore react negatively. Thus people may welcome or resist diversity in workgroups partly as a function of the levels of tolerance for ambiguity in their individual personalities.

While great care is advised in measuring personality, research has demonstrated that marked differences exist among people in their personality orientations toward out-groups. In the context of organization development for managing diversity, this fact is of some importance. To the extent that measurement concerns may be satisfied, organizations may wish to carefully screen-in persons with high-tolerance personalities and screen-out the lower-tolerance types. Also, since personality is to some extent changeable, organizations with diverse workforces may wish to invest in developing people to have antiauthoritarian personalities with high tolerance for ambiguity. In addition to the literature on the authoritarian personality and tolerance for ambiguity, readers interested in constructing measures of intrapersonal sources of prejudice may be helped by the work on measures of racial attitudes (e.g., the feeling thermometer, Campbell, 1971; the racism scales of McConohay, 1982, 1983; and the work on symbolic racism, Sears & Kinder, 1971; Weigel & Howes, 1985), by work on attitudes toward women (e.g., Shaffer, 1985), and by work on measuring attitudes toward persons with disabilities (e.g., Antonak, 1988).

Interpersonal Sources of Prejudice

Here I will deviate from the Trotman-Reid (1988) explanation of the sources of prejudice. The items that she classifies as interpersonal explanations for the existence of prejudice are: (1) socialization, (2) conforming to group norms, and (3) attribution theory. These factors do not work well in my view. Socialization is more of an organization-level factor, while norm conformity is perhaps a consequence but not a source of prejudice. Attribution theory is helpful to understanding some of the more subtle manifestations of prejudice and discrimination in organizations, such as the tendency to give greater weight to effort and ability when attributing positive work performance of men more so than for women (Deaux & Emswiller, 1974). However, it is not clear how it is useful to explain why prejudice and discrimination exist.

In lieu of the Trotman-Reid factors, I will emphasize here three interpersonal sources of prejudice that I view as more to the point: (1) perceived physical attractiveness, (2) communications proficiency, and (3) legacy effects from the history of intergroup relations.

Research has shown that favorable or unfavorable bias toward other people is influenced by their perceived physical attractiveness. In general, physically attractive people are viewed more positively than physically unattractive people (Bull & Rumsey, 1988). For example, it has been shown that attractive people are liked better and are assumed to have more social skills, more intelligence, and more competence (Yuker, 1988; Clifford & Walster, 1973). Further, research has shown that employment decisions are influenced by perceived attractiveness. For example, people with a physically unattractive appearance are viewed as less qualified than applicants with a more attractive appearance (Cash & Kilcullen, 1985). While standards of attractiveness vary, there are also clear culture-based preferences that tend to operate in a given society. Hence, the importance of physical attractiveness in interpersonal relations often leads to rejection of individuals from certain identity groups. Also, deviation from the norms of physical attractiveness has been cited as a causal factor in prejudice against persons with certain kinds of disabilities (Stone, Stone, & Dipboye, in press).

Interpersonal sources of prejudice also occur because of communication barriers that may be related to group identities. For example, negative attitudes toward persons with speech disabilities have been linked with the discomfort and frustration experienced by nondisabled persons in communicating with them (Yuker, 1988). The same response is shown to members of certain nationality or racioethnic groups for whom the primary language of an employer is a second language. In the United States, native English speakers often respond to non-native speakers with whom they experience communication difficulty by avoiding contact or shortening the length of contact with these persons. Often, the non-native speakers also feel the discomfort, both their own and that of majority group members, and respond by isolationist behavior or by seeking the companionship of others with whom they share the same first language.

Historical Legacy as a Source of Prejudice

My central thesis here is that contemporary feelings and attitudes of individuals toward others of a different culture group are very much influenced by the history of intergroup relations of the groups involved. There are two ways in which this sociocultural history effect is manifested. I will refer to them as a micro effect and a macro effect.

The *micro effect* refers to group identity–based experiences that many of us have in our own personal histories that partly shape our attitudes toward other groups. As an example, I can recall as a teenager growing up in a mostly White neighborhood being chased by carloads of angry White boys calling me names and threatening to do me bodily harm because I am Black. Many U.S. Jews recall being excluded from certain social clubs and even employment opportunities because they were Jewish. This was a major factor behind the emphasis among Jews on entrepreneurship and self-sufficient communities in the first half of the nineteenth century in the United States.

It is important to note that in these examples actions and experiences were explicitly tied to group identities and not individuality. This is quite different from overgeneralization based on a negative experience with one member of a group. In other words, individuals often have personal experiences in which the cause of behavior directed toward them is clearly based on their group identity, and where these behaviors are exhibited by groups or large segments of the whole society rather than by isolated individuals. These experiences therefore form a sociocultural background for future interactions among persons of the same group identities.

Because these kinds of personal experiences are numerous and vivid in the memory of most minority group members of our society, it is quite natural for them to acknowledge the impact of group identities on their relationships with majority group members. However, the same is not always true for majority group members (Alderfer, 1982). Peggy McIntosh (1988) has written some provocative material about the tendency of majority group members to be unaware of the effects of majority group identity on life experiences. In essence, she makes the point that the flip side of prejudice against a minority group is privilege for the majority group. Listed below are a few of the forty-six privileges of being White in U.S. social systems that McIntosh lists.

1. Educational materials consistently testify to the existence of my race and its contribution to country.
2. In virtually any geographic area I can find music, foods, and hairdressers who provide service appropriate to my cultural background.
3. I am able to take a job with an affirmative action employer without having co-workers suspect that the job was obtained based on race and not qualifications.
4. Being able to think over options for social, political, or professional activities without having to ask whether a person of my race would be accepted in the situation.

McIntosh's work also addresses what she calls "male privilege," and she makes the point that for most majority group members the positive bias associated with having a majority group cultural identity is invisible.

The above examples on the micro effect of sociocultural history illustrate how group identity–related events in the personal histories of individuals can impact on subsequent cross-group interpersonal relations. It should be emphasized, however, that it is not necessary for individuals to have personally participated in significant events in the history of intergroup relations in order for such events to affect how they think about people with a particular group identity. Significant intergroup historical events in which a given individual did not personally participate (macro effect) is also a source of prejudice. Some examples will be provided to clarify this.

The virtual confiscation of land from American Indians by early White settlers in the U.S. West and the fact that Whites forced the Indians to live on reservations, many of which offered poor opportunity for continuance of their preferred way of life, are major factors underlying negative attitudes toward Whites among Indians (Brown, 1970; Trimble, 1988). This does not mean that all Indians hate Whites. Nor does it mean that any particular interaction between an Indian and a White will suffer from the effects of this legacy of sour relations. But it is important to understand that this history of intergroup relations between Whites and Indians does predispose many Indians to take a dim view of Whites. Such predispositions can, of course, be overcome, but the likelihood of that will be greater if both parties understand how the historical context for their interaction may impact on their behavior.

As a second example, one might consider the chilling effect of the World War II internment camps on relations between Japanese Americans and Whites. For many Japanese Americans this is ancient history, but for a significant number of others it remains an important part of the backdrop for interactions with the majority group (Nakanishi, 1988).

The above examples assist us in making another point about the macro history effect of prejudice. The focus in discussions of prejudice often centers on prejudice by majority group members against members of minority groups. However, the previous examples make it clear that members of minority groups may also hold prejudices against majority group members (minority and majority groups are considered in the generic sense here and not as racioethnic groups). While understanding their history may give us insight into the sources of these prejudices, the fact remains that they become obstacles to effective interpersonal relations in diverse workgroups. Therefore, the investment in eradicating prejudice, including increasing self-awareness about our own attitudes and their sources, must be made by members of all identity groups and not just majority group members.

In summary, the sociocultural history source of prejudice emphasizes that individuals' attitudes and behavior toward people of different culture groups is partly determined by historical legacy effects of group identity–related transactions involving these groups in the past. Since these legacy effects are unique in some respects for any given set of identity groups, work toward improving intercultural relations must involve a combination of generic learnings and attention to the uniqueness of the particular bases of diversity at issue. For example, we can learn a great deal about Anglo-Hispanic relations from a careful study of the history of Black-White race relations in the United States, but there is also much of importance that we would not learn from such a study. A case in point is the story of Gregorio Cortez, a Mexican American of the early 1900s who essentially lost his freedom and ultimately his life largely due to a communication breakdown between himself and Anglo law enforcement officials (despite the presence of an Anglo interpreter of Spanish). This seemingly isolated incident had a profound effect on attitudes of Mexican Americans toward Anglos in the United States, especially in the state of Texas, but is rarely mentioned in historical accounts of race relations focusing on Blacks and Whites.

Societal Reinforcement as a Source of Prejudice

Finally, prejudice is often reinforced by societal forces. One obvious example is that for most of the history of the United States, prejudice based on identity groups was formalized in the laws of the country. Although this form of extreme societal reinforcement of prejudice was substantially reduced by the legal reform following the women's rights and civil rights movements, other forms of societal reinforcement remain. One is the bias in how members of various culture groups are portrayed in the media and in educational materials. For example, research indicates there are three times as many men on television as women and that young people and professional workers are represented in disproportionately high numbers (O'Guinn, Faber, Curias, & Schmitt, 1989). Thus the highly influential medium of television displays a world that is strongly demographically biased. Also, research on how women are portrayed in advertisements has been cited as a source of reinforcement for prejudice and unfavorable stereotypes of women (Goffman, 1979; Key, 1976; Millum, 1975; Boddewyn, 1991). Goffman (1979) identifies six specific ways in which he says the unfavorable portrayal of women consistently occurs in advertisements: (1) relative size (women are always smaller and standing in subordinate positions), (2) feminine touch (women portrayed as fragile and gentle), (3) function ranking (women are of lower authority, less knowledgeable than men), (4) family (bonds are portrayed as mother-daughter, father-son, and traditional gender roles in the home are reinforced), (5) ritualization of subordination (essentially a repeat of items 1 and 3 except more subtle), and (6) licensed withdrawal (the message is that it is okay for women to disengage psychologically from situations, perhaps leaving them to men to resolve). Bias has also been found in media portrayals of older people. For example, studies of the elderly on television indicate that they are often shown as lacking common sense, eccentric, and prone to failure (Arnoff, 1974; Gerbner et al., 1977)

One way in which educational institutions have contributed to the reinforcement of prejudice is by ignoring or portraying members of minority groups in stereotypical ways in textbooks. For example, a comprehensive review by thirty-two American Indian scholars of the portrayal of American Indians in textbooks used in the public schools in the United States found the following (Costo, 1970):

- Most of the books contained material judged to be derogatory to American Indians.
- Adjectives such as "primitive," "filthy," "warlike," and "savage" were often used in describing Indians.
- None of the books was judged to provide a suitable source of knowledge about the history and culture of American Indians.

Although many improvements have been made in this area in the twenty-two years since Costo's work was published, the influence of these materials on the current workforce in organizations should not be overlooked. Moreover, the portrayal of minorities in the media and in educational materials is of vital importance because of the great influence that they have in forming public opinion.

Is Prejudice Declining?

An important yet controversial issue concerning prejudice and discrimination against minority groups is whether or not they are declining over time. Since most of the available research on longitudinal trends in the magnitude of prejudice has focused on racioethnic minority groups, this will necessarily be the focus here. Concerning whether or not racioethnic prejudice is declining, there is evidence supporting both sides. For example, one study of prejudice against African Americans in the United States from 1972 to 1984 concluded that it declined significantly during that period (Firebaugh & Davis, 1988). On the other hand, the Southern Poverty Law Center reports that there were twenty-five bias-related murders in the United States in 1991 compared to eighteen in 1964, and a recent report on the impact of racioethnicity on treatment in the criminal justice system indicates that African Americans receive 49 percent longer sentences on average than Whites for similar crimes. This compares to 28 percent longer sentences ten years ago (*Wall Street Journal,* May, 1992).

Research also shows that the beliefs of majority and minority group members often differ markedly as to how much prejudice and discrimination has declined in recent years. For example, a recent survey of more than two thousand people showed that the African Americans were almost twice as likely as Whites to believe that racism actually increased during the 1980s.

While it is not clear whether prejudice is declining, what is clear is that a considerable amount of prejudice and discrimination continues to occur. Some evidence of this has already been presented. Additional examples abound. For instance, marketing research shows that in 1987 eight of the top ten most popular athletes were African American but only one of the top ten endorsement earners among athletes was an African American (Michael Jordan). Research in the medical field indicates that White men are twice as likely to get needed kidney transplants as African Americans (of either gender) and a third more likely than White women to receive them. Some of the research further shows that the difference in access to organ transplants cannot be fully attributed to socioeconomic factors (Blakeslee, 1989). In a different study focusing on access to housing for Whites and Hispanics in Michigan, trained testers found that thirteen of twenty housing sites discriminated in favor of White applicants, even though qualifications material submitted to the housing authorities was identical for members of the two groups (Cockrel, 1989). Discrimination against Hispanic Americans was also found in a recent study of promotion and other employment practices of the FBI ("Hispanics Harassed," 1988).

It should also be noted that the manifestation of prejudice in the 1990s is not limited to the United States. For example, prejudice against non-Whites is increasingly being witnessed in the cities of Europe ("Germans," 1991).

Subtle Discrimination: The Case of Double Standards of Behavior

Often in contemporary discussions of prejudice and discrimination the term *subtle* is used to refer to negative attitudes and behavior toward out-groups that are typically not overtly expressed. In many cases, the individuals are not aware of their own prejudices and discriminatory behaviors. One way in which subtle discrimination occurs is in different reactions to the same behavior or work style depending upon the identity of the person displaying the behavior.

I will give three examples. Research of attitudes toward persons with disabilities has shown that able-bodied persons are more likely to offer assistance to a person with a disability if the latter displays an unpleasant personality than a pleasant personality. By contrast, when responding to nondisabled persons, the subjects were more willing to offer help to someone who displayed a pleasant or friendly personality (Katz, Hass, & Bailey, 1988). The authors of the research interpret their findings as indicating that some of the subjects became annoyed or angry with the friendly disabled person because such friendliness violated their beliefs about how a disabled person is supposed to act.

A second example comes from Johnson and Johnson's study (1972) of the effects of race and attitude similarity on interpersonal attraction. Although they found that similarity of attitudes was more important than racioethnic identity to attraction, they also found that White men and women liked Whites better than Blacks when attitudes were not similar. In other words, there was an interaction between race and attitudes such that race didn't matter when attitudes were similar but did matter when attitudes were dissimilar.

A final example is the research on the effects of gender and leadership behavior. In one study women and men who had a participative orientation toward leadership were rated equally effective; however, women who favored more authoritarian leader styles were evaluated negatively whereas men displaying authoritarian styles were not (Jago & Vroom, 1982). This same pattern was found in a review of data from sixty-one research studies on gender and leadership by Eagly, Makhijani, and Klonsky (1992). These writers interpret the research as showing that "men may have greater freedom than women to lead in a range of styles without encountering negative reactions" (p. 16).

What these three studies, based on three different types of group identity, have in common is that the identity and the behavior combined (interacted) to influence how others responded to an individual. This research provides empirical evidence that members of minority groups may have a more limited range of acceptable behavior than majority group members. In all three cases, the *combination* of the type of behavior and the identity explained something in the responses of others that neither the behavior nor the identity revealed when examined by itself.

These findings have important implications for organizational practice and research. Members of organizations must be educated to be more aware of these subtle forms of discrimination. Reactions to behavior must be observed with greater insight and sensitivity. Behaviors in ourselves and others must be challenged when there is the appearance of a double standard about accepted behavior. Likewise, researchers must probe beyond simple cross-group comparisons on like behaviors and examine the interactions of style and personality with group identity.

Sexual Harassment

Legal interpretations of Title VII of the Civil Rights Act by the Federal Equal Employment Opportunity Commission and the

courts have classified sexual harassment as a form of sex discrimination. It therefore seems appropriate to address the topic of sexual
harassment in this chapter on prejudice and discrimination. Guidelines of the EEOC and court precedent have established a legal
definition of sexual harassment. It exists (1) when sexual activity is
explicitly or implicitly made a condition of employment; or (2)
when sexual conduct has the effect of interfering with a person's
work performance or creates an intimidating, hostile, or offensive
work environment.

The first form of harassment is generally referred to as "quid
pro quo" harassment and the second as the "hostile environment"
type. Three-fourths of the court cases on sexual harassment have
been based on the hostile environment form alone, with only about
6 percent based on quid pro quo alone and another 19 percent
alleging that both forms were at issue (Hamilton & Veglahn, 1992).
The courts have held that employers are accountable for harassment
behavior of employees when the behavior is known by the employer
or it is reasonable to expect that the employer should have known.
They have also held that employers are liable for harassment by
third-parties such as customers and suppliers (Winokur, 1992).

Frequency of Harassment

The frequency of occurrence of sexual harassment varies greatly by
the type of behavior. For example, Gutek (1985) found that only 3
percent of workers reported that sexual activity was tied to job consequences, while 24 percent reported sexual touching. It is clear that
the incidence of sexual harassment is rather pervasive worldwide. A
recent study by the International Labor Organization found that 21
percent of French women, 58 percent of Dutch women, and 74 percent of British women had experienced sexual harassment at work
(Abrams, 1992). Also, an often-quoted study of federal government
workers in the United States found that 42 percent of women and
15 percent of men reported that they had been sexually harassed at
work in the preceding twenty-four months (Tangri, Burt, & Johnson, 1982).

Although any employee may be a victim of sexual harassment,
research indicates that women are three to four times more likely
than men to be harassed (Terpstra, 1989). When men are harassed,

there is evidence that it is more often by another man than by a woman. For example, a study of harassment in the hotel industry found that 18 percent of men reported being harassed in their current job, but the harasser was a woman in only one case (Eller, 1990).

Contributing Causes

Experts agree that the two primary motivators behind sexual harassment behavior are sex and power. However, many believe that power is a more important factor than sex (Hemming, 1985). A typology of causes that readers should find useful is offered by Stringer, Remick, Salisbury, and Ginorio (1990). They have identified the following seven causal factors or motivations:

1. Abuse of power to obtain sexual favor
2. Sex used to gain power
3. Power used to decrease the power of a victim by reference to her or his sexuality and gender identity
4. Reaction to a personal crisis
5. Sexual attraction gone wrong
6. Genuine deviance
7. Result of confusion in dealing with new gender roles

The first case is the well-recognized scenario of a superior using organizational/personal stature to intimidate a subordinate into granting sexual favors or attention. This is a clear form of quid pro quo harassment. Power is central because the harasser by virtue of formal position has influence over both organizational rewards and punishments. The importance of this motive is indicated by the fact that two-thirds of sexual harassment complaints are filed against an immediate supervisor or someone in a higher management position of the firm (Sandroff, 1988).

The second case is also quid pro quo and concerns people who volunteer sexual favors as a career success strategy. Such behavior is as inappropriate as the abuse-of-power form but differs from it in that the victim can more easily reject the advances, since there is no career threat in doing so.

The third form typically involves the use of gender stereotypes and sexual inuendo by men to undermine the position of women in workgroups. The intent is not so much to elicit a sexual relationship as to de-legitimize the victim. This form is most common with women in traditionally male jobs and may also be applicable to prejudice against gays and lesbians. For a more extensive discussion of this motive for sexual harassment see Farley (1978).

Some people may react to a personal crisis such as divorce or money problems by inappropriately seeking sexual attention. Here the underlying motive may be to restore a sense of self-worth or attractiveness.

Sexual attraction gone wrong is typically a situation in which one party has lost interest in a previously mutual consent relationship. The jilted party may respond by harassing the former romantic partner. The legal interpretation of harassment is that the behavior must be "unwelcomed." These situations are difficult because a shift in response toward similar behaviors may occur, turning previously welcomed actions into unwelcomed behavior. Nevertheless, it seems clear that sexual advances will be interpreted as harassment if they continue *after* the person has expressed displeasure at the behavior.

Some harassment is undoubtedly due to psychological or substance abuse disorders, including alcoholism. Because the effect of alcohol on self-control is detrimental, one means of curtailing harassment behavior is for organizations to place strict limitations on its use in company-sponsored activities.

Finally, Stringer et al. (1990) suggest that some individuals act inappropriately out of confusion created by having to relate to the opposite gender in new roles in the workplace. For example, executives and workers in occupations that traditionally have been gender-segregated, who are accustomed to relating to the opposite gender mainly in a familial and social context, may have greater than average difficulty in making the transition to professional collegial relationships. Also, men are accustomed to viewing young single women primarily as dating partners and thus at work they may inappropriately attempt to sexualize relationships. Research supporting this conclusion indicates that young single women are especially likely to be victims of harassment (Terpstra, 1989).

Related to this last point, some experts have identified the "spill-over" of societal gender roles into the workplace as a primary contributor to sexual harassment behavior (Gutek & Cohen, 1987). These writers argue that the dominance of men and subordination of women is embedded in the social structure of many nations of the world and that sexual harassment is one result of the playing out of these societal gender roles in the organizational arena. They argue further that the occurrence of gender role spillover is greatly exacerbated by skewed gender composition in workgroups. Indeed, they present some empirical evidence that gender role spillover does not occur in gender-balanced workgroups.

Remedies for Sexual Harassment

It seems clear that both organizations and individuals bear responsibility for the elimination of sexual harassment in the workplace. On an individual level, two actions warrant special emphasis: (1) express a firm rejection of harassing behavior; and (2) if the harassing behavior cannot be resolved by expressing an objection to it, report it to internal or, if necessary, external authorities. Many behaviors that may be interpreted as harassment are simply insensitive remarks or actions by people who need to be educated. An important opportunity to provide that education rests with the victims. A simple, emphatic no or notification that the behavior is offensive will solve many potential harassment problems. Nevertheless, persistent behavior should not be ignored. Research indicates that ignoring the behavior usually does not solve the problem. Indeed, research suggests that in 75 percent of cases where harassment is ignored, it eventually worsens (Hemming, 1985). At the same time, there is evidence that 95 percent of all persons who experience or observe harassment are reluctant to complain due to fear of retaliation and loss of privacy (Sandroff, 1988).

Individual employees should assume some responsibility for eliminating harassment. Steps that individuals should take include keeping a diary and talking to others who may have observed harassing behavior or may later be in a position to witness such behavior.

Organizational leaders must also address this challenge. Steps that organizations should take include:

- Training for all employees
- A written policy on sexual harassment with guidelines as to what behaviors may be considered harassment
- A procedure for filing complaints that protects the confidentiality of the grievant to the greatest extent possible
- Creation of a position or committee for employees to contact for information or to file a complaint

Concerning training, it is important to design and deliver the training in an impactful way. In one organization in which I recently worked, nearly one in three managerial and professional workers in a sample of three hundred reported that they had not received training despite the fact that the organization had recently offered a "mandatory" training course on harassment. Furthermore, survey data indicate that nearly three-fourths of the companies that have used training have limited it to management employees. This seems questionable in view of the fact that nearly a third of harassers are not superiors (Sandroff, 1988). According to some estimates, an initial training program for a large company can be provided for about $200,000 (Sandroff, 1988).

Regarding the use of grievance committees or omsbudspersons, it is noteworthy that the courts have formally recognized differences between women and men in how they view sexual harassment. In the case of *Ellison* v. *Brady,* the U.S. Court of Appeals for the Ninth Circuit held that the traditional interpretation of the law, based on the premise that the "reasonable person standard" is gender-neutral, is flawed. The court found that "the traditional model tends to be male-biased and tends to systematically ignore the experiences of women" (Simon, 1991, p. 71). This finding highlights the criticalness of adequate female representation on all grievance boards that will address sexual harassment issues in organizations.

Impact of Prejudice on Career
Outcomes in Organizations

As this chapter has indicated, much of the available theory and research on prejudice and discrimination have focused on the society at large rather than on organizations. Since organizations take their members from the broader society, this fact does not mean that the research is not useful. Nevertheless, I would like to focus more specifically in this last segment on implications of prejudice for employment experiences.

I begin with the observation that a majority of executives apparently believe that prejudice and discrimination *do* influence career outcomes in organizations. For example, a recent study by the consulting group Catalyst of 241 U.S. CEOs found that 80 percent believed there are identifiable gender-related barriers to the success of women in organizations and 81 percent of that group stated that the principal barriers are stereotyping and preconceptions about women (Fierman, 1990). This is consistent with my own recent research in which in-depth interviews with 50 middle and senior managers in a division of a Fortune 500 firm revealed that 80 percent believed that experiences at work were influenced by group identities such as racioethnicity and gender.

The specific ways in which prejudice might impact career experience and success are numerous, but I will focus here on four examples: (1) the effect on interpersonal trust, (2) the effect on individual motivation and performance improvement, (3) self-fulfilling prophesy effects, and (4) the effects of sexual harassment.

Effect of Prejudice on Trust

Interpersonal trust is an important ingredient of effective human relations and performance in organizations. Although many factors influence trust, the existence of prejudice and discrimination takes a heavy toll. Recalling the examples given in our discussion of the sources of prejudice, one can easily understand why trust is harder to build across culture groups than it is within them. For example, the micro and macro sociocultural history of relations between Anglo Americans and African Americans has certainly created a trust barrier to successful interaction and communications.

The following quotation, taken from an African American female's comments about her experiences working in all-Black versus racioethnically mixed project groups, provides an example of this: "I had the luck to be in an all-Black female group once. I felt that cohesiveness was definitely enhanced. I felt much more free to express my opinions and ideas off the cuff without having done a lot of internal pre-screening or self-censorship which I tend to do in order to not seem too radical in other groups. In same race groups of mixed sexes, I again tend to feel free to express myself more than in majority (White) groups, male or female." This person is clearly expressing behavioral differences (between the same and mixed racioethnicity groups) that are related to her own racioethnic identity and that represent obstacles to effectiveness in diverse groups. Because majority group members are often unaware that this kind of self-censorship is occurring, the losses to the group generally go unnoticed.

Effect on Motivation

One of the most difficult problems that the existence of prejudice and discrimination presents for members of minority groups is what I term *attribution uncertainty*. This refers to the added complexity of determining the cause of events and life experiences. For members of groups that have been victims of prejudice and discrimination, there is always the problem of whether or not a particular experience or result is due to discrimination or to other factors. We can readily see the magnitude of this problem by considering two crucial organizational processes: processing feedback and employee motivation.

Processing Feedback. When negative feedback is received on performance results, the typical response is to accept it at face value and strive to improve in that area. To the extent that prejudice is the cause, however, this "normal" method of processing feedback breaks down. When a person believes that the feedback received is a mixture of prejudice and realistic performance evaluation, it is difficult to sort out what to change and what not to change. This kind of interpretive confusion is one of the most vexing problems that minorities have to deal with in organizations.

One strategy widely cited for dealing with this problem is to develop such strong credentials for ability that the impact of prejudice would be eliminated and therefore would no longer have to be considered. Although this approach is to be recommended, members of minority groups inevitably find that no matter how good their credentials or past success, the prospect of identity group discrimination cannot be ruled out. The dilemma is summarized well by the renown entertainer Sammy Davis, Jr.: "Racism had a profound effect on me. In one respect it was good for me because I used it as a motivating force. But it was also negative, because it made me get too deeply involved in trying to play a game that's impossible to play . . . pretending that if you get fame or if you become well known, it will eradicate the prejudice. Because there's no such eradication" (*Ann Arbor News*, May 20, 1990).

Employee Motivation. One of the most popular and heavily re searched theories of employee motivation is the expectancy theory (Vroom, 1964; Lawler, 1973). This theory holds that the motivation to perform on a job is a function of three factors: (1) the perceived probability that a given effort level will produce the desired performance level, (2) the belief that achieving a prescribed performance level will result in certain outcomes (e.g., a raise or promotion), and (3) the value placed on the outcomes in the personal need structure of the individual.

If we examine the implications of prejudice and discrimination in the context of this theory, problems are evident in factors 1 and 2. To the extent that group-based discrimination exists, individuals may not believe that performance ratings will adequately reflect effort and therefore motivation may suffer. Even if the evaluation of performance is not influenced by group identities, motivation will still be hampered if employees believe that outcomes are not strictly performance-based but somewhat dependent on group identity prejudice. The importance of perceptions in this regard was illustrated in some recent data I collected in a Fortune 500 company in which women had significantly lower responses than men on a measure of perceived fairness in the performance evaluation process despite the fact that actual performance ratings of women (according to personnel records) were higher than for men in the most recent rating period. If the impact of prejudice on the evaluation process is perceived as severe, the lower expectancy probabilities may collectively account for a large motivational loss.

Self-Fulfilling Prophesy

While the issues of trust and motivation discussed above are vitally important, prejudice may do its greatest damage to organizational performance by means of the self-fulfilling prophesy (SFP) phenomenon. The term itself refers to a sequence of events in which expectations of a result induce behavior that increases the likelihood of the result occurring (Merton, 1948; Eden, 1990). Research on SFP has shown that the performance of individuals is indirectly influenced by the expectations of those in positions of influence or authority. For example, managers in organizations and teachers in schools have been found to inadvertently change their behavior toward employees or students as a consequence of their preconceived ideas about the ability of the individuals.

One of the most dramatic examples of the operation of prejudice with SFP implications occurred in the experiments of Jane Elliot with schoolchildren as described in the classic book and film *A Class Divided*. Children were divided into blue-eyed and brown-eyed groups, and the "out-group" wore a collar to make a clearly visible identification. The teacher (Elliot) then told the children that the brown-eyed out-group was inferior and reinforced this by various actions such as the distribution of certain privileges based on eye color. On the second day, the roles were reversed with the blue-eyed children placed in the "inferior" group. The "superior" group proceeded to discriminate against the "inferiors," calling them names and otherwise ostracizing them. One of the most interesting aspects of the experiment, however, was that the classroom performance of the so-called inferior group declined markedly after just a few hours of the discriminatory treatment. Test scores of the students went up on the day they were in the advantaged group and down on the day the same students were in the disadvantaged group. The change in behavior of the teacher and classmates had an immediate impact on the performance of the students.

The magnitude of the SFP effect on performance can be staggering. Indeed, research has shown that managers unwittingly implement different leadership behaviors toward subordinates in accordance with their expectations (Eden & Shani, 1982). In one experiment, trainees in a command course of the Israeli Defense Forces were identified to instructors as having either high, regular, or unknown command potential. In reality, the trainees were randomly assigned to the three levels. Results indicated that the expectancy induced by the identifications potentially accounted for 73 percent of differences among trainees in objective measures of performance in the course. In addition, the trainees identified as having high aptitude reported higher satisfaction and more motivation to continue to the next course of instruction (Eden & Shani, 1982).

Some experts have suggested that leader expectations are communicated to subordinates in four specific ways: (1) the overall climate set (favorable tone, positive responses, and so on), (2) amount of input given (information relevant to getting the job done), (3) amount of feedback given, and (4) amount of output (or whether goals are challenging and confidence is shown in the individual's ability to achieve high results) (Rosenthal, 1974).

It is important to note that the SFP factor can operate negatively as well as positively. In the context of workforce diversity, prejudice in favor of in-group members and against out-group members may manifest itself as lower expectations for members of minority groups. In fact, a specific case of the SFP, labeled the "Golem effect," has been identified in which members of minority groups underachieve in schools and at work because they are expected to do poorly by teachers and supervisors (Eden, 1990).

When we consider the SFP phenomenon in the context of a social system in which identity-group prejudice operates, the potential for substantial adverse effects on the performance of minority group members of organizations is quite apparent.

Effects of Sexual Harassment

Finally, several specific effects of sexual harassment on work outcomes may be noted. First, in terms of the affective outcomes of the IMCD model, research has shown that harassment takes a severe personal toll in terms of stress and psychological damage. Some of the specific effects along this line include anxiety, tension, depression, and physical and mental illness (Hadjifortiou, 1983). These affective outcomes translate into first-order organizational performance measures, as is easily demonstrated by data on losses in productivity, turnover, and absenteeism. For example, the economic cost of sexual harassment to the typical Fortune 500 company due to these outcomes has been estimated at $6.7 million per year (Sandroff, 1988). These numbers may be understatements in view of evidence that an amazing 10 percent of American women and 6 percent of German women report they have quit at least one job because of sexual harassment (Gutek, Cohen, & Konrad, 1990; Abrams, 1992).

Summary

This chapter has examined prejudice and discrimination and offered examples of how they are manifested in organizations, including several examples of subtle forms of discrimination. Although it is difficult to prove that any given event or experience in the workplace is due to identity group discrimination, there is ample empirical evidence that discrimination continues to occur. The discussion of the impact of prejudice on career outcomes makes it clear how organizational performance is directly and indirectly hampered by personal prejudices, especially among those in managerial jobs. As readers use the information of this chapter, it is hoped that they will use it not to focus blame but rather to build self-awareness and understanding. This insight into personal attitudes and behaviors is a critical part of developing multicultural organizations.

Propositions for Discussion

In conclusion, based on the theory, research, and discussion presented in this chapter, the following summary propositions are offered:

Proposition 5.1:   Prejudice and discrimination based on culture group identity continue to be manifested in many societies of the world and in their organizations.

Proposition 5.2: Personality traits such as authoritarianism and tolerance for ambiguity will partly determine levels of effectiveness in working in and managing culturally diverse workgroups.

Proposition 5.3: Group identity–related prejudice among employees will hinder effective interpersonal relations and ultimately organizational performance.

Proposition 5.4: Discrimination among persons in positions of power toward a particular identity group will have an adverse effect on the career outcomes of members of that group.

Proposition 5.5: The sociocultural history of intergroup relations among groups at personal, organizational, and societal levels will have an impact on contemporary relationships between members of those groups.

Proposition 5.6: Intergroup attitudes including prejudice are heavily influenced by societal forces such as portrayals of culture groups in the media and in educational materials.

Proposition 5.7: Prejudice is often manifested in responses based on the interaction of behavior and group identity. This often means that members of minority groups must act within a more restricted range of acceptable behavior in performing their jobs.

6

Stereotyping

Stereotyping is a perceptual and cognitive process in which specific behavioral traits are ascribed to individuals on the basis of their apparent membership in a group. Although closely related to prejudice, especially in its effects, we may distinguish between the two terms. *Stereotyping* is a process by which individuals are viewed as members of groups and the information that we have stored in our minds about the group is ascribed to the individual. Thus while the emphasis in prejudice is on attitudes and emotional reactions to people, the emphasis here is on processes of group identity categorization and on the assumed traits of these categories. One way in which the distinction becomes meaningful is that while prejudice does not necessarily decrease (and may even increase) with increased time of contact, the use of stereotypes is normally expected to decline as the duration or closeness of association lengthens (Eagly, 1983).

Stereotyping is widely practiced as a means of simplifying the world and making perceptual and cognitive processes more efficient (Allport, 1954). Research has demonstrated that stereotyping is a pervasive human tendency and that in socially diverse settings, people routinely process personal information through mental filters based on social categories (Taylor, Fiske, Etcoff, & Ruderman, 1978). Extensive research has shown that stereotyping impacts interpersonal relations based on gender (Hoffman & Hurst, 1990), age (Cleveland & Landy, 1983; Rosen & Jerdee, 1976), physical ability (Lester & Caudill, 1987), and racioethnicity and nationality (Allport, 1954; Lobel, 1988). There is even evidence that stereotypes of overweight people exist and that such stereotypes do impact their career opportunities (Everett, 1990).

Stereotyping appears to be a worldwide phenomenon. As just one example of the pervasiveness of stereotyping worldwide, consider a recent study about gender stereotypes in which eight-year-old children in twenty-three countries were read stories and then asked to identify the gender of the characters based on the traits displayed in the story. Table 6.1 lists the set of traits that were identified as female and male by at least 60 percent of the children in twenty or more of the twenty-three countries (Best, 1985).

Why Do People Stereotype?

Several explanations have been offered for the widespread use of stereotyping. Already mentioned is the utility of stereotyping for visual and mental efficiency. The advantages and drawbacks of stereotyping as a tool for simplification of environmental stimuli may be illustrated with the following example of buying a dog. Assume you are looking for a dog for your child and that one of your concerns is to select a dog with a gentle, congenial disposition—one that is unlikely to bite even when provoked. You are aware that some breeds of dogs, such as the collie, have a reputation for being good with children. Therefore you focus your search on collies. In doing so, you are making your search easier by narrowing it to one breed. You might search the newspapers and call for prices and other information only when you see collies listed. This would potentially cut down considerably on your search time. Further, to

Table 6.1 An International Study of Gender Stereotypes.

Female Traits	Male Traits
Weak	Strong
Soft-hearted	Cruel
Meek	Aggressive
Gentle	Loud
Appreciative	Coarse
Emotional	Independent
Excitable	Boastful
	Severe

Source: Adapted from Best, 1985.

the extent that the reputation for gentleness is accurate, the probability of finding the type of dog you want is indeed greater if you limit your search in this manner. Thus we can see the potential advantages of holding and acting on your stereotype about collies.

On the other hand, two critical pitfalls must be acknowledged in the use of stereotypes as a mental efficiency tool. First, it is vitally important that your assumptions about the characteristics of the group are accurate. In the dog illustration, it would be good to ask oneself, where did the idea that collies are good with children come from? Is it based on a truly systematic study of the breeds of dogs or on relatively untested impressions that may have been formed by folklore or the media? One example of an untested impression that is widely believed is that older workers have lower capacity to learn new methods and jobs than younger workers. In fact, the data indicate that learning capacity generally does not show any noticeable decline before the age of seventy (Kauffman, 1987).

As a second example, employers have traditionally resisted hiring persons with disabilities partly because of the belief that they pose safety risks, increase health-care costs, and have higher absence and lower productive capacity than nondisabled workers. However, an analysis of data shows that these stereotypical assumptions are unfounded (Stone, Stone, & Dipboye, in press). Specifically, an extensive review of ninety empirical studies has revealed that compared to other employees, disabled employees (1) do not have higher turnover and absence rates or less job-assignment flexibility, but (2) do have better safety records (Greenwood & Johnson, 1987). Moreover, a study by Dupont of their 1,452 workers with disabilities ranging from epilepsy to blindness revealed that 91 percent of the workers were rated as average or above average on overall job performance. As for health care costs, experts say that hiring disabled persons will not normally increase them and may, due to the better safety record and various forms of incentives for hiring, actually improve overall costs.

A second pitfall of stereotyping is the assumption that any particular member of a group will be characteristic of the group. Again, using the dog analogy, if the stereotype of collies is used in isolation, we may select a dog that does not meet our needs at all, or may overlook an even more ideal dog of another breed.

The preceding discussion highlights two crucial distinctions that should be made between stereotyping behavior and acknowledging group difference in a "valuing diversity" context. Unlike stereotyping, the latter (1) bases beliefs about characteristics of culture groups on systematic study of reliable sources of data, and (2) acknowledges that intragroup variation exists. A third equally important difference is that contrary to valuing diversity, stereotypes represent not merely an acknowledgement of differences but also an evaluation of them. Thus many common stereotypes are words or phrases with built-in negative connotations. For example, Table 6.2 lists stereotypes elicited from one of my recent MBA classes when a culturally diverse group of twenty-one students was asked to post labels containing stereotypes they were aware of. The identity groups represented in the table are those represented in the class.

As Table 6.2 indicates, a majority of the descriptors listed as stereotypes familiar to the students are negative for all groups. Interestingly, this includes White men. It is not clear whether this result occurred because the word *stereotype* itself was interpeted by the students as meaning negative descriptors or simply because a majority of known stereotypes are negative. The point is that in most cases stereotyping means not only acknowledging differences of other groups but also judging them as somehow inferior or undesirable. One of the challenges for organization and individual change in diverse organizations is therefore to create the ability to acknowledge differences in positive or neutral terms.

Beyond the perceptual efficiency rationale, several other explanations for stereotyping have been offered. Jussim, Coleman, and Lerch (1987) discuss three alternative explanations for stereotyping: (1) complexity-extremity theory, (2) assumed characteristics theory, and (3) expectancy violation theory. Complexity-extremity theory holds that stereotypes result from the differences in levels of contact individuals have with members of their own in-group compared to members of various out-groups. Since contact with out-group members is low, there is a tendency to evaluate them along fewer dimensions (low-complexity evaluation), which in turn leads to more extreme evaluations of out-group members as either very favorable or very unfavorable. As evidence of this perspective, the authors cite research showing that White evaluations of Blacks in-

Table 6.2. Sterotypes of Various Groups.

Jews	Blacks	White Men	White Women	Japanese Men	French Men	East Indian Women
Rich	Athletes	Responsible for all of society's ills	Bad at math and science	Meticulous	Good lovers	Analytical
Miserly	Underqualified	Competitive	Emphatic	Studious	Frank	Passive
All support Israel	Good dancers	Intelligent	Easy	Humble	Dry-humored	Submissive
Money-grubbing	Greedy (food)	Insecure	Passive	Workaholics	Romantic	Alway wear saris
Penny-pinchers	Uneducated	Racist	Money-hungry	Dedicated	Harass women	Very feminine
Well-educated	Expressive in communication	Power-hungry	Ruining the traditional American family	Polite	Egotistical	Religious
Complainers		Manipulative		Family-oriented	Drink wine all the time	Quiet
Stingy	Poor	Insensitive	Competitive	Highly intelligent	Suave	Overachieving
Cheap	Militant	Aggressive	Change their minds frequently	Racist	Sexy	Subservient to men
Unified	Untrustworthy	Ignorant		Anti-American	Do not shower much	Class-oriented
Family-oriented	Volatile	Clannish	Talkative	Single-minded		Mothering type
Good at business	Low IQs	Arrogant	Timid	Business-oriented	Superior attitude	Tradition
Run New York City	Clannish	Not really perceptive	Selfish	Nationalistic	Hate Americans	Uneducated
Self-centered	Hate Whites		Nasty	Disciplined	Arrogant	Not ambitious
Status-conscious	Lazy	Domineering	Ambitious	Unemotional	Extremely eccentric	Too concerned with social status
Hard to get in social circle	Laid back	Like to brag	Individual-oriented	Demanding	Individualistic	
Racist	Defensive	Like beer	Gullible	Sexist	Unfaithful	
Snobbish	No Ambition	Wear Dockers	Trusting	Drink a lot, especially scotch	Proud of country	
Hates other religions	Unmotivated	Not literate	Flaky	Productive		
Take care of their own	Have lots of friends	Cold	Shallow	Power-hungry		
	Content with life	Handed everything on a silver platter	Non-aggressive	Vindictive, hold grudges		
Manipulative	Love talking	Oppressive	Do not care about careers	Good at math and science		
Nonrythmic	Oversexed	Greedy		Secretly envious of American life style		
Girls are JAPs—Jewish American Princesses	Violent	Always trying to keep non-Whites down		Defer to authority		
	Very emotional			Cameras		
Separatists	Warm	Out for themselves				
Cliquish	On welfare	Elitist				
Too sensitive to group criticism	Funny	Dishonest				
	Spendthrifts, too much concern about clothes	Backstabbers				
		Opportunistic				

volve fewer dimensions and are more extreme than their evaluations of individual Whites (Linville & Jones, 1980).

Assumed characteristics theory essentially states that stereotypes occur as a way to fill in information voids about people. According to this perspective, in the absence of information to the contrary, people generally assume that others of dissimilar group identities possess less favorable traits. Accordingly, the tendency to stereotype is correctable by providing information. Some research showing that bias against out-group members declines when a person believes they hold values and behavioral orientations similar to those of the in-group is offered in support of this theory. Implicit here is that stereotyping will only be reduced if the groups are culturally similar. In culturally dissimilar groups, which is the essence of cultural diversity, we would expect stereotyping to continue and perhaps even increase as more knowledge about other groups is gained.

Expectancy violation theory suggests that stereotyping occurs as an overreaction to behaviors that do not match our expectations. For example, when a member of an identity group performs at a higher level than we expect, we may react with a positive stereotype, whereas no stereotype would be applied if the same behavior came from members of a group expected to show the behavior. It is conceivable that this perspective might be applicable to the generally positive stereotypes that have been applied to Asian Americans (Sue & Kitano, 1973).

Impact of Stereotypes on Career Outcomes

It seems almost tautological to say that stereotyping will adversely affect the organizational career experience of members of the target groups. I will comment here on several specific ways in which this impact on careers occurs.

Organizational Entry

Stereotypes may hinder members of certain identity groups who wish to be hired for certain jobs. For example, during an interview with a partner of a Kansas law firm, a Black applicant was told that the recruiter was reluctant to hire him because "he had never seen a Black patent attorney" (*Wall Street Journal,* Feb. 2, 1989). Also, stereotypes have been cited as obstacles to hiring overweight people (Everett, 1990) and, as mentioned before, to hiring persons with disabilities (Lester & Caudill, 1987; Schweltzer & Deely, 1982; McCarthy, 1985).

Shaw (1977) presents a discussion and some data indicating circumstances under which gender stereotypes have a negative impact in the selection of applicants for scientific and engineering jobs. Since we have established that stereotyping is widely practiced, it is logical to assume that many hiring decisions are impacted by preconceived notions about the skills and competencies of particular groups. As indicated in the above examples, the impact of stereotyping in the recruitment process is seen not only in rejected applicants but also in the restrictions on the types of jobs that an individual might be considered for. This subject will be addressed further in the next section.

Postentry Effects of Stereotyping

Gregory's discussion (1990) of the impact of gender on organizational experiences includes a list of eight specific ways that stereotypes impact postentry career experience:

1. Role status incongruence
2. Role conflict
3. Career mobility
4. Evaluation
5. Power differences
6. Differences in training and development
7. Feedback differences
8. Job segregation

I will briefly comment on each of these.

Role Status Incongruence. Social status is given a great deal of importance in many nations of the world, including Japan, most of Europe, and the United States. In organizations, status is often attached to formal organizational roles such as the level of authority in a chain of command. As a result of stereotyping, group identities such as gender, racioethnicity, and age are utilized as "diffuse status characteristics." This means they are attributes that form the basis for beliefs about a person's value and competence over a wide range of social situations (Eagly, 1983). Thus, in much of the world, men of the majority racioethnic group are accorded higher social status than women and minority group men in matters relating to business and economics. Older people are also granted a higher status than younger people in many parts of the world. The existence of multiple sources of status sets up the potential for situations of status incongruence. For example, the placement of women, who stereotypically have lower status than men in society, in senior management positions creates a status incongruence in the minds of many. Because stereotyping is often done unconsciously, people are usually unaware that this kind of mental inconsistency is influencing their thinking and possibly their interaction with other people. Therefore, stereotypes create role-incongruence barriers that members of particular identity groups must overcome in order to be accepted in leadership roles in organizations.

One of the ways that this is manifested, according to working women with whom I have talked, is that men often try to relate to them as if they were their wives or daughters instead of as professional colleagues.

Role Conflict. A different kind of conflict occurs when roles that a person is expected to perform outside of work conflict with the expectations on the job. The most obvious example of this is women with young children who are also engaged in managerial and professional career roles in which long hours, extensive travel, and geographic mobility are expected. Despite the changes of recent years, women continue to bear the responsibility for the majority of child care and home care (Powell, 1988). As a result, job demands for long hours and extensive travel create severe role conflicts for many people. The association of women with child rearing and homemaking is part of the traditional group identity of women in most nations of the world. As a result, this type of role conflict is prevalent. Two facts make it is especially severe in the United States.

First, the United States is among the leaders in the world in participation rates of women in the workforce (Johnston, 1991), and, second, U.S. firms trail many other nations of the world in providing childcare and other kinds of family support to workers.

Career Mobility. An example of the potential impact of stereotypes on career mobility has already been given in the earlier discussion of the relative absence of Asian Americans from leadership positions in U.S. organizations. The upward mobility of Asians has sometimes been limited by stereotypes that they are technical wizards with little interest and ability in management (Sue, Zane, & Sue, 1985; Khoo, 1988). Stereotypes are also partly to blame for the well-documented "glass ceiling" effect for women in majority-male organizations (Morrison, White, & VanVelsor, 1987). One of the ways that this glass ceiling is perpetuated is by defining leadership competence as consisting mostly of masculine traits (Powell, 1988). Since the job of manager itself is stereotyped in predominantly male terms, it is little wonder that women have a harder time advancing in organizations. This is discussed further in Chapter Thirteen.

Evaluation. One of the most revealing research examples on how stereotypes impact the evaluation of performance in organizations is that done on performance attributions. Rather than focusing on performance ratings themselves, this research addresses the assumed causes of attained performance levels. The reason that causes are important is that research has shown that a given performance level is more likely to yield a good promotion rating if it is assumed to result from ability and effort rather than more fortuitous factors like luck or sponsorship (Green & Mitchell, 1979; Heilman & Guzzo, 1978). Therefore some have reasoned that due to preconceptions about ability and effort, performance attributions may be different for minority group and majority group members. Empirical research has shown that performance attributions are indeed influenced by both gender and racioethnic identities of workers. For example, it has been found that successful performance by women on tasks traditionally done by men was attributed to luck, whereas for men it was attributed more to ability (Deaux & Emswiller, 1974; Cash, Gillen, & Burns, 1977). Likewise, a recent study conducted in three large U.S. firms revealed that the performance of Black managers was less likely to be attributed to ability and effort and more likely to be attributed to help from others than the performance of White managers (Greenhaus & Parasuraman, in press).

This work on performance attributions is extremely useful in helping expose one of the most subtle ways in which stereotypes influence career experiences and outcomes of people in organizations. It clearly shows that culture group identities may impact performance evaluation even when the ratings themselves do not differ by group. Additional examples involving the impact of group identity on performance ratings are given in Chapter Thirteen.

Power Differences. Stereotypes may impact the distribution of power in organizations for essentially the same reasons that were given in the discussion of role-status incongruence. Preconceptions about the ability or suitability of persons of certain culture groups to lead may limit their opportunity to serve in positions of high authority. For the same reason, it may be difficult for members of minority groups in organizations to exert influence over decision processes in organizations even among colleagues. For example, observers have noted a pattern in group meetings in which ideas offered by non-majority-group members get less response than ideas from majority group members (*Managing Diversity*, 1987). Research has also shown that women are interrupted more frequently than men (Tannen, 1990). This problem of stereotyping is not limited to majority group members. For instance, in a recent focus group meeting I conducted with six randomly selected entry-level women at a manufacturing plant, all six stated that men made better supervisors than women and that they preferred to report to a man. One explained this by saying that women become too emotional and this interferes with the job. Another said that women are more prone to favoritism in making decisions.

Differences in Training and Development. Stereotyping may also impact career development opportunities in organizations. The issue of upward mobility has already been mentioned. Another example of this is reluctance to retrain older workers due to a belief that they lack the capacity or the will to learn new techniques or technologies. For example, a recent research study shows that training is less likely to be recommended for older workers who have performance problems than for younger workers with the identical problems (Dietrick & Dobbins, 1991).

A final example is that negative stereotypes of persons with disabilities have been cited as a major impediment to their training and development opportunities (Stace, 1987). Experts have also noted the tendency for persons with disabilities to engage in self-limiting behaviors such as unecessarily narrow definitions of viable career options (Curnow, 1989). In order to address this limitation, career counselors need to encourage broader definitions of career goals among the disabled and to seek organizational support for necessary training accommodations to include disabled persons. For example, for years IBM has sponsored programs to train deaf persons for jobs as computer programmers (Schein, 1975).

Feedback Effects. Performance feedback is critical for all workers as a basis for planning self-improvement. Unfortunately, many managers are not skillful in giving performance feedback, especially when there are problems with performance. This general problem may be exacerbated by group stereotypes. For example, women (Best, 1985) and persons with disabilities (McCarthy, 1985) are often stereotyped as fragile and overly emotional. Because of these stereotypes, managers may withhold negative performance feedback or give them less complete feedback than they give to majority group employees with the same development needs. When this occurs, the individuals involved have an information disadvantage that may contribute to continued sub-par performance. A vicious cycle sometimes occurs when the continued substandard performance becomes a reinforcement for doubts about the ability of women or persons with disabilities to work at the standard set for men and the nondisabled.

Job Segregation. Perhaps the greatest impact of stereotypes on career experiences is the tendency for members of certain culture groups to be segregated into certain job categories in organizations. Some have argued that occupational segregation related to identity group is so prevalent in U.S. society that there is a castelike dual labor market in which women and non-White men work disproportionately in occupations and industries with lower prestige, status, and compensation. Within organizations they typically work in jobs and departments that are less influential, with lower status than White men (Johnson, 1987; Buono & Kamm, 1983).

Some progress has been made in terms of group identity-related job segregation in recent years. For example, the percentage of women in management and professional jobs has increased from around 20 percent in 1972 to between 33 and 40 percent, depending on the source of information, today. Nevertheless, overall levels of job segregation based on group identities like gender and racioethnicity remain extremely high. A recent study of gender segregation in a diverse sample of California jobs concluded: "In the few instances in which men and women perform similar work roles, the jobs are typically done in distinct organizational settings, and when an enterprise employs both sexes in the same occupation, men and women are usually assigned different job titles. The findings are consistent with the theory of statistical discrimination, which posits that employers reserve some jobs for men and others for women" (Bielby & Baron, 1986, p. 759). The reference to "statistical discrimination" is a direct association of the existence of job segregation with the cause of gender stereotyping. These same authors state that in order to achieve gender-neutral distributions across different job categories in the United States, 60 to 70 percent of all workers would have to be reclassified to different occupational categories.

It should be noted that the existence of occupational segregation based on identity groups does not in itself indicate effects of stereotyping. Indeed, with regard to women in particular, it has been argued that much of the occupational distribution reflects their own preferences and not stereotype-driven job placement decisions by organizational managers. There is even some research supporting the conclusion that occupational preferences are influenced by group identities such as gender and racioethnicity (Bailyn, 1987; Bigoness, 1988; Brenner & Tomkowicz, 1982). Thus, occupational segregation is due to some extent to personal choice factors. It is also due to some extent to differences in educational specializations. For example, while more than half of all bachelor's degrees now go to women, they represent less than 20 percent of engineering graduates. Despite these caveats, there is evidence that a significant part of the occupational segregation occurs as a direct result of management staffing decisions, which are often influenced by gender, racioethnicity, and other group identity factors.

One of the most revealing empirical studies along this line is Sharon Collins's study (1989) of seventy-six high-level Black executives employed in predominantly White corporations in the Chicago area. She found:

- Sixty-six percent of the executives were career-tracked into jobs created to handle pressures on their corporations related to civil rights.
- A majority (59 percent) of the executives specifically held jobs in affirmative action or urban affairs. Of these, half were working in more mainstream areas of the organization when approached by company management to take the affirmative action/urban affairs jobs.
- Black managers were asked to take jobs related to affirmative action or urban affairs without regard to their educational and work backgrounds. For example, a majority of the executives with technical backgrounds such as chemistry, accounting, or engineering were recruited to fill affirmative action or urban affairs jobs.

A similar conclusion was reached by Daniel Levinson in an indepth study of the careers of forty-five women. He reports that the women who were in managerial careers were mostly in staff and not line positions and that "when women do reach top executive positions they are often pigeonholed into certain departments to perform women's work" (quoted in Johnson, 1987, p. 37).

Summary

This chapter has defined stereotyping and explained how it impacts behavior in organizations, especially the career experiences of minority group members. As a pervasive activity of people, stereotyping is a major factor in the diversity climate of organizations. Reduction of stereotyping behavior is therefore important for developing personal and organizational effectiveness with diverse work-groups. Various techniques have been used to increase awareness of stereotyping and help people reduce its occurrence. Two basic suggestions are awareness training and the auditing of career paths and job placement decisions by identity group to detect involuntary job segregation. Also, Loden and Rosener (1991) discuss several good ideas in their recent book.

Propositions for Discussion

Proposition 6.1: Stereotyping behavior is prevalent in organizations and, where present, adversely impacts the career experiences of members of the stereotyped groups.

Proposition 6.2: Due to power imbalances, members of culture minority groups will be more affected by stereotypes than will majority group members.

Proposition 6.3: Stereotypes will be manifested in organizations by such things as lower acceptance of out-group members as leaders, job segregation based on identity group, and differences in the causal attributions for both hiring and performance (between majority and minority group members).

PART THREE

GROUP AND INTERGROUP FACTORS IN UNDERSTANDING DIVERSITY

As previously indicated, the Interactional Model of Cultural Diversity posits that various aspects of individual and organizational career experience are at least partly attributable to effects of culture group identities. Further, I have argued that these group identity effects operate at three different levels of analysis. In Part Two, we considered how group identities operate through the individual-level mechanisms of culture identity structures, prejudice, and stereotyping. In Part Three, attention is turned to the group and intergroup factors of the IMCD model. Specifically, this section addresses the topics of cultural differences between groups, ethnocentrism, and intergroup conflict. On each subject, definitions and examples of the terms are provided, along with a discussion of how they impact human behavior in organizations.

7

Cultural Differences

If the immigrant who comes here in good faith becomes an American and assimilates himself to us he shall be treated on an exact equality with everyone else. But this equality is predicated on the man's becoming in very fact an American and nothing but an American. There can be no divided allegiance here. Any man who says he is an American but something else also, isn't an American at all.

The above quotation from a 1919 speech by the president of the United States, Theodore Roosevelt, exemplifies a perspective on cultural difference that I find is still widely embraced today. The quotation indicates that "American" meant a monolithic culture identity based on nationality and nothing else. In contrast to this philosophy, a major principle of this book is that America, like many other nations of the world, is really a macroculture within which many microcultures exist. In many situations, these microcultures provide alternative norm systems for guiding behavior. A knowledge of intergroup cultural differences has often been cited as important for understanding diversity in organizations, but exactly what these differences are and how they are relevant to behavior in organizations have not been well articulated in the literature. Therefore, in this chapter, numerous examples of specific cultural differences are provided.

Culture Identity Groups

In accordance with the emphasis in the book and also in line with the available research on intergroup cultural differences, this chapter will focus on the identities of nationality, racioethnicity, and gender. Chapter Four established that for many people racioethnicity has cultural as well as physical significance. Here I want to address the distinction between nationality identity and racioethnic identity. This is more complicated than it seems in countries such as the United States, which have a large number of immigrants. Roughly one-fifth of the net growth in the United States labor force in the past twenty years has been immigrants, mostly from Latino and Asian countries. Because these immigrants are under enormous pressure to assimilate to the host culture as a matter of economic survival, they invariably represent a mixture of two or more national cultures. One way to segment these cultures is to distinguish between nationality culture and racioethnic group culture. Thus many Asian Americans, Hispanic Americans and African Americans identify with cultural systems of both the United States and one or more Asian, Latino, or African countries. American Indians have the distinction of representing the original "American" culture as well as significant identity with the Euro-American tradition that supplanted it beginning in the 1500s.

An understanding of the reality and importance of microcultures within the macroculture of a nation is crucial to the development of competency to work in and lead diverse workgroups.

While the importance of cultural distinctions among racioethnic groups is often poorly understood, there is even less recognition of the cultural significance of gender. Some researchers have stressed that norm and value differences between women and men are relatively minor (e.g., Powell, 1988; Epstein, 1988), while others argue that they are quite significant (e.g., Henning & Jardim, 1976; Gilligan, 1982; Helgesen, 1990). Based on my review of the available evidence, including my own research and experience, I conclude that gender does indeed represent a cultural category. Evidence indicates that the socialization of people in most societies of the world is greatly influenced by gender, so that women, as a group, hold a distinctly different worldview from men. Among the specific ways that socialization is different are different ways of learning and creating knowledge (Belenky, Clinchy, Goldberger, and Tarule, 1986), playing differently and other childhood socialization experiences (Tannen, 1990; Fottler & Bain, 1980; Rosener, 1990), differences in role modeling of behaviors for each gender by fathers (with whom boys identify more readily) and mothers (with whom girls identify more readily), and differences in the way men and women are portrayed in the media (see Chapter Five).

Some have argued that repeated treatment of gender as a sociocultural category in the literature reinforces the problems of gender difference because such categorization inevitably leads to ranking and women will be lower than men. The following quotation is illustrative of this view: "Dichotomous distinctions rarely avoid creating ranked comparisons, and, in the case of female-male, whatever characteristics are ascribed to each gender, those associated with men rank higher" (Epstein, 1988, p. 233).

The case for ignoring or minimizing cultural distinctions between women and men has merit, but there are also significant problems with it. First, the position that men and women are culturally the same does not square with the evidence. In addition to the above references, some specific examples will be presented in the sections to follow. Indeed, both Powell (1988) and Epstein (1988) concede that there are gender differences in behavioral norms and values, but they find them to be far outweighed by the similarities. Moreover, the relevance of a social category like gender to life experiences has been shown to be so widespread in human society that the approach of minimizing differences has something of the quality of denying reality (Taylor, Fiske, Etcoff, & Ruderman, 1978). Second, in the context of organizations, differences may be thought of as representing opportunities instead of problems. Thus I disagree with the suggestion made explicitly by Schwartz (1989), and strongly implied by Epstein, that the solution to discrimination against women in male-dominated organizations is for women and men to become culturally indistinguishable over time.

One other point worth noting is that much of the research that minimizes the cultural relevance of gender is based on managerial and professional employees of organizations, whereas much of the work advocating the gender-as-culture perspective is based on a broader slice of the population. For example, the work by Belenky et al. (1986) was based on in-depth interviews with college students and workers in a community outreach agency. In view of the organizational history of women conforming to organizational cultures dominated by men, one might raise questions as to whether research done on current managers is representative of women who are entering organizations in the 1990s and beyond. This is particularly true given that increasing participation of women suggests that a broader spectrum of women may be hired and advanced. It should also be noted, however, that current gender differences are based on past socialization. Therefore, to the extent that men and women have similar sociocultural experiences in contemporary times, the cultural differences between them may decline in the future. As already noted, it is questionable whether such a convergence of cultures would be desirable.

Unlike gender and racioethnic identities, the cultural importance of nationality is rarely questioned. Indeed for many people, cultural difference is *always* interpreted in terms of nationality. However, the following sections offer evidence that this view is too narrow.

Examples of Cultural Differences

In order to lend credence to the premise that gender, nationality, and racioethnic groups differ culturally, specific examples will be discussed in six areas of behavior with relevance to organizations:

1.   Time and space orientation
2.   Leadership style orientations
3.   Individualism versus collectivism
4.   Competitive versus cooperative behavior
5.   Locus of control
6.   Communication styles

Each of these will be discussed separately below.

Time and Space

Edward T. Hall (1976, 1982) has contributed much to our understanding of cultural differences and the importance of culture as an influence on human behavior. His cross-cultural research includes work on differences in orientations to time and space. For example, he reports that the norms for physical distances between persons conversing in public places vary widely. In many Arab countries, for example, the norm is for persons to stand much closer together than is typical in Western societies such as the United States (Hall, 1976). I have learned from discussions with persons from South and Central American countries and Mexico that standing or sitting close together and physical touching during conversation is characteristic of many Latino-based cultures. By contrast, most Americans prefer more distance, and both Anglo Americans and the French frown on touching except by the closest of friends or family. Violation of space norms creates psychological discomfort, and Americans often move away to create the distance that they are comfortable with. Such movements may be interpreted as rude by persons from other cultures and set the stage for interpersonal misunderstanding.

Orientations toward time also vary across culture groups. One framework for characterizing time orientations that has proven useful in cross-cultural research identifies three distinct time orientations: linear-separable, circular, and procedural (Graham, 1981). Linear time orientation is characterized by viewing time as consisting of past, present, and an infinite future, with emphasis on the future. It also views time as separable into quantifiable, discrete units with fixed beginnings and endings for events. People with a circular time orientation experience time as determined by repeated cycles of activities such as the planting, cultivating, and harvesting cycles of agriculture. The circular orientation does not see time as stretching into the future but rather focuses on the past and present. Procedural time orientation essentially treats time as irrelevant. Behavior is activity-driven and takes as much time as is needed for its completion.

Application to Organizations. Cultural differences in space orientations may manifest themselves in such things as different perceptions of comfortable office sizes and layout and the requirements for privacy in work stations. Indeed, Hall's book *The Hidden Dimension* (1982) deals almost exclusively with cross-cultural nuances related to space. One of his observations is that reactions to a workplace in which walls are torn down to create an open "bullpen" effect will partly depend on culturally defined preferences

about human density, privacy, and territorialism. Workplace archi-
tecture therefore needs to have an appreciation of cultural
differences, especially in multinational companies.

Regarding time orientation, it has been noted that the Euro-
Anglo culture that predominates in American organizations favors
a linear orientation toward time (Cote & Tansuhaj, 1989; McGrath
& Rotchford, 1983). In organizations, this orientation is manifested
in such things as the great emphasis placed on scheduling appointments, the specification of starting and ending times for events, a
preoccupation with promptness and deadlines, and the extensive
use of long-range planning. By contrast, research indicates that
many Americans of African, Mexican, Asian, and Arab descent have
cultural traditions with circular or procedural time orientations.
For example, in a recent study of students from three countries,
Thais and Jordanians scored significantly lower than a sample of
predominantly White Americans on a measure of linear time orientation (Cote & Tansuhaj, 1989).

Most Black Americans are descendants of tribes of West Africa.
In his discussion of the philosophy of these tribes and its effects on
the psychology of Black Americans, Nobles (1972) reports that the
time orientation recognizes only the past and present dimensions,
not the future. He states in regard to this: "What had no possibility
of occurring immediately or had not taken place already is considered in the category of no time" (p. 22).

Nobles also refers to "elastic time" as an expression of the fact
that relatively little consideration is given to time considerations per
se. These are activity-based cultures. As one evidence of this, he
notes that in Swahili, a major language of West Africa, there is no
clear distinction between past and present. A similar analysis is
offered by Asante and Asante (1985), who add that "there is always
a concern about the feasibility of long-range planning" (p. 129).

This description fits closely a blend of the circular and procedural orientations for time as defined above. That this African
cultural heritage survives in the contemporary African American
culture is indicated by such phenomena as the frequent absence of
specific ending times for social events planned in the Black community and the existence of "CP (colored people) time," a colloqui-
alism meaning that scheduled starting times for events and

appointments are treated with a great deal of flexibility. Indeed, at some events, such as social parties, arriving late is clearly the norm.

Scholars on Hispanic culture, in particular Mexican and Cuban American cultures, also report a more circular time orientation than is typical in the Euro-Anglo cultural tradition (Szapocznik, Scopetta, & King, 1978; Ramirez, 1988).

The fact that most racioethnic minorities, especially those who work for predominantly White American organizations, have adapted to the more rigid linear time orientation should not be taken as an indication that their time orientations are the same as that of White Americans. The continued differences in the use of time among racioethnic groups in social settings make the distinction in time orientation clear. This is but one of many examples of how members of a minority culture group have adapted their behavior in order to be accepted and successful in majority-dominated organizations.

Leadership Style Orientations

Another dimension of behavior along which distinctions among culture groups might be drawn is the preferred style of leadership. Styles of leadership have typically been categorized along dimensions such as task versus relationships orientation and democratic versus autocratic orientation. The task-orientated person approaches the job in a very instrumental fashion, focusing foremost on completing assigned duties. The relationship-oriented person places primary emphasis on creating and maintaining strong interpersonal relationships (Bateman & Zeithaml, 1990). This does not mean that the relationship style is unconcerned with tasks, but rather that relationship building is considered of primary importance in task accomplishment. For the task-oriented person, relationship building is secondary and may not occur at all if it seems that goals can be accomplished without it.

One example of cross-cultural differences in leadership style orientations is provided by research on Mexicans, Mexican Americans, and Anglo Americans in a predominantly Anglo-American bank by Zurcher, Meadow, and Zurcher (1965). In their assessment of the extent to which the employees emphasized friendship and relationships over institutional procedures, these writers found that both Mexican and Mexican American employees scored significantly higher than the Anglo Americans. This difference has also been cited by experts on international business relations, who have noted that when doing business in Mexico one must spend time to build a rapport before moving to a discussion of the business at hand (e.g., *Going International*).

Again, it is important to acknowledge that the cultural traditions of Mexico are still very much alive in the behavioral preferences of Americans of Mexican descent as indicated by the Zurcher et al. research. Therefore Mexican Americans may experience business transactions with Anglo Americans as too abrupt and lacking a personalization they would prefer. Alternatively, Anglo Americans may experience interactions with some Mexican Americans as unnecessarily drawn out or difficult to proceed to closure. Since the influence of culture on human transactions is mostly invisible (Hall, 1976), neither party is likely to understand the underlying reasons that the interaction is not more satisfying or easily consummated.

Some experts have also suggested that women are more relationship-oriented in their approach to work than men (Rosener, 1990; Helgesen, 1990; Henning & Jardim, 1976). In the book *Women's Ways of Knowing*, Belenky et al. (1986) offer a cogent explanation for why women might place more importance than men on building relationships at work. They conducted an in-depth study of the life histories and self-concept of 135 women using a seven-category structured interview method. One of the seven categories was "relationships." They compared their findings with in-depth studies of men that examined some similar categories. They concluded that women are motivated more by a "morality of responsibility" than a "morality of rights" (male orientation), and that women more often than men define themselves in terms of their relationships and connections to others. Men, they argue, think of themselves in more autonomous terms. These research-based observations seem to fit with anecdotal evidence such as the idea that women are generally more sociable than men.

Empirical evidence on whether women are more relationship-oriented than men is somewhat inconsistent at least among management personnel of organizations. From his review of the available research, Powell (1990) concludes that women and men managers do not differ in task versus relationship orientations to leadership. However, along the dimensions of democratic versus autocratic orientations to leadership, the evidence on gender differences is more clear. Based on a review of data from 162 different studies, Eagly and Johnson (1990) concluded that women are significantly more likely than men to manage in a democratic way.

Application to Organizations. Aside from the obvious point that men and women may take different approaches to leading workgroups based on their cultural backgrounds, the above discussion suggests some possible difficulties for women in male-dominated organizations. The preferred and expected styles of leadership will tend to be defined by men. Women therefore may be more likely to encounter pressures to change their natural style. In light of this, some writers have suggested that women managers often experience conflict between their gender role and their leader role (see Eagly & Johnson, 1990, for a summary). The situation is further complicated, however, by evidence (cited in Chapter Five) that women are more likely than men to receive negative reactions when they display more directive leadership styles.

As a final comment, it would seem that the current emphasis on employee empowerment and involvement would favor a democratic style of leadership. Therefore, to the extent that this style is more natural for women, they may be better positioned to lead in the 1990s, and their presence and involvement in positions of leadership should facilitate cultural change toward a more relationship-oriented, democratic climate in organizations.

Individualism Versus Collectivism

Probably the most heavily researched dimension of cultural differences relevant to impact of diversity on organizations is that of individualism-collectivism. Compared to individualists, collectivists place greater emphasis on the needs and goals of the group, social norms and duty, and cooperation behaviors. Collectivists are also more likely than individualists to sacrifice personal interests for the attainment of group goals, to have a stronger family orientation, and to be more satisfied with team-based rewards (Cox, Lobel, & McLeod, 1991).

Self-reliance and autonomy are two of the dominate values of British business ideology in which the economic systems of much of the Western world are grounded (Jenner, 1984). It is therefore not surprising that cross-cultural researchers have found that value orientations among Anglo Americans tend to be highly individualistic. In a widely cited series of studies on cross-national cultural differences, subjects from the United States scored the highest on individualism among respondents from fifty-three different countries (Hofstede, 1980, 1984). Hofstede's research also shows patterns of individualism among nations that are helpful in uncovering differences among culture groups represented in the United States. For example, his cultural maps show the United States grouped with countries like Britain, New Zealand, and Australia at the high end of the individualism scale, with most West African, Latino, and Asian countries much lower on the scale (Hofstede, 1984). This suggests that many U.S. racioethnic minority groups have historical roots in nations with more collectivist cultural traditions. Hofstede's conclusions are collaborated by a number of other scholars. For example, a primary distinction between Chinese and North American cultures is the collective orientation of the former and the individualistic orientation of the latter (Tse, Lee, Vertisnsky, & Wehrung, 1988; Chan, 1986). Chung's analysis (1988a) of Chinese culture states emphatically that the "individualism so stressed in the United States is alien to the Chinese mentality" (p. 155).

Also, discussions of the impact of culture on counseling and mental health have highlighted the importance of group membership in the self-concept of African Americans (Babaron, Good, Pharr, & Suskind, 1981). Nobels (1972) states that a key aspect of the African worldview embraced by many African Americans is that the self comes into being only in the context of the group, "Thus I and we cannot be meaningfully separated." Others who confirm cultural differences in individualism-collectivism among Hispanic, Asian, and Black Americans include Kagan (1977), Marin and Triandis (1985), Triandis, McCusker, and Hui, (1990), and Foeman and Pressley (1987).

Finally, there is evidence that American Indians may also be more collectivist in orientation than Euro-Americans. For instance,

Indians as a rule do not acknowledge individual rights to land-ownership or to capital for investment. Such rights reside with the tribe, the collective body. Thus, contrary to Euro-American culture, in Indian culture, the primary unit of analysis is the tribe, not the individual (Cohen, 1988; Kallen, 1958).

Application to Organizations. The relevance of different values about individualism for organizational behavior is easily demonstrated. Organizations are increasingly extolling the virtues of teamwork, but organizational reward systems often are not aligned with this goal and continue to foster individualism. Although I have found dissatisfaction about the failure of organizations to emphasize teamwork among workers of all identities, work organized in a way that emphasizes the individual contributor is likely to be least satisfying for members from Asian, African, Hispanic, or American Indian backgrounds.

Differences in individualism-collectivism orientation may also be manifested in how managers prefer to allocate organizational rewards or in how employees prefer to receive them. For example, Leung and Bond (1984) found differences in reward allocations between Chinese and a group of predominantly White Americans. The Chinese subjects favored an equality norm in which all members of a workgroup would participate equally in the rewards, whereas the White American subjects favored an equity norm in which rewards depended much more on the individual contribution of each member. Such differences suggest that employees may react differently to compensation plans and promotion criteria of organizations due partly to cultural differences.

Competitive Versus Cooperative Behavior

Individuals of different culture groups have also been found to differ in terms of the extent to which they have a competitive versus a cooperative orientation toward interactions and toward the performance of tasks. In particular, there is research evidence that while Anglo Americans, especially Anglo American men, tend to be highly competitive in social interaction and task performance, the microcultures of Mexican Americans, African Americans, and Chinese Americans favor a more cooperative approach. For example, using a two-party prisoner's dilemma game, Cox, Lobel, and McLeod (1991) showed that Americans of African, Asian, and Latino descent responded more cooperatively in the game. We not only found that members of these three racioethnic minority groups were more cooperative individually but also that heterogeneous groups of Asians, Whites, Blacks, and Hispanics gave significantly more cooperative responses than homogeneous, all-Anglo groups. The magnitude of difference in cooperative behavior between the Anglos and the members of the other groups increased when the game was changed to create the expectation that the cooperative behavior would be reciprocated by the other party. The all-Anglo groups were the only groups whose members did not increase their cooperative responses when the game was changed so members would expect cooperation.

In another study involving the use of a cooperation-competition game with children from three culture groups, Kagan and Madsen (1971) found that Mexican children were the most cooperative, followed by Mexican American children. The Anglo American children responded most competitively among the three groups. The authors concluded that children in the United States are socialized to be competitive starting at a very early age. They interpreted the fact that the scores on competition of the Mexican Americans (who had attended Anglo schools from an early age) were intermediate between the scores for Mexicans and the scores for Anglos as evidence of this. They further concluded from their research that if the norm to compete is strong, that people will often engage in competitive behavior even when the structure of the task makes it irrational to do so.

DeVos (1980) offers a theoretical explanation for the differing propensities to compete among Americans of Anglo, African, and Mexican descent. He argues that Anglo Americans tend to have a cognitive style that is "field-independent," a style that he says encourages autonomous decision making and individual competition in social interaction. By contrast, Mexican Americans and Black Americans tend to think and respond in a "field-dependent" manner, leading them to employ more interdependent and cooperative personal styles.

The theoretical argument of DeVos certainly fits the data cited earlier. In addition, although DeVos builds his arguments on the cognitive style and socialization literatures, his conclusions are very reminiscent of the work of Edward T. Hall on high- and low-context cultures (1976). As explained by Hall, in high-context cultures the meaning of events is heavily dependent on the circumstances, and thus attention to details of context is crucial in forming one's response to them. In low-context cultures, on the other hand, events are often considered in a more isolated decontextualized way, leading to, for instance, an embracing of universal principles. Hall compares the legal systems of several countries to illustrate his ideas, arguing that in many parts of the world, including Japan, nearly anything is admissible as evidence in a trial. Great attention is paid to the background against which an action was carried out. This he contrasts with the "just the facts, please" approach that is prevalent in the United States. The field-independent notion of DeVos appears to correspond very closely to what Hall calls low-context, while field-dependent aligns rather well with Hall's concept of high-context. Thus these two streams of work seem to have pursued divergent paths to reach very similar conclusions.

Another culture identity that has been found to exhibit differences in cooperation and competition is gender. Specifically, some research has shown women to be more prone to cooperative social value orientations while men are more prone to competitive orientations (McClintock & Allison, 1989). Individuals with a cooperative social value orientation approach tasks with the goal of maximizing the welfare of others jointly with their own. By contrast, individuals with a competitive orientation are prone to maximize the difference between their own outcomes and those of others (Messick & McClintock, 1968). One of the behavioral implications that has been found to be associated with these different social value orientations is the likelihood of engaging in helping behaviors. Not surprisingly, cooperatively oriented individuals engage in more helping behaviors than competitively oriented individuals.

Application to Organizations. One illustration of how cultural differences in competitive-cooperative orientations may affect organizational behavior is the use of ranking systems for promotion. In these systems, the suitability of individuals for leadership is judged by the extent to which they stand out from others. The individual contributions of one member are compared to those of other members in order to determine a hierarchy of contributions. The process generates major pressures toward individualized competition.

My experience in U.S. companies is that such systems are disliked by a large percentage of employees of all culture groups. However, members from cultural backgrounds that are less competition-oriented are likely to be especially uncomfortable with ranking systems. As we have seen, there is evidence that this includes White women as well as many Asian Americans, Hispanic Americans, and African Americans.

Locus of Control

Locus of control (LOC) refers to beliefs about the causation of life events. Persons with an external LOC believe that the primary determinants of life events are external, often uncontrollable forces, whereas persons with an internal LOC tend to believe that they themselves are the primary cause of events in their lives (Rotter, 1966; Spector, 1982). There is some evidence that members of different culture groups differ in LOC orientations. Specifically, Anglo Americans tend to have internal LOC orientations, whereas Mexican Americans (Ramirez, 1988) and African Americans (Helms & Giorgis, 1980) tend to hold a more external LOC orientation. In addition, members of some Arab and Asian cultures have been found to have significantly more external LOC orientations than Anglo Americans (Cote & Tansuhaj, 1989).

We get clues to the underlying reasons for these differences in LOC from an understanding of what is generally called fatalism. Fatalism may be used to label a variety of belief systems that embrace the predetermination of events and/or the control of events by God. Cross-cultural research has shown that fatalism is much stronger in the cultures of many Arab, Asian, African, and Latino cultures than it is in most European cultures (Tse, Lee, Vertinsky, & Wehrung, 1988; Delgado, 1981; Asante & Asante, 1985; Redding, 1982). The idea that an external LOC for African Americans is related to cultural traditions that stem from roots in African culture is further reinforced by research showing that Black Africans tend to have more external LOCs than White Africans (Orpen & Nko-hande, 1977) and that Black Africans tend to have more external LOCs than Black Americans (Helms & Giorgis, 1980).

Finally, it seems logical that members of racioethnic minority groups may have a more external LOC than majority group members because they are much more sensitive to the influence of racioethnicity on life events. This same logic applies to women and members of other low-power groups. Obviously, to the extent that career opportunity and success are influenced by identity factors such as gender, racioethnicity, physical ability, or professional discipline, they are not internally controlled.

It should be noted that the existence of affirmative action has led some White men, in organizations historically dominated by White men, to believe that they are disadvantaged by their group identity. Thus majority group members may be more prone to have an external LOC under affirmative action. However, I have found that members of the traditional low-power groups believe there is more influence of racioethnicity and gender on work experiences even in organizations with active affirmative action programs. Table 7.1 gives a sample of data on which I base this conclusion.

Application to Organizations. As indicated by the Table 7.1 data, LOC differences between culture groups may be manifested in belief systems about the effects of group identity on advancement opportunity. Thus, members of out-groups may experience frustration

Table 7.1. Ratings of the Perceived Importance of Race and Gender to Promotion Opportunity for Executive Jobs (by percent).

	White Men (N = 123)	*White Women (N = 76)*	*Non-White Men (N = 52)*	*Non-White Women (N = 17)*
Race	26	62	75	76
Gender	31	87	71	82

Note: Table values are the percentages saying that race or gender was important or very important.

Source: 1992 survey research of a group of 268 managerial/professional personnel from a Fortune 500 company by Taylor Cox, Jr.

and disillusionment due to their belief that their accomplishments are influenced by factors other than their ability and effort. Likewise, as suggested in our earlier discussion of the effect of prejudice on work motivation (Chapter Five), LOC differences may affect behavior in organizations by creating differences in work outcome expectancies. Readers will recall that expectancy theory holds that the motivation toward work will be determined by effort-performance and performance outcome expectations (see Chapter Five). Earlier I argued that both may be related to group identities through the behavioral manifestation of prejudice. The same argument applies here. Motivation and reward systems of organizations tend to be built on assumptions of an internal LOC. That is, they are based on the premise that employees basically control their rewards by the level of performance they achieve. Indeed, research has shown that both the effort-performance (probability of meeting performance standards given a strong effort) and the performance outcome (belief that achieving prescribed performance levels will lead to desired outcomes) dimensions of expectancy theory are positively related to internal LOC scores (Broedling, 1975; Szilagyi & Sims, 1975). To the extent that members of minority groups in organizations hold more external LOC orientations, they may experience lower work motivation. It is also likely that reward systems designed using the internal-LOC assumptions of expectancy theory may not have the same impact for out-group members.

Communication Styles

The final area of cultural difference to be discussed in this chapter is communication styles. Examples will be given from theory and research on cross-gender, cross-national, and interracioethnic diversity.

In her book *You Just Don't Understand,* Deborah Tannen (1990) discusses differences between men and women in communication styles. Some of these differences are summarized in Table 7.2.

Tannen argues that differences between men and women in communication styles are outgrowths of gender differences in childhood experiences and the use of language in those experiences. For example, she notes that young girls and boys spend most of their

**Table 7.2. Some Differences in Communication Styles
Between Men and Women.**

Men	*Women*
1. Conversations are negotiations in which people seek the upper hand in a hierarchical social order.	1. Conversations are negotiations for closeness in which people seek to share support and reach consensus.
2. Communication emphasizes independence.	2. Communication emphasizes intimacy.
3. Inclined to resist doing what he is asked to do; perceives requests as orders.	3. Inclined to do what she is asked to do; does not perceive requests as orders.
4. Talk is for information.	4. Talk is for interaction

Source: Adapted from Tannen, 1990.

playtime in same-gender groups, with boys tending to play outside in large groups that have a definite status structure and acknowledged winners and losers. She also says that boys use talking as a means of gaining attention. Girls, on the other hand, play in small groups or in pairs, and often play games such as jumprope and house in which there are no winners or losers.

The differences in styles are also suggested to explain some common behavioral differences between men and women. One example Tannen uses that many people I have talked to identify with is the reluctance of men to ask for directions when traveling. Men will often drive around for a considerable length of time and only stop to ask directions as a last resort. Alternatively, women drivers will ask for help right away if they are unsure of the right direction. Further, when women are traveling companions to male drivers, they often suggest stopping long before the man does so. Tannen's analysis offers two explanations for this. First, men, more so than women, may view asking directions as diminishing their independence and competency. The fact that the female companion suggests stopping to ask directions may make the man even less likely to do so, because he does not want to feel as though he is taking orders, especially from a woman. Second, asking for information concedes status to the informant as a possessor of knowledge.

Tannen argues that men are more prone than women to treat transactions in terms of status effects and thus are more likely to resist asking for help because they view it as conceding status to another at the expense of their own.

Another example of how gender differences in communication styles are manifested is the way in which women and men identify a problem. According to Tannen, women often acknowledge problems in an effort to solicit confirmation, support, and discussion of the issues. Men often respond with a strongly worded piece of advice on how to solve the problem. This asymmetry in conversation is traceable to items 1 and 4 of Table 7.2.

Differences in communication styles also occur between people of different nationalities and different racioethnic groups. For example, Chung's work (1988b) on cultural effects on business negotiations indicates that even when parties share a common language, information is often presented and interpreted differently by persons of different culture groups.

Another example is that, in cross-group interactions, Asians are often affected by "speech anxiety," or verbal inhibitions and reserve (Morishima, 1981). It is often manifested in such behaviors as reluctance to speak out at meetings or in classroom settings, a reluctance to complain about ill-treatment, a reluctance to ask questions, and hesitancy to ask directly for improvements in conditions such as a raise in salary. Although these behaviors are frequently attributed to low ability, incompetence, or poor language skills, they are often the result of specific cultural differences between Anglo Americans and Asians. Specific cultural traits of Asian and Pacific Americans that underlie speech anxiety include shyness, deference to authority figures, and reserve (Morishima, 1981). Similar observations have been made about the Japanese cultural traditions of *enryo*, which requires, among other things, modesty in the presence of one's superiors (Kitano, 1976).

It is important to understand that within the Asian cultures that subscribe to *enryo*, modesty, deference, and reserve are highly valued and appreciated. As a result, Asians often experience the communication styles of Anglo Americans, African Americans, and others in group settings as rude and inhibiting. The following Asian American's reaction to a group meeting of MBA students working on a class project illustrates the point: "As someone who prefers to listen and provide input in an orderly manner, I found it difficult to contribute to the group discussion because some people would speak up right away without soliciting other people's opinions. One person realized this occurring and attempted to draw me into the discussion, but the discussion always seemed to degenerate into a free-for-all."

This Asian American viewed the form of discourse not only as different but as inferior to the more polite style he would have preferred. Of course, I do not rule out the possibility that this student's reaction had little to do with Asian culture, since many Anglo Americans react similarly. The point, however, is that there are definite cultural reasons that may explain why this particular student would react differently from others to the group process.

Scholars have also noted distinct differences in preferred communication styles between African Americans and Anglo Americans. For example, style preferences of Blacks are characterized as highly assertive, even bold, by Anglo standards. Communication in Black communities is characterized by such things as forthrightness, high responsiveness from listeners, and the expression of emotion (Foeman & Pressley, 1987, Kochman, 1981).

In addition, African American culture, especially among men, is high on verbal bravado and attention-seeking behavior. Style, in the sense of behavioral distinctiveness, is highly prized as a form of self-expression and identity. Forthrightness is expressed in preference for direct confrontation as a method of resolving conflicts, and a high value is placed on the integrity of communication. By integrity I mean that actions and words align perfectly with beliefs. Relating to this point, Nobles (1972) has noted that in traditional West African culture and language, no distinction was made between actions and beliefs. Actions were assumed to accurately reflect beliefs. This fact is potentially helpful in explaining the disdain of many Blacks for rhetorical communications and verbal expressions that are not followed through with actions. The saying "actions speak louder than words" is often heard in the Black American community and is one expression of this emphasis on the alignment of communication with one's innermost beliefs.

Responsiveness refers to a propensity to react extensively to the communications of others. Foeman and Pressley (1987) report that Blacks are more likely than Whites to make confirming responses as listeners, whereas the Anglo norm is one of verbalizing response only when there is disagreement.

Differences among culture groups have also been observed in nonverbal communication. For example, the use of eye contact varies from culture to culture. In some Asian cultures (e.g., Japan), direct eye contact in discourse among people of unequal status is considered rude. This contrasts sharply with the American tradition of "look me in the eye." Some studies of African American communication styles suggest that high eye contact is preferred of speakers but less is preferred of listeners (Foeman & Pressley, 1987). Ignorance of cultural differences such as these in communication styles creates a high potential for misunderstanding and dissatisfaction with interactions in the workplace. In the next section, a few specific applications to the organization setting will be considered.

Application to Organizations. The implications of cultural differences in communication styles for behavior in the workplace are numerous. Several examples will be given here that illustrate great potential for miscommunication among individuals of different culture groups. As mentioned earlier, a classic asymmetry in communication between women and men is that women often communicate problems in an effort to obtain support and a sharing of ideas, while men often interpret the mention of a problem as a request for them to solve it (Tannen, 1990). In organizations, this difference may manifest itself when a woman shares a problem with a male colleague and he responds with what she interprets as telling her what to do. The woman goes away frustrated and a little angry at being misinterpreted while the male colleague feels satisfied that he has been helpful. He may even wonder if the woman lacks the confidence and competence to solve problems on her own. The career implications of this scenario will be exacerbated when the man is the woman's boss. Since the vast majority of managerial and professional women in organizations have male bosses, the high potential for career damage from such misunderstandings is quite clear. My purpose here is not to place blame on men for poor communication but rather to point out that unacknowledged cultural differences may detract from working relationships. It is therefore important for both parties to understand the differences in order to achieve maximum effectiveness of interaction at work.

Here is another example of how miscommunication can sometimes be traced to cultural differences in communication styles. In a recent workshop that I conducted, a Black woman stated that she became upset when an Asian colleague refused to look at her when he talked to her. She took the lack of eye contact as an insult. As we have seen, it may well have been just the opposite, a show of respect. These kinds of misunderstandings are potentially numerous in groups with diverse cultures and underscore the need for knowledge of cultural differences.

A second example of how cultural differences in communication styles can affect workplace interaction concerns the effects of speech anxiety. Although a common phenomenon in some Asian cultures, several features of American business practice tend to place persons with the cultural characteristics that underlie speech anxiety at a disadvantage. These include the great importance placed on verbal glibness and polished oral presentations, the relevance of self-promotional activities to achieving success, the use of brainstorming, and the norm of aggressive competition for "airtime" in meetings.

From my interviews with dozens of Asians and others for whom English is a second language, I am convinced that the potential organizational contributions of many of them are underappreciated due to insistence on skill in oral presentations. I have had a number of Asians tell me that their work has sometimes been presented by others in meetings with senior managers because of concerns that they would not speak well enough to present it themselves. These were not people who did not know how to speak English but rather people who had not mastered all the nuances of the language. In such cases, these persons are denied an important opportunity to give visibility to their ideas. In addition, when verbal skill is emphasized, nonnative speakers often feel intimidated by native speakers, who tend to dominate the discussion regardless of the comparative quality of their ideas.

In the context of diverse workgroups, greater patience and acceptance of different standards of oral communication efficiency may pay dividends in the quality of problem solving and innovation. Since immigration continues to supply roughly one fifth of the annual labor force growth in the United States and cultural differences between Asians and Anglos have been found to persist even after several generations (Kitano, 1976), the research on cross-national differences in communication styles has implications for workforce diversity in domestic operations of U.S. firms as well as international ones.

Before leaving the topic of speech anxiety, something more should be said about norms of obtaining airtime in meetings. In the United States, norms of participation in meetings often favor those who are very forceful about getting their points heard. Typically, one obtains airtime by jumping in as soon as the current speaker pauses. Since a pause may or may not signal the completion of a person's intended contribution to the discussion, people are routinely cut off prematurely. This type of communication is difficult for many people, but it is especially difficult for those from cultural backgrounds where speech anxiety resulting from modesty or reserved behavior is operative. There may also be a gender effect here in that men, more so than women, are culturally conditioned to use communication to gather and hold attention in groups (Tannen, 1990) and are more prone to dominance behavior in groups (Adams & Landers, 1978).

In addition to Asians and White women, members of any minority culture group will have more difficulty participating under conditions of open competition for airtime. The higher visibility that accompanies minority identity, especially when an individual is the only person of a particular identity group in the meeting, increases the barriers to participation. Members of minority groups are therefore more likely to feel that they must think ideas through fully and be sure before they speak. Under norms of highly competitive airtime, the extra time that many members of minority groups take before speaking severely limits their participation. Often the result is that they are assumed to have little to contribute and the potential benefit of their ideas is lost.

As a final example, let us consider the implications of forthrightness, discussed above in reference to African Americans. It was explained that this cultural trait reflects in part a preference by Blacks for direct confrontation to resolve conflict. However, Anglos (Foeman & Pressley, 1987), many Asians (Kitano, 1976), and many Hispanics (Hall, 1976) prefer more indirect methods for resolving conflict. For example, Hall states that a key feature of Spanish

American culture is "avoidance at all costs of face-to-face confrontation or unpleasantness with anyone with whom you are working or with whom you have a relationship" (1976, p. 158). The result is that the direct approach of African Americans may be perceived by others as inappropriately hostile or militant behavior, a perception that is reinforced by stereotypes of Blacks as being prone to violence.

A related point is that communication differences can hamper the building of interpersonal trust. In order to illustrate how this might occur, recall the earlier reference to the cultural trait in African American communication of alignment of communication and other actions with beliefs. This is an aspect of forthrightness that is highly valued in the Black community. Unfortunately, one of the perceptions that is widely held among Blacks is that Anglo culture does not place a high value on forthrightness as defined here. A prominent historical source of this perception is the perpetuation for centuries of a formal creed that espoused human equality but coexisted with slavery and with legally enforced racial inequality in the postslavery period. In the organizational context, some observers have argued that an absence of forthrightness is manifested by managers (most of whom are White) when they talk around a problem or discuss it with a worker's manager or colleague rather than with the worker (Dickens & Dickens, 1982).

One result of all this is that Blacks are often distrustful of communications that come from Whites and sometimes withhold information or deliberately alter their viewpoints as an expression of this distrust. Stanbeck and Pearce offer an extensive discussion of these dynamics in their article "Talking to the Man" (1981). Kochman (1981) also offers an analysis of this.

Summary

Cultural differences potentially explain a great deal about the less than fully satisfactory experiences of employees in diverse workgroups. In the increasingly global economy, the importance of cultural differences among people of different nationalities is becoming more obvious. However, most of us have only a cursory knowledge of what these differences are and how they may affect behavior. Moreover, it is widely believed that cultural differences exist only between people of different nationalities, whereas the message of this chapter is that there are significant culture group differences within societies. The chapter has identified numerous cultural differences among culture groups of the United States and discussed their implications for organizational behavior. It should be noted that in many cases the behavioral norms discussed here will not be manifested in organizations because individuals have learned to suppress them in order to fit in and survive in an organizational (macro) culture that may be quite different from their preferred culture. In addition, as noted previously in our discussion of culture identity structures, members of an identity group vary in the extent to which they embrace, or are even aware of, the cultural nuances of the culture groups. The important related topic of cultural fit is addressed in Chapter Ten. Suffice it to say here that leaders and others in organizations must understand these cultural differences, not necessarily so that they may be eliminated, but so that interpersonal relations between co-workers can be based on mutual understanding and respect and therefore be more effective.

Propositions for Discussion

Proposition 7.1:   In culturally diverse organizations, members will have significant group identity–related differences in norm and value orientations in such areas as time and space, leadership styles, individualism-collectivism, cooperation-competition, locus of control, and communication styles.

Proposition 7.2:   Ignorance of cultural differences is a source of ineffectiveness in the work performance of diverse workgroups. Likewise, a knowledge of the cultural differences in diverse workgroups will enhance work relationships and workteam effectiveness.

Proposition 7.3:   In traditional assimilationist-oriented organizations, cultural differences between majority and minority group members will create barriers to full participation of minority group members.

Proposition 7.4:   In pluralistic/multicultural organizations, cultural differences among members will be utilized to enhance creativity, problem solving, and marketing to diverse constituencies.

8

Ethnocentrism

In Chapter Seven, evidence was given of cultural differences among different gender, racioethnic, and nationality groups of the workforce. In this chapter we discuss one of the phenomena of social relations that make such differences important in organizations. *Ethnocentrism* has been defined as a proclivity for viewing members of one's own group (in-group) as the center of the universe, for interpreting other social groups (out-groups) from the perspective of one's own group, and for evaluating beliefs, behaviors, and values of one's own group somewhat more positively than those of out-groups (Shimp & Sharma, 1987). Like many of the sociopsychological phenomena discussed in this book, ethnocentrism has been extensively addressed in the social psychology literature but not in the context of organizations.

Previous research indicates that ethnocentric attitudes and behaviors are widespread in human society. For instance, some research on Caucasian Americans indicates that they tend to be highly ethnocentric about nationality in their thinking (Sigelman, 1982). Likewise, there is evidence that the Chinese are strongly ethnocentric on nationality (Fitz, 1985), and studies of Black college students revealed evidence of racioethnic ethnocentrism among Black Americans (Chang & Ritter, 1976). Indeed, some writers characterize ethnocentrism as a universal tendency (e.g., Shimp & Sharma, 1987).

There is, however, some research in the business arena that suggests Anglo American managers are more ethnocentric than their counterparts in other parts of the world, such as mainland Europe, Australia, and Britain (Jenner, 1984; Edfelt, 1986).

Ethnocentrism as a Factor in Interpersonal Relations

In many ways ethnocentrism is a group-level version of individual prejudice, which was discussed in Chapter Five. In fact, the overlap between the two is such that their treatment as different concepts is potentially confusing. For my purpose here, ethnocentrism will refer to two aspects of human behavior that are not ordinarily associated with prejudice. The first is that in-group/out-group bias may occur on the basis of nearly any group identity and is not limited to cross-group interaction with a long history of prejudice, such as racioethnic, gender, or nationality group relations. Second, ethnocentrism can be distinguished as a milder form of in-group favoritism than the more extreme forms of hostile bigotry such as are frequently associated with the terms racism and sexism. Each of these will be discussed briefly.

Pervasiveness of In-Group/Out-Group Bias

Although ethnocentrism has traditionally been applied to cross-national diversity, it is clear from the research that people define group boundaries on the basis of numerous criteria and then tend to make distinctions between themselves and others on the basis of these boundaries. Thus ethnocentrism potentially explains why members of organizations often respond ethnocentrically based on group boundaries such as work function, organizational level, and academic discipline. These kinds of group boundaries are often the basis for stereotypes, status hierarchies, and other phenomena that are typically associated with physical-culture identities like gender.

One startling illustration of how readily the dynamics of in-group/out-group bias can be established is the classic experiment of educator Jane Elliot with young school children referred to previously. As noted in Chapter Five, Elliot divided the children by eye color and manipulated their privileges based on the eye-color groups in order to teach them what it felt like to be discriminated against on the basis of an outward appearance factor. These experiments provided several relevant insights on ethnocentrism. The children almost immediately changed their behavior to favor their own group and tease and denigrate the out-group. In one incident, a fight broke out between two of the children over the use of the scurrilous nickname "Brown-Eye." In another case, a member of the superior group suggested that a ruler be used to apply discipline to the brown-eyed kids, who could be expected to misbehave. A second very important result for the general topic of this book was that the class performance of the kids dropped when they were in the so-called inferior group and improved when they were identified with the superior group.

Among the many revealing aspects of this work by Jane Elliott is that she was able to create the main dimensions of ethnocentric behavior in a matter of hours on the basis of a group separation that was essentially arbitrary.

Ethnocentrism as In-Group Favoritism

Although all forms of group identity–related prejudice involve some degree of favoritism toward the in-group and less favorable attitudes toward out-group members, I believe it is important to acknowledge that ethnocentrism need not mean hostility or hatred toward out-groups. It is conceivable that it need not even require that one think of one's group as superior in any objective sense. In its mildest form, ethnocentrism may simply indicate an all-other-things-being-equal preference to interact with others with whom we readily identify and whom we perceive as being most like ourselves. The other-things-equal part bears special emphasis because I am not suggesting here that most people would prefer to work with others of their own group identities even if they have lower skills. Nor am I suggesting that shared group identities are necessarily a primary factor in forming attitudes toward work colleagues. But when all other things are equal, as they frequently are in recruiting and promotion decisions, for example, some degree of in-group favoritism is likely to be manifested. Working with others whom we view as similar to ourselves does create certain benefits. Among them are the following:

- It gives us a sense that the behavior of others is less uncertain and more predictable.

- It removes one alternative for attributing the causes of actions or reactions from that person.
- To the extent that we are instrumental in providing economic opportunity for others of our group, there may be some psychic payoff for our need to give back or promote the well-being of the group.
- It may make it easier to establish rapport and provide another basis on which to establish a relationship.

In my view, a recognition of this aspect of ethnocentrism is extremely important for building commitment to address diversity issues in organizations, especially for majority group members. Among other things, it is of great value in addressing opposition to affirmative action initiatives, which are increasingly a source of intergroup conflict in organizations.

Sources of Ethnocentrism

We find assistance in understanding the basis of ethnocentric behavior in the literature on personality theory and attribution theory, just as we did when learning about prejudice. Personality theory indicates that authoritarianism and stage of moral development are two aspects of personality that are highly correlated with ethnocentrism (in the range of .5–.8). Persons who are high in authoritarian personality and low in moral development tend to be less tolerant toward, and hold less favorable attitudes toward, members of out-groups, especially minority group members (Adorno, Frenkel-Brunswik, Levinson, & Sanford, 1950; Ijzendoorn, 1980).

The second stream of literature, attribution theory, takes a more cognitive-information processing approach to ethnocentrism in in-group/out-group behavior. Taylor and Jaggi (1974) developed the theory that causal attributions are biased by ethnocentric tendencies. Specifically, they hypothesized that when judging in-group members, internal attributions are made for positive outcomes and external attributions are made for negative outcomes. The opposite attribution pattern was hypothesized for judging members of out-groups. Thus, for example, obtaining a promotion is more likely to be attributed to merit and less likely to be attributed to organizational politics when the appointee is an in-group member. Taylor and Jaggi present empirical support for their theory. Subsequent work by Hewstone and Ward (1985) generally supported the ethnocentric attribution hypothesis, with the caveat that the tendency may not be a universal one but rather may be influenced by the cultural and sociopolitical context. They studied ethnocentricity in attributions by a sample of Chinese and Malays in Malaysia and Singapore. Ethnocentric behavior was much higher among the Malays and also was stronger in Malaysia than it was in Singapore. The authors reasoned that the differences were due to the more multicultural environment in Singapore, as well as to differences between Malays and Chinese in socioeconomic status and political power in the two countries.

Application to Organizations

One way in which ethnocentrism may affect the career experiences of organization members is that persons in authority positions may rate the performance and organizational contributions of in-group members more favorably than those of out-group members (Brewer, 1979). An empirical study of 227 American adults in an intermediate skiing class supports this conclusion (Downing & Monaco, 1986). The subjects are assumed to be White, although the author did not specify in the article. The subjects were randomly assigned to either a "blue" or "green" group and asked to wear appropriately colored racing ties for identification at a distance. They were then taught a turning maneuver by the ski instructor. After a period of practice, each subject was asked in random order to execute the maneuver and the quality of their performance was rated by all other subjects. Results revealed that the average ratings of in-group members were significantly higher than those for out-group members. In other words, the "blues" rated the blues higher and the "greens" rated the greens higher. This research suggests that in-group favoritism may operate in performance ratings even when the definitions of group boundaries are largely arbitrary. When group boundaries are based on more meaningful criteria such as professional affiliation or gender, one would expect ethnocentric bias to be more severe.

In another study, researchers tested the impact of racioethnicity and gender on performance attributions. Using data from a sample of 748 Black and White managers from three large U.S. companies, they found that among White managers, the performance of Blacks was less likely to be attributed to ability and effort and more likely to be attributed to help from others than the performance of the White managers (Greenhaus & Parasuraman, 1991). No test of attributions by Black managers for White subordinates was possible because there were insufficient numbers of cases where this relationship occurred.

Ethnocentrism may also manifest itself in how members of organizations relate to customers of a different culture group. For example, Clark (1975) found that White bank tellers in banks with strict check-cashing policies were more likely to bend the rules to cash out-of-town checks for White customers than for Black customers. He concluded that "White individuals in institutionally defined roles behave differently toward members of their own race, particularly where their role behavior is clearly prescribed" (p. 433).

Summary

I have noted in this chapter that ethnocentric behavior is typical of many culture groups and is by no means limited to majority group members. Nevertheless, it is important to consider the effects of ethnocentrism in the context of the distribution of power among culture groups in organizations. In most U.S. organizations, ethnocentrism by White male Americans will have a far greater impact on career outcomes than the ethnocentrism of other culture groups. In New Zealand, ethnocentrism by the Pakeha majority will have more impact than that of the Maori minority. In Singapore, the ethnocentric behavior by the ethnic Chinese will have much more impact on career experiences than that of the Malays because they represent nearly 80 percent of the population and are overrepresented among the highly educated and in large businesses (Hewstone & Ward, 1985). In light of this understanding of the impact of ethnocentrism, the IMCD conceptual framework on which this book is based refers especially to the level of ethnocentrism among majority group members.

Propositions for Discussion

Proposition 8.1:

To the extent that the cultural majority group in organizations may be appropriately characterized as the in-group with power and other culture groups are to some degree viewed as out-groups, members of minority culture groups will be disadvantaged by the ethnocentric behavior of the majority group. Ways that this disadvantage may be manifested include:

Proposition 8.1a:

Minority group members may receive lower performance ratings or less credit for positive performance or accomplishments than majority group members.

Proposition 8.1b:

Minority group members may receive lower compensation or promotion rates. These effects may be manifested either directly or indirectly through lower performance ratings.

Proposition 8.1c:

In the absence of affirmative action, members of minority groups with qualifications equal to those of majority group members will have a lower probability of being hired.

Proposition 8.2:

The effects of ethnocentrism, as described in propositions 8.1a–8.1c, will not be limited to racioethnic, gender, and nationality identities, but will include such identities as job level, professional discipline, and geographic region of birth. This will be especially true where specific identities on these dimensions are dominant in organizations (e.g., where a particular discipline is especially powerful in an organization).

9

Intergroup Conflict

While the presence of cultural diversity offers a number of potential benefits for organizations, it also presents certain difficulties that must be given attention in the management of diverse workgroups. One important way that this occurs is that group identity-based conflict may occur in diverse groups. In this chapter I will first provide a definition of intergroup conflict in the context of diversity in organizations. I will then discuss various sources of conflict among culture identity groups with specific examples of each. Finally, ways that intergroup conflict is manifested in organizations will be explored and some suggestions for their minimization will be offered.

Intergroup Conflict Defined

Although writers have offered numerous different definitions of conflict, they seem to agree that conflict is an overt expression of tensions between the goals or concerns of one party and those of another. Thus the core of conflict is opposing interests of the involved parties (Rummell, 1976). In this chapter we are concerned with conflict between groups. Since all groups are composed of individuals and conflict behavior is frequently enacted by individuals, intergroup conflict may be conceived as a special case of interpersonal conflict. Intergroup conflict in the context of cultural diversity has two distinguishing features: (1) group boundaries and group differences are involved, and (2) the conflict is directly or indirectly related to culture group identities.

Concerning the second point, there are at least two reasons why a great deal of observed interpersonal conflict may be analyzed from an intergroup perspective. First, as we noted in Chapter Four, group identities are an integral part of the individual personality. Therefore, much of what is commonly referred to as "personality clash" may actually be a manifestation of group identity–related conflict. Second, there are clear cases in which the basis of conflict is endemic to the groups as well as, or instead of, the individuals involved. For example, considerable conflict has arisen in parts of Florida and California over the extent to which education will be conducted exclusively in English. The main parties to the conflict are Hispanic Americans (the majority of whom are bilingual but have Spanish as their first language) and non-Hispanic Americans, who by and large are monolingual English speakers. In this instance, the source of the conflict itself has roots in the different culture identities of the parties.

Also in the context of cultural diversity in organizations, it may be useful to note that intergroup conflict occurs between the majority group and the various minority groups represented as well as among the minority groups themselves. In the following section, sources of intergroup conflict in the context of cultural diversity in organizations will be addressed.

Sources of Intergroup Conflict

As indicated in the definition above, the core element of conflict is opposing interests. A study of literature on intergroup dynamics in organizations reveals myriad issues, attitudes, and behaviors around which opposing interest may develop (Alderfer, Alderfer, Tucker, & Tucker, 1980; Landis & Boucher, 1987; Arnold & Feldman, 1986; Daft & Steers, 1986). In the context of cultural diversity in organizations, however, five stand out to me as particularly important. They are:

1.   Competing goals
2.   Competition for resources
3.   Cultural differences
4.   Power discrepancies
5.   Assimilation versus preservation of microcultural identity

Reflecting back on the earlier categorization of conflict as either majority-minority or minority-minority, the first three sources of conflict listed apply to both. Sources 4 and 5, however, are most often sources of majority-minority conflict.

In the sections that follow, each of these will be briefly discussed.

Competing Goals

As previously indicated, common goals is one of the defining characteristics of culture groups. Indeed, this characteristic applies to groups of any kind. In multicultural social systems, the various groups represented may develop competing goals which then become the basis of intergroup conflict. This insight into intergroup conflict has been addressed extensively by Campbell (1965) and by Sherif (1966) in their discussions of "realistic group conflict theory."

To the extent that organizations may be portrayed as macrogroups within which many microgroups operate, the potential for goal conflict among the microgroups is huge. Examples abound. As a staffperson working in the production control section at a plant site for a Fortune 100 company, I observed the following example firsthand. It was a jobshop plant, and each order had a promised delivery date that was given to marketing and ultimately passed on to the customer. While both marketing and production were ostensibly interested in customer service, they were focused on different goals. Marketing's objective was to achieve the earliest possible delivery date to give to the customer, while production was more focused on controlling costs. One visible manifestation of the clash of goals was in the approach to job expediting. In an effort to respond to customer requests, marketing continually pressured production for delivery-date improvements. Such expediting, however, created major headaches for production because it meant completing some jobs in less than the scheduled lead times, and because the jobs required constant monitoring to ensure that they were moving from station to station at the accelerated pace. The conflict was exacerbated by the fact that marketing was not formally measured on production costs and production was not formally measured on lead times. As a result, the reward system offered little direct incentive for one department to pay attention to the goals of the other (Cox, 1985).

Similar examples are well known to those who have followed the recent emphasis in the management development field on improving cross-functional cooperation. The point to be made here is that organizational functions are often characterized by very different systems of norms, goal priorities, work styles, and so on. In other words, they may be viewed as having different occupational cultures. The difference in cultures between them, partly manifested in different goals, sets the stage for intergroup conflict.

Competition for Resources

A second source of intergroup conflict is disagreement about the allocation of resources. In some cases, such as conflict between American Indians and White Americans, the bases of these conflicts are embedded in the history of intergroup relations. In other cases, such as tensions between men and women over access to executive jobs, the conflict is more directly embedded in organizational issues. Several examples will be offered.

Intergroup conflict over resources is illustrated by a recent consulting project I was involved in at a plant site of a large international telecommunications company. Several years ago, the plant hired a significant number of Laotian immigrants. Subsequently there was a major downsizing in which several hundred employees were relocated or lost their jobs. Many of the local Laotian workers survived these cuts. In interviews with African American, Hispanic Americans, and White American workers at the plant, all of whom are native-born, a great deal of resentment was expressed toward the plant's management and toward the Laotians themselves over the loss of jobs to "outsiders." The Laotians that I talked to were also aware of this resentment and held a certain amount of hostility of their own toward what they regarded as unfair treatment by the native-born Americans. The conflict had persisted over a period of several years and was a hindrance to the effective functioning of self-managed workteams that the plant was trying to implement.

The resource in contention in the above example (jobs) is

frequently a source of intergroup conflict related to diversity. This can be seen, for example, in the recent events in European cities where immigrants, most of them non-White, are increasingly being harassed by natives who view them as unwelcome outsiders who are threatening their access to employment (see, for example, "Germans," 1991). It has also been identified as a major source of conflict between Black and White Americans as well as between Blacks and other racioethnic minorities. For example, Rosenbloom (1973) studied employment patterns in seventy-five Federal agencies to determine the extent to which Blacks gained employment at the expense of job losses by members of other racioethnic minority groups. He found that in twenty-three of the agencies there was at least partial interminority group competition. In 8 percent of the agencies, increases or decreases in the employment proportion of non-Black minority groups were due entirely to changes in the employment percentage of Blacks. Most of the interminority competition occurred between Blacks and Hispanics.

A second example of competition for resources as a source of intergroup conflict is seen in the history of relationships between Euro-Americans and American Indians. Trimble (1987) and Brown (1970) provide excellent discussions of the importance of conflict over land and its use in Anglo-Indian relations. Indeed, control over natural resources is at the center of intergroup conflict in relationships between indigenous populations and ,colonial powers in many places around the world. As noted in Chapter Five, in our discussion of macrolevel sociocultural history as a source of prejudice, such historical, societal-level events do play an important role in contemporary intergroup relations. The mistrust and hostility that is engendered in disputes such as the one between the Sioux and the American government over the Black Hills creates a grim foundation on which to build favorable relationships between groups. Organizations are not immune from this reality.

Tensions over the allocation of economic resources have also been cited as central in intergroup conflict in other parts of the world, such as between the Maoris and Pakehas in New Zealand (Howe, 1977; Armstrong, 1987) and the Malays and Chinese in Singapore and more so in Malaysia (Provencher, 1987).

Cultural Differences

Intergroup conflict between diverse groups may also occur because of misunderstandings and misperceptions that are related to the different worldviews of culture groups. For example, Alderfer and Smith (1982) and Daft and Steers (1986) are among those citing cognitive differences between groups as a primary source of potential conflict. Alderfer and Smith describe the nature of these differences in the following way: "[Groups] condition their members' perceptions of objective and subjective phenomena and transmit a set of propositions . . . to explain the nature of experiences encountered by members and to influence relations with other groups" (p. 40).

Alderfer and Smith provide one of the most startling examples of different cognitive orientations between groups from their data on perceptions of race relations in a large organization. In a study of 2,000 managers in a large corporation, they found that perceptions between Whites and Blacks were dramatically different. For example, they found that while 62 percent of Black men and 53 percent of Black women agreed that qualified Whites were promoted in the company more rapidly than equally qualified Blacks, the percent agreement among Whites was only 4 and 7 percent respectively for men and women. They also asked the same subjects if they agreed that qualified Blacks are promoted more rapidly than equally qualified Whites. Here the percentages tended to be reversed, with agreement by only 12 to 13 percent of Blacks versus 75 to 82 percent of Whites. Since the statements are mutually exclusive, these data give a striking portrayal of how members of different groups in the same organization can see events very differently. Another revealing finding from this study concerns perceptions of the nature of two support groups in the organization. The Black Managers Association was composed of Black managers of all organization levels and restricted its membership to Blacks. The Foreman's Club was composed of first-level supervisors, nearly all of whom were White; however, membership was open to anyone at the specified organization level. Nearly half of the White women (45 percent) and more than half of the White men (64 percent) viewed the Black Manager's Association as "essentially a racist organization." This compared to only 25 and 16 percent respectively for Black women and men. Alternatively, a majority of Blacks (both men and women) viewed the Foreman's Club as essentially racist, while less than 20 percent of Whites held this view. One could argue that the differences in eligibility criteria between the two support groups left the Black Managers Association more vulnerable to charges of racism, but the point here is to note how differently Whites and Blacks viewed the two organizations.

These types of organizational support groups have become increasingly common in recent years (Cox, 1991) and therefore these data are relevant to one of the most ubiquitous consequences of cultural diversity in organizations. I contend that it is not the existence of such organizational support groups per se that creates conflict but rather the differences in how they are perceived. Reconciling such differences in perceptions therefore is a critical challenge for organization development work related to cultural diversity.

The findings of Alderfer and Smith are reinforced from many sources. One is the recent work of Judith Lichtenberg (1992), who reports that Black and White Americans have two different "languages of race." A key manifestation of these differences is the definition of racism itself. According to Lichtenberg, Whites tend to view racism narrowly as "explicit, consciously held beliefs in racial superiority," while Blacks tend to define it more broadly as a "set of practices and institutions that result in the oppression of Black people." This distinction potentially sheds light on why majority group members often see incidents of racioethnic injustice as "isolated occurrences" while many minorities see them as single events in an overall pattern of oppression that is embedded in the social system itself.

In closing this section, I should point out that many other examples of conflict caused by cultural differences in worldviews could be cited. Virtually all of the differences mentioned in Chapter Seven are potential sources of intergroup conflict. I have chosen to examine differences is perspective on majority-minority relations here, using racism as the principal example, because in my view it is one of the most important for us to understand and address if intergroup relations are to be maximally effective in organizations.

Power Discrepancies

Majority groups as defined in this book hold advantages over minority groups in the power structure of organizations. As numerous writers have noted, this discrepancy of power is a primary source of potential conflict (Landis & Boucher, 1987; Alderfer & Smith, 1982; Randolph & Blackburn, 1989). The logic of this is straightforward. Stated simply, the "power approach" argues that intergroup hostility and antagonism are natural results of competition between groups for control of the economic, political, and social structures of social systems (Giles & Evans, 1986). On a general level, a core manifestation of the power perspective is tension between minority groups and the majority group over whether to change or preserve the status quo. Examples at the societal level are readily seen in the interethnic conflict of countries such as South Africa (Blacks versus Whites) and Malaysia (Malays versus Chinese).

An example of the change versus no-change problem from the organizational setting is shown in Table 9.1, which records results of interviews done with thirty middle- and senior-level managers in a Fortune 100 company. Respondents were asked how much change would be needed to create an organization in which persons of all cultural backgrounds could achieve to their full potential unhindered by group identities such as gender, nationality, and race. Response categories were a small amount, medium amount, or large amount of change. As the table shows, there was a substantial difference between members of the majority group (nine White men) and non-majority-group members (eight White women, ten non-White men, and three non-White women). Members of minority groups were three to five times more likely to perceive the magnitude of change needed as large. Such differences in perception about the fundamental issue of the need for change represent a major obstacle to organization development work on managing and valuing cultural diversity.

On a more specific level, the power approach to explaining intergroup conflict is illustrated in tensions between majority and minority group members over the use of affirmative action in promotion decisions. Most minority group members are favorable toward affirmative action as one method to promote a redistribution

Table 9.1. Perception That a Large Change Is Needed (by percent).

	Overall (N = 30)	Majority Group (N = 9)	Nonmajority Group (N = 21)
Interpersonal attitudes	40	11	53
Management practices and policies	47	11	62
Organization culture	50	22	62

of power in organizations, while many majority group members oppose it as an unwarranted and misguided policy of reverse discrimination. The question of reverse discrimination will be taken up in more detail in Part Five (see Chapter Fifteen). Suffice to say, however, majority group backlash against affirmative action and similar practices are among the most serious forms of intergroup conflict in organizations.

The notion that disagreement over the redistribution of power is central to differences between majority and minority group members over affirmative action is supported by research on minority group density. Some of this research will be briefly reviewed in the next section.

Minority Group Density. *Minority group density* refers to the percentage representation of a minority group in the total population of a social system. A considerable amount of research in the political science and social science fields has addressed the effects of minority group density on majority-minority relations in diverse groups (Blalock, 1967; Giles & Evans, 1986). Much of the research has focused on how minority group density affects the behavior of majority group members toward minorities. Specifically of interest has been the "minority-group-size-inequality hypothesis" (MGSI) which holds that majority group members tend to lower levels of support for, and increase levels of discrimination against, minorities when their percentage representation increases beyond a certain, relatively low, threshold (Blalock, 1967; Blau, 1977). The essence of the argument is that majority members are less favorable toward minorities when their numbers are relatively large because they perceive them as a threat to their established power.

Blalock's empirical data on the MGSI hypothesis were largely taken from records of voting behavior among Whites, and on educational and economic inequality between Blacks and Whites in the southern United States. He concluded that the level of educational and economic disadvantage for Blacks, and the level of support for politically conservative candidates among Whites, was systematically related to the percentage representation of Blacks in the local area. Consistent with the MGSI hypothesis, Blalock concluded that the aforementioned conditions were more favorable toward Blacks in those areas where they had small representations (Blalock, 1967).

A somewhat similar analysis, which focused specifically on attitudes toward affirmative action–related initiatives, was conducted by Giles and Evans (1986). Based on survey data of 1,032 Whites, they found that Whites living in counties with high concentrations of Blacks were significantly more intolerant toward Blacks and more opposed to government policies designed to assist them than were Whites living in areas with low concentrations of Blacks. The government policies tested included efforts aimed at ensuring equal job opportunity.

Research on organizations has also supported the MGSI hypothesis. For example, in a survey of 230 women in a federal bureaucracy, South, Bonjean, Markam, and Corder (1982) found that density of women was negatively associated with frequency of contact with, and amount of social support from, the male majority. In addition, they found that the amount of encouragement from men for the promotion of women was negatively associated with the proportion of women in the workgroup.

A second example is Ott's study (1989) of 297 women in two Dutch police departments. Ott found that male attitudes toward the presence of women shifted from neutral to negative when their numbers reached a critical mass (15–20 percent).

In another relevant study, Hoffman (1985) examined communications patterns in ninety-six groups with varying percentages of Black and White government-agency supervisors. He predicted that communication would improve in higher-density groups because there would be less isolation and stereotyping of Blacks in groups where they represented a larger percentage of the group. He found, however, that only formal communications such as in staff meetings increased in the higher-density groups. Communication on the interpersonal level actually declined as the percent non-White increased.

Finally, Toren and Kraus (1987) studied 171 Israeli faculty members and found that the proportional representation of women was inversely related to their achievement in terms of academic rank.

The interpretation of some of this research on the MGSI hypothesis is complex. For example, measures of discrimination are necessarily indirect, and support for the progress of nonmajorities is easily overstated in self-report research. Also, it is difficult to separate the decline in overt support of minorities by majorities in high-density groups which is due to power threat from that which may be due to an assumption that less support is needed. These explanations would not, however, explain the findings of increased hostility or more negative attitudes among majority group members in high-density minority settings.

Collectively the theory and research of MGSI provide considerable support for the idea that the distribution of power is key to majority-minority group conflict. Promotion decisions are a primary mechanism by which organizations define participation in the formal influence structure, and therefore changes here simultaneously pose a threat to the existing power structure and an opportunity for those who are relatively powerless.

Conformity Versus Identity Affirmation

The final source of interconflict to be discussed here is the tension between majority and minority group members over the preservation of minority group identity. One perspective on this source of conflict that I have found very useful is provided by Ashforth and Mael (1989) in their discussion of high-status versus low-status groups in organization: "The identity of a low-status group is implicitly threatened by a high-status group. . . . A high-status group, however, is less likely to feel threatened and thus less in need of positive affirmation. Accordingly, while a low-status group may go to great lengths to differentiate itself from a high-status group, the latter may be relatively unconcerned about such comparisons and form no strong impression about the low-status group. This indifference of the high-status group is, perhaps, the greatest threat to the identity of the low-status group because the latter's identity remains socially unvalidated." (p.33).

Status is not defined by the authors but, based on the examples they give, appears to be closely related to the relative power and prestige of groups. Thus the majority group in an organization has higher status than minority groups by definition. Having made this clarification, we can identify several important insights in the above quotation. First, it points out that minority groups will usually be much more aware of, and more concerned with, the preservation of group identity than majority group members will. Not feeling a need for "positive affirmation" themselves, they often will not understand or appreciate that members of minority groups do feel this need. The constant efforts of minority groups to affirm themselves may annoy majority group members, who view these efforts as needless differentiations that serve no useful purpose. A prime example of this in organizations is the reaction of majority group members to support groups formed by minority group members. For instance, in companies such as Xerox, Michigan Bell, Avon, and U.S. West, there are a number of informal groups whose membership is defined by a culture group identity such as gender or racioethnicity. Likewise, on many college campuses there are Hispanic student organizations, Black student associations, associations of foreign-born students, and so on. Many majority group members view these organizations with disdain. The difference in perspective regarding the need for, and desirability of, such groups often becomes the focus of intergroup tensions.

The prevalence of minority support groups throughout history attests to the fact that minority group members in majority organizations often feel a need to form such groups and their purposes are often expressly understood to include protection against a perceived threat to survival of the group (i.e., the groups are to some degree a reaction to being in a lower-status situation). Thus, in the groups of which I have been a member or had occasion to observe, the role of the group in identity affirmation has been explicitly acknowledged. On the other hand, my experience has been that majority group members often fail to realize that their opposition to minority support groups is, in part, a result of their insensitivity to the identity threat that minorities feel. The last statement of the Ashforth and Mael quotation gets at this. They refer to the indifference of the high-status group toward efforts of minority groups to differentiate and affirm themselves. As suggested previously, I have observed numerous cases where the attitude has gone beyond indifference to a hostility toward efforts of the minority group to differentiate itself. The refusal by members of a majority group to acknowledge the need for support groups leaves differences unvalidated, which minorities are quite sensitive to but majorities, by and large, are not. Thus Ashforth and Mael have hit upon an important, albeit subtle, insight into sources of intergroup conflict in organizations related to identity preservation.

Another example of conflict related to conformity versus preservation of identity can be seen in the tension between French Canadians and Anglophone Canada. Canadian scholars have reported that despite the formal recognition of pluralism in Canada, many of the French Canadian minority group perceive a threat to their identity from pressures to assimilate to Anglophone culture and language. A not infrequent French Canadian response has been to advocate separating into their own subsociety (Breton, Burnet, Hartmann, Isajiw, & Lennards, 1975). Conflict related to identity preservation within Canada has also been reported for minority groups of Canadian Indians (Wong-Reider, 1983) and for non-Canadians studying in Canadian universities (Wong-Reider, 1982, 1984).

A final example of intergroup conflict related to identity preservation is the frequent disagreement over the use of non-majority-group languages in organizations. In my own work, this was illustrated most recently in interviews at the plant site of a large telecommunications company, referred to earlier, that employs a significant number of Laotians. Considerable tensions between Laotian and non-Laotian members of the organization existed. As previously reported some of this was due to conflict over jobs. However, a second dimension was the preference among many of the non-Laotian members for the use of English only in communications in the workplace. Some Laotians felt that this represented an unwarranted denial of their opportunity for cultural expression as well as simply a loss of communication facility when conversing with others who knew their native language. The basis of concern among some about the use of the Laotian language revolved around a discomfort with not being able to understand proximate communication, even when it was directed to someone else, and a concern that it tended to interfere with developing English language skills.

This is but one of numerous examples of intergroup conflict with language differences at the root. In addition to disagreement over the use of nonnative languages, language nuances are often the source of misunderstanding between native and nonnative speakers. The following story illustrating this was recently told to me by an American manager working in a Japanese-owned manufacturing company. He said that in conversation with employees he would often respond to ideas they offered by saying something like "That's a good idea." His Japanese superiors overhearing this would be distraught, because they took this response to mean that he was committing the company to using the idea, whereas no such commitment had been made. He explained that such expressions are commonly made in the United States as a simple affirmation of valuing the employees' input but did not necessarily imply a commitment to adopt an idea. Such misunderstandings are often easily cleared up, but their pervasiveness should not be underestimated. A Chinese American colleague with whom I have done consulting work confided to me that he still feels insecure about knowledge of the English language despite his twenty-plus years of residence in the United States and wide acclaim as an effective public speaker.

Approaches to Managing Intergroup Conflict

Thus far in this chapter I have reviewed five primary sources of intergroup conflict related to cultural diversity in organizations. There is no question that the potential for increased conflict is a possible downside of increased diversity in workgroups. However, since diversity in many situations is a fact of life and not a choice, and since the potential benefits of diversity appear to be greater than the potential costs (Cox & Blake, 1991), the challenge for organizations is to manage the conflict. In this final section, I will briefly discuss suggestions for minimizing diversity-related intergroup conflict.

Management writers have identified common approaches to the resolution of intergroup conflict in organizations (Arnold & Feldman, 1986; Randolph & Blackburn, 1989). Table 9.2 shows a list of the most commonly mentioned strategies, along with my assessment of the sources of diversity-related conflict that they are most effective in addressing.

Competing Goals

As Table 9.2 indicates, most of the strategies offer some potential for addressing conflict resulting from competing goals. I will discuss two examples. Competing goals between marketing and manufacturing might be addressed by restructuring the organization into cross-functional workteams whose organizational rewards depend upon collaboration and joint outcomes. One of the most promising resolution techniques is to get both departments to focus attention on superordinate organizational goals such as profits and market share rather than on those of their individual departments. As a final example, bargaining and mediation have historically been used to resolve competing interests of management and labor groups, although not always successfully, especially in recent years.

An application of superordinate goals and of smoothing that seems especially pertinent to gender, racioethnic, and nationality diversity in organizations is to capitalize on the shared group identity of the common employer. To do this successfully, minority as well as majority members of organizations have to identify with the employer and have some degree of confidence that the goals of the organization and those of the microculture group are compatible if not mutually supportive.

Table 9.2. Managing Conflict in Diverse Workgroups.

Resolution Strategies	Source of Conflict				
	Competitive Goals	Resources	Cultural Differences	Power Discrepancies	Identity Affirmation
Collaboration/negotiation/bargaining	X			X	X
Alter situation/context (e.g., organization redesign)	X	X		X	X
Procedures/rules/policies		X		X	X
Alter personnel			X		X
Alter/redefine the issues of contention	X		X	X	
Hierarchical appeal	X				
Smoothing (emphasize similarities, play down conflict)	X				
Superordinate goals	X	X			
Structured interactions	X	X	X	X	X
Integrative problem solving (mediation + compromise)	X				X

Competition for Resources

As noted earlier, one of the most common manifestations of re-source competition in the context of cultural diversity is competition over jobs. Obviously a great deal of conflict potential is eliminated when jobs are more plentiful. Thus to the extent that overall job opportunities can be expanded, the climate of inter-group relations will be improved immeasurably. Unfortunately, the expansion of resources is often not possible, especially in the short term.

In many organizations, hiring policies—such as Xerox's Bal-anced Workforce Plan—attempt to formally acknowledge group identities such as gender, racioethnicity, and nationality in regulat-ing the competition for jobs. The goal is to ensure equal compe-tition, although, as noted in previous chapters, the reaction to such plans among majority group members often heightens intergroup conflict related to job competition. Xerox has been somewhat suc-cessful at minimizing and resolving conflict related to their plan partly by paying a lot of attention to how the plan has been communicated.

The utility of superordinate goals for resolving resource-based conflict can be illustrated by considering the case of two depart-ments vying for a larger share of a limited training budget. If both can be encouraged to plan on the basis of the training priorities of the overall organization, it may help to resolve the conflict.

Finally, as with all of the sources of conflict, structured inter-action to discuss the points of contention, gain a better appreciation of the other party's perspective, and promote mutual understanding is a potentially valuable tool for resolving conflict based on resource competition.

Cultural Differences

Here I recommend three strategies for conflict resolution related to cultural differences, beginning with altering personnel. One way to achieve this goal is by educating existing personnel to obtain a better knowledge of cultural differences. Another way is to hire and promote persons with tolerant and flexible personalities who will productively support cultural-diversity change initiatives in the organization. Stated simply, people who are more tolerant and accepting of difference will produce less conflict when confronted with cultural differences than people who are not. The problem of intergroup conflict is partly due to emotional or affective reactions of individuals.

Redefining issues can also aid in cultural conflict resolution. An example of this is promoting the mindset that cultural differences present opportunities rather than problems to be solved. For example, Blau (1977) argues that increased intergroup experience stimulates intellectual endeavors. One way that this kind of redefinition is illustrated in the language of organizational relations is in the preference for the "valuing" of diversity rather than "tolerating" diversity.

Structured interaction is also usable in resolving conflict related to cultural differences. An example is the use of interdepartmental task forces. Although such groups normally have a specific work task to accomplish, time may be spent initially on activities designed to help representatives of the various departments get to know the culture of the other departments better. Familiarity with the language and norms of the other groups is likely to facilitate the work on the task. Even informal meetings may be of great value. For example, during a recent consulting project with a research and development firm, several engineers and scientists spoke about how some of them had used cross-disciplinary meetings as a means of gaining understanding about the differences between their functions and how they viewed their role in the overall mission of the firm. These persons reported that the meetings had proved valuable in reducing misconceptions between the groups and that joint projects and cross-functional communications had increased as a result.

Power Discrepancies

The earlier discussion of this factor made it clear that power differences between majority and minority members of organizations are perhaps the most deadly of the conflict sources. Power discrepancies are sometimes resolved by negotiations, such as those currently under way between the government of South Africa and the African National Congress over representation of Black and White South Africans in the new government under a democratic model. Power differences may also be resolved by policies, such as designated representation of minority groups in government bodies. For example, a minimum of four seats are reserved for Maoris in the New Zealand legislature.

Another policy with obvious power redistribution objectives is affirmative action in promotion decisions. Although controversial, there is no denying the impact of affirmative action in changing and diversifying the authority structure of an organization. The substantial results of Xerox's Balanced Workforce Plan and U.S. West's Pluralism Performance Effort are two cases in point.

An example of an organization redesign to assist in resolving intergroup power conflicts is the creation of diverse groups of advisers to give direct input to senior management. U.S. West and Equitable Life Insurance are examples of companies that have created these. To the extent that such groups address issues beyond diversity, they hold the potential to make modest shifts in the power structure of organizations, even though they do not change the fundamental authority hierarchy per se.

It may also be useful to redefine issues as a means of conflict reduction. For example, what is the primary motive for using affirmative action in promotion decisions? Is it to right the wrongs of past discrimination, to address the discrimination of the present, to meet social responsibility objectives, or to meet economic responsibilities of the organization? Further, is the effect of promoting a woman to a higher-level group that has historically been nearly all-male of importance only to the promotee and others at her new level, or does it have important ramifications on the ability of the organization to attract and retain talented women much farther down in the organization? I submit that how these questions are answered, and the extent to which their answers are understood and embraced by members of organizations, has much to do with the success in resolving power-based conflict in organizations.

Finally, planned interactions between groups to discuss the

existence of power discrepancies, their effects, and what to do about them are advised for majority-minority situations of all kinds.

Conflict over Conformity Versus Affirmative Identity

In this last category, a number of strategies are indicated in Table 9.2 as potentially effective. First, since some combination of assimilation to majority group norms and preservation of microculture norms is expected, the techniques of negotiation and compromise seem at least theoretically relevant. One example is the extent to which organizations adapt the work environment to accommodate a particular disability of an employee or potential employee. In many instances the level of accommodation will not eliminate all barriers to full participation. However, some compromise may be reached that reduces the potential for conflict between persons with disabilities seeking accommodation and fully able members who may feel that the cost of accommodations places an undue burden on the financial and social resources of the firm.

In some instances, mediation may be of help in resolving intergroup differences related to conformity. One example is when consultants on workforce diversity are asked to assist in improving relations between identity-based employee support groups and the senior management of organizations. This work includes increasing awareness among senior management of the importance of identity affirmation by members of minority groups, as well increasing sensitivity among support-group members of senior management concerns over the existence and purposes of these groups.

An example of a structural/environmental change that organizations can make to alter conflict potential related to conformity is the selection of a mode of acculturation. This is discussed in detail in the next chapter, but suffice to say here that an organization's choice of whether to approach acculturation using a pluralism or a traditional assimilation model has many implications for the identity-based conflict under discussion here.

Another type of identity-related conflict that was discussed above is disagreement over the use of alternative languages. Organizations may wish to address this type of conflict by establishing a policy statement about the use of alternative languages in the workplace that is sensitive to the concerns of both groups. Companies such as Esprit De Corp., Economy Color Card, and Pace Foods are examples of firms that have taken what I consider to be a sound approach by supporting the learning of alternative languages by English-only speakers and the formal use of non-English languages under some conditions such as in published policy manuals (Cox, 1991).

Concerning altering personnel, the same points made earlier in this section about cultural differences apply here. Intolerant, narrow-minded people will tend to expand the scope of behaviors for which pressure is applied to conform to the norms of the majority group. It is true that restricting the hiring of persons in minority groups to those who do not have a strong concern with the preservation of microcultural identity may eliminate some potential intergroup conflict by creating a more culturally homogeneous organization. This approach is not recommended, however, because it is out of step with worldwide labor-force demographic trends and because it brings other, unaffordable costs, such as the loss of divergent cultural perspectives to enhance problem solving.

Summary

This chapter has considered the nature and sources of intergroup conflict that may arise in culturally diverse groups. The potential for such conflict as a possible downside of diversity should not be ignored by organizations but rather should be recognized as an important element of managing diversity. Numerous suggestions for minimizing this conflict were offered to assist organizations with meeting this important challenge.

Propositions for Discussion

Proposition 9.1: When all other things are equal, the potential for intergroup conflict is greater in organizations/workgroups with culturally diverse workforces than in orga-

nizations/workgroups that are culturally homogeneous.

Proposition 9.2:   Conflict will be less when (a) competing
                               goals are reconciled, (b) resources are
                               plentiful, (c) cultural differences are
                               lower or are well understood, (d) power is
                               distributed in a representative manner,
                               and (e) the identity of minority group
                               members is affirmed.

PART FOUR

ORGANIZATIONAL CONTEXT FACTORS IN UNDERSTANDING DIVERSITY

In Part Four, the aspects of the organizational environment that are especially critical to cultural diversity in the workforce will be addressed. We begin by considering organizational culture as a backdrop against which all organization behavior is enacted. Thus, in some ways everything about an organization is part of its culture. However, the focus here is on dominant themes in the content of culture and on processes by which culture is transmitted and cultural differences resolved (i.e., socialization and acculturation processes in organizations). We then consider the structural integration (Chapter Eleven), informal integration (Chapter Twelve), and institutional bias (Chapter Thirteen) dimensions of the IMCD framework. Each of these factors will be defined and illustrated with specific examples.

10

Organizational Culture and Acculturation

Celia V. Harquail and Taylor Cox, Jr.

In this chapter we will consider how the culture of organizations and the processes of member socialization and acculturation combine to explain certain effects and implications of cultural diversity in workgroups. First, organizational culture will be explained. Then, the closely related processes of organizational socialization and member acculturation will be explained. Next, we will consider how these three organizational factors interact with the culture identity of organization members to determine employee behavior and individual career outcomes. Finally, in line with the other chapters of the book, we conclude with a set of propositions that summarize the major points presented.

Organizational Culture

The concept of culture was defined in Chapter One as the system of values, beliefs, shared meanings, norms and traditions that distinguish one group of people from another. A group's culture is manifested in what members of that group think, believe, understand, and do. As the discussion in Chapter Four made clear, boundaries of culture groups may be defined on the basis of many dimensions, including nationality, socioeconomic class, gender, and racioethnicity. Likewise, the organization itself may be specified as a group boundary.

In line with this, the term *organizational culture* has been defined as the "underlying values, beliefs and principles that serve as a foundation for the organization's management system, as well as the set of management practices and behaviors that both exemplify and reinforce those principles" (Denison, 1990, p. 2).

Organizational cultures are part of a network of embedded cultures. Earlier we discussed macroculture and microculture in terms of majority and minority groups. On one level of analysis, we can think of organizational culture as a macroculture within which identity group cultures exist. On another level, we can think of organizational culture as a microculture within a larger societal culture. For example, IBM has a particular culture that is also significantly American, Nippondentsu has a specific organizational culture that is heavily influenced by Japanese culture, and so on. Organizational cultures are thus embedded in larger national cultures and are also influenced by the regional, social class, racioethnic, and gender cultures of their members.

Some work has been done to compare organizational cultures with each other and to determine which kinds of cultural characteristics seem to promote organizational effectiveness. We may likewise think in terms of types of cultures that are more suitable for culturally diverse workforces. Some thoughts along this line will be given in this chapter and in Chapter Fourteen. In order to facilitate this discussion, it will be helpful to identify some relevant dimensions of organizational culture. This subject is addressed next.

Dimensions of Organizational Culture

Two primary dimensions along which organizational cultures can be described and compared are strength and content.

Culture Strength. With regard to organizational cultures, *strength* has generally been defined as a combination of the extent to which norms and values are clearly defined and the extent to which they are rigorously enforced (Denison, 1989; Mitroff & Kilman, 1984; Pascale, 1985; Weiner, 1988). Strong cultures provide more cues on how to behave, more reinforcing information about what is right to do, and may have higher penalties for nonconformity. Mischel (1977) suggests that a strong culture is one in which everyone construes a situation similarly; thus the situation induces uniform expectancies and a uniform response. Conversely, when organizational culture is weak, there is less direction and less approbation when behaviors are "incorrect." Mischel notes that when organiza-

tional culture is weak, identity-related behaviors are more prominent. That is, when organizational culture does not provide a strong
sense of how to behave, people invoke their own identities for
modes of behaving. Thus one implication of this definition of weak
culture is that people with different perspectives, norms, and values
can more easily enact them. On the other hand, low enforcement
may mean that even essential values are not shared by members, and
the extreme of weak culture is organizational chaos.

Content of Organizational Cultures. Particular organizational norms
compose an organization's culture. Thus the *content* dimension of
culture refers to specific values, norms, and styles that characterize the
organization. Since content elements are often derived from analyses
of specific organizations, they may not always be comparable to other
organizations. However, some organizational researchers have identified content dimensions that can be compared across organizations.
For example, O'Reilly, Chapman, and Caldwell (1991) list flexibility,
rule-oriented, people-oriented, and competitive among 54 items that
they found useful for analysis of cultural content in organizations.
Likewise Hofstede's (1980) work on cross-national culture analysis
utilizes power distance, uncertainty avoidance, masculinity-feminin-
ity, and individualism-collectivism as four core content areas. As a
third example, in his competing values model, Quinn (1988) advocates that organizations be described and compared on the four dimensions of (1) predictability-spontaneity, (2) internal focus–external
focus, (3) order-flexibility, and (4) long-term or short-term focus.

    Researchers have also established types of organizations that
share similar clusters of content dimensions. For example, Sonnenfeld, Peiperl, and Kotter's typology (1988) of organizational culture
as a baseball team, an academy, a club, and a fortress.

    Dimensions of content can be further distinguished by the
centrality or importance placed on these characteristics. For example, Schein (1971) distinguishes between values that are "relevant"
(desirable but not mandatory) and "pivotal" (vital for career survival). A cultural gaffe or conflict on relevant norms will evoke far
less conflict than will differences on pivotal norms. For example,
if the organizational norm for attention to detail is pivotal and the
norm for promptness is relevant, a member exhibiting carelessness

will feel more pressure to adapt than one who is habitually late. Schein lists such things as dress and decorum as relevant norms. However, the notions of pivotal and relevant may be applied to any set of norms. Thus, for example, a respect for authority may be treated as a relevant norm in one organization and as pivotal in another.

In combining the cultural characteristics of strength and content, Cox and Finley-Nickelson (1991) have suggested that there are two distinct types of strong organizational cultures. In one type, the range of core norms and values is more restricted and thus the organization exerts heavy pressure for conformity on core values but not on more peripheral norms and values. They call this the Type 3 culture. In the other type of strong culture, conformity is expected in a wide range of behavioral domains. One might think of this as either an expansion of core values or high enforcement of both core and peripheral values and norms. Cox and Finley-Nickelson refer to this as the Type 4 culture. They note that the Type 3 culture is more suitable for diverse groups because it is less prescriptive and allows for more expression of difference on behaviors where uniformity is not critical to organizational results.

Finally, it may also be useful to acknowledge aspects of culture content that do not fit neatly into a specific research framework, such as the extent to which frequent interruption is the norm during meetings or what time people leave work at the end of the day.

Organizational Socialization

Organizational socialization is the process of conveying the organization's goals, norms, and preferred ways of doing things to members. Through the socialization process, members come to understand the values, abilities, expected behaviors, and social knowledge essential for assuming a specific organizational role and for participating as an accepted member (Louis, 1980; Van Maanen & Schein, 1979).

There are three relatively distinct aspects of organizational socialization: (1) the development of work abilities, (2) the acquisition of appropriate role behaviors, and (3) the adjustment to the workgroup's norms and values (Feldman, 1981). Research on organizational socialization has tended to focus on the first two aspects (Van

Maanen, 1975). In discussions of diversity, however, the often over-looked third stage is particularly critical. The third stage is when the newcomer, who may be by then be an "old-timer," "acquires organizationally appropriate attitudes and behaviors, resolves intra-, and interorganizational conflicts and begins efforts to individualize his or her organizational role" (Jablin, 1987, p. 694). It is in this third stage of ongoing small-scale socialization, that the intimate knowledge—the unspoken, unwritten, and sometimes most critical information—about getting along in an organization is transmitted. These unspoken rules and norms may be more difficult for culturally different members to learn, especially when these members are not part of the informal social networks of their organizations.

Research on organizational socialization has also tended to focus more on specific job settings than on the organizational culture as a whole, and since the term often refers only to cultural transmission to newcomers, more attention is paid to the members' initial introduction to the organization than to their ongoing participation and education within the organization (Jablin, 1987). It is also important to note that socialization often represents an adjustment of individuals to group norms in outward behaviors without necessarily changing their points of view. Employees often resist changing their values, especially when their sense of self-control and self-determination is threatened (Feldman, 1981).

There are a variety of mechanisms used for the transmission of culture during socialization, ranging from more informal methods such as rituals, stories, language (e.g., jargon), and role modeling to more explicit and formal methods such as training, performance appraisal, and promotion decisions (Smircich, 1983).

Traditionally, the objective of the socialization process has been complete alignment of the individual with the norms of the organization. Thus socialization, as it has typically been defined, is closely linked to acculturation processes, as will be made clear in the following section.

Acculturation

A second process related to organizational culture and cultural diversity is acculturation. Acculturation refers to the process for resolving cultural differences and of cultural change and adaptation between groups, especially when one group is being merged into a larger, more dominant group (Berry, 1980). In discussing acculturation in the organizational context, determining the point of reference for the dominant group is somewhat problematic. It is possible to think of the parties to a cultural "merger" as being the organizational culture and the cultural backgrounds of its entering employees. However, there is also typically a dominant culture group within organizations. In the United States, this is comprised of White, fully able-bodied, male Americans. To the extent that the organizational culture and the culture of White male Americans are different, some conceptual confusion exists about acculturation. For our purposes here, we will treat acculturation in the organizational context as a process that is manifested in mergers between organizations with different cultures (Malekzadeh & Nahavandi, 1990), and in the cultural exchange between entering members and the organizational culture of their employers (Cox & Finley-Nickelson, 1991). This understanding acknowledges that there is an acculturation process for White males in large U.S. organizations just as there is for members of other culture identity groups.

Acculturation processes present alternative strategies for handling intercultural relationships that produce specific outcomes for both the organization and individual employees. One recent typology of acculturation alternatives describes four modes, or types, of acculturation processes in organizations: (1) assimilation, (2) separation, (3) deculturation, and (4) pluralism (Cox & Finley-Nickelson, 1991). Assimilation is a one-way adaptation in which an organization's culture becomes the standard of behavior for all other cultures merging into the organization. The goal of assimilation is to eliminate cultural differences, or at least the expression of the different (nondominant) cultures, at work. To accomplish this, entering members who are culturally different from the organization's culture must reject or at least repress the norms, values, and practices of the socioculture from which they have come.

Separation refers to cultural merger situations in which the entering members are unwilling or unable to adapt to an organization's culture and seek some autonomy from it (Cox & Finley-Nickelson, 1991; Berry, 1980). Cultural exchange is minimal. Although the existence of separation is more easily seen at the societal level than within organization, a limited form of it is sometimes manifested in organizations in the segregation of members of minority culture groups into certain job categories. A separation strategy may also be pursued by minority groups through voluntary isolation from members of the power structure of the organization in an effort to maintain some cultural autonomy.

Deculturation occurs when neither the culture of entering members nor that of the organization is influential or highly valued in framing the behavior of incoming members. In this circumstance, the culture identity of members is ill-defined. This may occur with minority group members who have severed ties with their original sociocultural group but have not been successful in forming new ties with the dominant culture or have been rejected by it. In the organizational context, deculturation is inconsistent with the notion of strong organizational culture.

Pluralism refers to a two-way learning and adaption process in which both the organization and entering members from various cultural backgrounds change to some degree to reflect the cultural norms and values of the other(s). Pluralism emphasizes interdependence and mutual appreciation among cultures and the importance of preservation of microculture group identity. Moreover, in terms of the centrality-of-content dimension of organizational culture, pluralism is an acculturation process in which the entering members assimilate a limited number of core behaviors and values while preserving important differences along other dimensions.

This taxonomy of acculturation processes was developed to describe cultural relationships between two merging cultures, such as the merger of Rolm and IBM or the hiring of Chinese Americans by predominantly White organizations. There is, however, additional complexity involved in organizational acculturation processes, such as that occurring due to the presence of multiple conflicting sociocultural groups of different racioethnic, socioeconomic, and gender backgrounds. In addition, as noted in Chapter Four, each member of an organization has many group identities. Thus, members may be seeking resolution between the various cultures they represent and the culture that dominates in the organization. Another aspect of this complexity is that the organization's culture may also be influenced by the microcultures represented within it.

Organizational Culture and Diversity

Having explained our terms, let us consider how the organizational culture and its attending processes of socialization and acculturation interact with member diversity to affect the work experiences and outcomes of employees. Two principal ways that this occurs are (1) the impact of specific cultural content and (2) cultural fit.

Impact of Specific Cultural Content

Certain cultural content dimensions, general enough to be found across a variety of organizations, would seem to take on particular importance in light of cultural diversity in the work force. Two examples are tolerance for ambiguity and the degree to which cultural diversity is valued.

Tolerance for Ambiguity. In Chapter Five, tolerance for ambiguity was discussed as an individual personality trait that is relevant to diversity impact. Meyerson and Lewis (1992) have shown how tolerance for ambiguity can be construed as a cultural theme of organizations. At the organizational level, they consider it as "an organization's assumptions about whether ambiguities are legitimate and normal" (p. 12). One manifestation of levels of ambiguity tolerance might be the preferred modes of member acculturation. An organizational culture with a high tolerance for ambiguity will exert less pressure for convergence and will tolerate more divergence. Thus these organizations might be more inclined to favor pluralism as an acculturation mode. Conversely, organizations low in tolerance for ambiguity will have a stronger need for gaining clarity and control. Such organizations might be expected to favor assimilation and separation as efforts to manage sociocultural differences in the organization.

In a situation where various sociocultures are intermingling, how the resulting ambiguity is interpreted becomes important. In organizations with high tolerance for ambiguity, sociocultural conflicts would be viewed as normal and potentially useful rather than as dysfunctional and to be avoided.

Degree to Which Cultural Diversity Is Valued. Studies of organizational mergers among companies with different cultures have found that the extent to which diversity itself is valued in an organization will influence the organization's acculturation mode (Nahavandi & Malekzadeh, 1988; Malekzadeh & Nahavandi, 1990). In applying these findings to cultural diversity within organizations, Cox and Finley-Nickelson (1991) argue that organizations that do not place a high value on cultural diversity tend to impose pressure on all members to conform to a single system of existing organizational norms and values, thus imposing an assimilationist approach to acculturation. Conversely, an organization with a strong valuing diversity norm might welcome the cultural exchange and interaction that is at the core of the pluralism mode of acculturation.

The Low-Prescription Culture. The discussion of tolerance for ambiguity and valuing diversity, along with other aspects of culture discussed in this book, suggests that organizations that are highly prescriptive of member behavior will be less suitable for diverse workgroups than those with low-prescription cultures. By *high-prescription culture* we mean a culture that is characterized by the following:

- A narrow view of right or good behavior
- A prevalence of evaluative, judgmental behavior and people who are quick to express criticism
- Risk-aversion
- A general intolerance of mistakes and more managerial response to mistakes than recognition of positive contributions
- Management, especially senior management, that not only defines broad goals and strategies but also prescribes methodological and tactical details of how work is performed

By contrast, a *low-prescription culture* is one in which:

- Except for core values like integrity and quality, a wide range of work styles and behaviors are defined as right, good, or appropriate.

- Members refrain from evaluating ideas until they are clearly understood and are able to react to ideas in ways other than by evaluating them as good or bad.
- Taking calculated risks is tolerated and even encouraged. Failure, within limits, is viewed as a learning opportunity and an inevitable cost of innovation.
- Positive deviations from performance norms receive equal or greater management attention than negative deviations.
- Within the constraints of integrity, safety, and ethics, individuals have great latitude to create their own approaches to their work.

Based on hundreds of interviews with employees in a variety of organizations in recent years, we find that many American firms are high prescription when they need to be low prescription in order to get the most out of a diverse workforce. This cultural gap establishes the basis for an organization transformation that will be necessary in many organizations in order for effectiveness with a diverse workforce to be realized. Further, this cultural transformation simultaneously addresses changes that are necessary to pursue total quality and to effectively use self-managed workteams.

Cultural Fit

Cultural fit refers to the degree of alignment between two or more cultural configurations. One way in which this concept is applicable to cultural diversity in organizations is that subcultures may exist within the organizational culture. Siehl and Martin (1984) offer a taxonomy of subcultures based on how the norms and values of subcultures compare to the organizational culture. They propose that an *enhancing subculture* is compatible with and strongly reinforces the norms and values of the organizational culture. *Orthogonal subcultures* share many of the basic assumptions and values of the dominant culture but also hold some that are unique. These unique elements may be consistent with the elements in the dominant culture or they may be norms that the dominant culture does not share. For example, according to some analysts, the Puerto Rican culture features a strong orientation toward both individualism and passivity (including deference to others). The former is common to the culture in the typical U.S. firm, but the latter runs counter to the value Americans place on aggressive behavior (Ghali, 1977). Finally, a *counterculture* is one in which basic assumptions and norms are predominantly in conflict with the organizational culture. In sum, subcultures may reinforce, refine, or challenge a dominant organizational culture.

A related concept for analysis of cultural fit is cultural overlap. *Cultural overlap* refers to the extent to which the norm sets of two or more culture groups are similar (De Anda, 1984). In the context of this book, the term refers most specifically to the similarity in norm systems between the organizational culture and the prominent microcultural identity groups of its members. One implication of overlap for employee experience is that assimilation is made easier by high overlap, because members already possess many of the cultural norms common in the organization. Further, organization members from the sociocultural group that predominates in the power structure of the organization are more likely to be easily assimilated into the organization, since they are more likely to have a microculture that is similar to that of the organization. Conversely, members from nonmajority cultural backgrounds would be expected to have a more difficult time with assimilation. *Cultural distance,* a correlative term, refers to the amount of difference in average scores on specific dimensions of culture content. The meaning of the two terms can perhaps be clarified by an example.

Figure 10.1 is based on data from a study of three culture groups. The Anglo American group predominated in the U.S. bank from which the data were taken. The overlapping circles represent normal distributions of scores on a measure of universalism-particularism for the three groups. The assumption that the Anglo group most closely represents the organizational culture of the bank was supported in the research by the fact that employee alienation was lower for employees who were high on universalism (the Anglo norm). Areas of overlap are indicated by the shading. If we assume that the Anglo American norm is closest to the organizational culture, the figure illustrates a greater degree of cultural overlap for the Mexican Americans than for the Mexican employees. This is consistent with previous research indicating that Mexican Americans

**Figure 10.1. Research-Based Example of the Cultural Overlap
and Cultural Distance Concepts.**

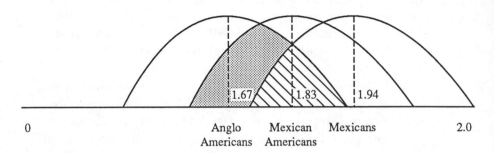

| 0 | | Anglo
Americans | Mexican
Americans | Mexicans | | 2.0 |

Universalism
(Bureaucratic norms of
impersonality, rationality,
and adherence to rules)

Particularism
(Emphasis on personal
alliances—higher emphasis
on friendship than on
obligation to institution)

Source: Created using data from Zurcher, Meadow, and Zurcher, 1965.

have assimilated more to Anglo norms than Mexicans. The cultural
distance is indicated by the differences in average scores between
groups (represented in the figure by the dashed vertical lines). In
mathematical terms, the cultural distance between Mexican Americans and Anglo Americans on this dimension of culture content
was .16, a difference that was statistically significant in the sample.
In more practical terms, the larger cultural distance for the non-
Anglos suggests that they will have a greater burden of conformity
during socialization to the organization, a problem that will be
exacerbated if the organization has a Type 4 culture that enforces
norm conformity on a wide range of behaviors.

The above discussion helps us to understand how, because of
cultural fit, as measured by degrees of overlap and distance between
the culture of the organization and that of its members (or between
two competing organizational cultures in an organizational merger
situation), members of the majority group may have a different level
of cultural comfort than that of other identity groups in an organization. It must also be recognized, however, that cultural fit also

occurs at the individual level and that within any culture group there is a range of behavior around the group norms. The Figure 10.1 presentation also helps to illustrate this aspect of intercultural dynamics in organizations in that the distribution around the averages for each group makes clear that members vary within the group along the culture dimension being measured. Thus the greater cultural distance for the group as a whole and individual variation within the group are both accurate descriptions of how cultural fit operates in organizations. Impersonality is a prominent norm among the Anglo Americans in the sample, but certainly not all Anglos displayed this style. At the same time, it is also true that the norm for the Anglos is different from the norm for the Mexican Americans, and that the cultural distance between the organization and the subgroup is smallest for the Anglo employees and greatest for the Mexican employees.

Results similar to those of Figure 10.1 occurred in data collected in recent diversity-awareness workshops conducted by one of the present authors in a large predominantly White male organization in the United States. In an exercise designed to illustrate the concepts of cultural fit and acculturation, participants were asked to give two ratings of culture along each of seven content dimensions. The content dimensions were partly selected on the basis of knowledge of cultural differences and were presented as polar adjective pairs (see Table 10.1 for the dimensions). The first rating was for perceptions of the current organizational culture and the second was for the norms of the identity group that they represented in the exercise. A measure of cultural distance is derived from the difference between the two ratings. The workshop design focused on the gender and racioethnic dimensions of diversity and therefore the groups were formed along these lines. The groups sometimes had difficulty giving responses on the basis of what they thought represented the norms of their identity group. When this difficulty could not be resolved by discussion, some groups resorted to averaging the ratings of individual members to create the identity group norm. Two observations I have made conducting the exercise with many groups are: (1) there was a great deal of consensus among all groups on the content ratings of the company culture, and (2) in most cases, the norm for the White male identity group was closest to that of the company culture as perceived by the participants. The data in Table 10.1 is a sample result of the exercise from one of the workshops. There was one group of each of the identities noted containing two to six members in each group.

The Table 10.1 data clearly indicate that in this sample the cultural distance scores for the two White male groups were considerably smaller than for the other groups. However, even within the White male identity group, being Jewish made a difference in some of the culture content scores. Again, it should be emphasized that all groups tended to view the corporate culture similarly. Specifically, the organization was perceived as having a strong task orientation; a time orientation that focused on the present; and values favoring aggressiveness, self-promotion, competitive behavior, and individualism and opposing the expression of emotions at work. Although this information is presented to illustrate the concepts

Table 10.1. Sample Workshop Data Illustrating Concepts of Culture Fit.[a]

	WM[b]	WJAM	WW	CA	AA	HA
1. Emphasis on task more than on relationships	1	0	6	3	7	7
2. Time focus on present more than on the future	0	2	2	2	1	2
3. Aggressiveness versus nonaggressiveness	0	1	6	6	7	5
4. Self-promotion versus modesty	1	0	7	5	7	6
5. Competitive versus cooperative	1	0	1	3	1	6
6. Emotional expression at work is dangerous versus is desirable	1	6	7	3	6	7
7. Predominance of the individual versus of the team	0	3	6	3	6	2

[a] Entries = difference between rating of organization and personal preference on a scale of 1–7.

[b] WM = White men, WJAM = White Jewish American men, WW = White American women, CA = Chinese American, AA = African American, HA = Hispanic/Latino American.

being discussed and not as irrefutable "proof" of conclusions, it is very consistent with a number of points made in the book. One such point is that the organizational culture tends to reflect the values of the dominant identity group. Another is that there are important *cultural* differences even within nationality groups.

Research on value congruence has shown that the degree of cultural fit between employees and their organization impacts a variety of work outcomes, including organizational commitment, job satisfaction, efficiency in organizational socialization, and employee turnover (Chatman, 1991; O'Reilly, Chapman, & Caldwell, 1991). As noted above, in organizations that have been historically dominated by members of one culture group, we would expect the organizational culture to be heavily determined by the norms of that group. Thus we would expect cultural distances among nonmajority members of organizations to be generally higher than among majority group members. Thus, cultural distance may be an important explanatory factor in the less favorable career experiences and more limited opportunity to contribute to organizational goals of minority group members.

Summary

This chapter has explained how organizational culture and the socialization and acculturation processes in organizations explain an important part of the impact of cultural diversity. Other important concepts that were introduced are cultural fit, cultural overlap, and cultural distance. When cultural distances are greater due to backgrounds that diverge from the organizational norm, a differential burden of conformity is created for entering members. While cultural profiles vary within as well as between identity groups, being a member of a minority group does increase the probability of cultural distance. How cultural distances are closed in organizations depends a great deal on the operative mode of acculturation. In assimilationist organizations, the burden of change falls completely on the entering member, whereas in more pluralistic climates, more of a two-way influence process may be expected. Organizations with diverse workforces are advised to study the content of their cultures, to seek to create Type 3 rather than Type 4 strong cultures, to develop low-prescription cultures, and to assume some of the burden of change imposed by the intersection of different cultures in one social system.

Propositions for Discussion

Proposition 10.1:   The specific culture content of organizations is an important factor in evaluating the effectiveness of organizational climates for diverse workgroups.

Proposition 10.2:   Organizations that are (a) highly prescriptive or (b) Type 4 will be less effective for diverse workforces than those that are the opposite of these.

Proposition 10.3:   Cultural overlap facilitates organizational socialization, and the higher the overlap the more easily member socialization will occur.

Proposition 10.4:   In traditional assimilationist-oriented organizations, cultural distance will be inversely related to positive member career outcomes.

Proposition 10.5:   As a group, members of nonmajority culture identity groups will tend to have higher cultural distance scores than members of the majority group.

11

Structural Integration

In the context of the IMCD framework of diversity in organizations, *structural integration* refers to levels of heterogeneity in the formal structure of an organization (Cox, 1991). As one of the organization-level variables of the model, this term captures the type of organizational profile analyses that have traditionally been emphasized in equal opportunity/affirmative action work. Levels of structural integration are typically measured along two principal dimensions: (1) overall employment profile and (2) participation in the power structure of the organization. This chapter will discuss structural integration using these two dimensions.

Overall Employment Profile

The *overall employment profile* refers to proportionate representation of various culture groups in the total work force of an organization. Traditionally, in the practice of equal opportunity efforts, organizations have been analyzed in terms of percent women, percent Hispanic, and so on. We may also describe organizations on the basis of structural integration of other group identities, such as by percentage of persons with disabilities and age demographics.

Group Composition

Theory and research on group composition assist us in understanding the importance of proportionate group size as an influence on the organizational experience of members of culture groups. For example, research has shown that Black and White Americans have different preferences for group composition, with Blacks favoring an equal representation norm while Whites prefer a proportional representation norm (Davis, 1985; Davis & Burnstein, 1981). In practical terms, the difference between these perspectives is the creation of racially balanced groups versus representation of each race in accordance with their proportion in the total national population. There appear to be several factors underlying these preferences. One is an assumption that racioethnic identity is relevant to the position that group members take on at least some of the issues to be addressed by the group. This assumption is consistent with a central idea of this book as well as other writings on diversity—namely, that the group identities of people have a significant influence on their worldviews (Jackson, 1991; Alderfer, Tucker, Morgan, & Drasgow, 1983). A second factor is what Davis (1980) describes as the "psychological minority phenomenon." According to Davis, when a group has held a dominant position in a social system over a long period of time, members of the group experience psychological discomfort when the percentage of minority group members exceeds about 20 percent. Because the 20 percent represents such a drastic change from what is customary, majorities may *feel* outnumbered even though the minority percentage remains far below 50 percent. For group identities for which representation in the society at large is unevenly distributed, the proportionate representation norm ensures a dominant position, both psychologically and numerically, for the majority group.

This work adds further insight into why members of minority groups often lobby organizations to increase the representation of their culture group in the organization, while members of the majority group often resist such efforts. In practice, organizations sometimes display a proportionate representation norm in forming committees and in staffing decisions. In such cases, attention is given to having a representative number of women, non-White men, and other minorities. It is also true that in many organizations, especially smaller ones that do not have active affirmative action programs, neither an equality nor a proportionate norm is operative. The use of equality norms is less frequent partly because of the constraints created by the demographic imbalances in the society. Two exceptions, however, are (1) diversity task forces, for which a concerted effort is often made to have approximately equal numbers of majority group members and representatives of various minority groups, and (2) certain groups in which efforts are made to balance gender, for example, in selecting informal team leaders to coordinate self-managed workteams.

Token Representation

There is some evidence that the inability or unwillingness of organizations to achieve balanced group representation in workgroups has some important consequences for organizational experience. One example is the theories and research on tokenism. This research highlights the ways in which being one of kind or one of a few (an O in a field of X's) creates certain obstacles to full participation and success (Kanter, 1977a, 1977b; Pettigrew & Martin, 1987). Kanter (1977b) argues that acceptance in a group and the ability to achieve to one's full potential are enhanced if group composition is "balanced" (approximately equal representation of group types), but it suffers somewhat in titled groups (minority representation of 15 to 35 percent) and greatly in skewed groups (minority representation of less than 15 percent). Her conclusions were based largely on research with women in predominantly male organizations and indicate that subtle discrimination against minority group members occur in skewed groups due to several phenomena related to their low proportionate representation in the group. The high visibility of tokens leads to such things as a tendency for them to be viewed as representatives of their culture group rather than as individuals, as well as a tendency for their performance, good or bad, to be magnified because of the extra attention that their distinctiveness creates. Polarization also occurs and refers to the tendency of majority group members to become more aware of the differences of out-group members and the similarities shared by in-group members. One result is social isolation of minorities in skewed groups. Finally, stereotyping behavior (which Kanter calls assimilation) is increased, with one manifestation being perceptual distortions of actions of minority group members to fit preexisting assumptions about group traits. An example might be characterizing a Hispanic who delivers an animated presentation as overly emotional and lacking poise.

Kanter's theory about composition is that subtle discrimination, at least in the forms previously noted, is minimized in groups where minority representation approaches a critical mass of 15 to 20 percent. However, as was noted in our Chapter Nine discussion of the minority-group-size inequality hypothesis, subsequent research indicates that the advantages gained by critical mass may be outweighed by a heightened sense of threat to power and control over resources among majority group members. Taken together, the work on tokenism and the work cited earlier on the minority-group-size inequality hypothesis raise questions as to whether increased perceived threat is an inevitable consequence of increased proportionate representation of minorities or whether this relationship is influenced by other situational factors. It would seem, therefore, that an important challenge in managing diversity is to create and implement strategies for achieving critical mass while minimizing the extent to which majority group members feel threatened by these strategies. Some thoughts about this difficult mission are offered in Part Five.

Effects on Performance Evaluation and Compensation

A third line of research illustrating the practical importance of proportionate group size is the research on the effects of proportionate group size on performance evaluation and compensation in jobs.

For example, research has shown that performance ratings of in-group members increased and ratings of out-group members decreased as distinctiveness of group differences was made more salient (Sherif, Harvey, White, Hood, & Sherif, 1961). Certainly identity salience is affected by group density. If we accept Kanter's conclusion that salience of minority identity is higher in low-density situations, then we would expect discrimination against minorities in performance ratings to be greater when their proportional representation is low.

A second example is the research on the effects of gender composition of jobs on status ratings, prestige, and earnings received (Taylor, Fiske, Etcoff, & Ruderman, 1978; Buckley, 1971; Touhey, 1974; England, 1984; Pfeffer & Davis-Blake, 1987). In general, this research indicates that as the percentage of women in an occupational category increases, status, prestige, and earnings decline (Konrad & Gutek, 1987). For instance, in one study, college students rated slide and tape presentations of teacher groups on overall competence and organization. The researchers found that ratings became more positive as the percentage of men in the teacher groups was increased (Taylor et al., 1978). Similarly, a study of *1983 Current Population Survey* data shows that the average earnings of both women and men were positively related to the percentage of men employed in the occupations, even when labor market and individual experience and education factors were held constant (Konrad & Gutek, 1987). This research suggests that a status hierarchy exists for group identities themselves, and that these status designations, which exist in the society at large, are manifested in ways that are relevant to work experiences in organizations.

A final example of the effects of proportionate group size on employee experiences in organizations is related to the occurrence of sexual harassment of women: this phenomenon appears to be directly related to the proportion of women in a workgroup (this conclusion may also apply to men, but the research on this point has largely been done on women). For instance, using an analysis of data from telephone interviews of 827 women and 405 men, Gutek and Cohen (1987) concluded that a major cause of sexual harassment in the workplace is gender role spillover. As previously explained, spillover refers to the tendency for gender roles in the society to extend into the workplace. These writers argue that spillover rarely occurs in gender-balanced groups because distinctions of gender roles is deemphasized. A similar conclusion was drawn from cross-cultural research showing that friendly and equitable relationships between men and women tend to occur when they have equal power in a social system (Hemming, 1985; Sanday, 1981). The most compelling evidence of the connection between gender distribution and sexual harassment is data from 160 Fortune 500 companies on formal complaints, which shows that the rate of complaints is directly related to gender density. For companies in which women make up less than 25 percent of the workforce, the complaint rate was 2 per 1,000 women. The rate fell by 50 percent when the proportion of women in the corporation was 50 percent or more (Sandroff, 1988).

These data strongly support the conclusion that the isolation of women in predominantly male workgroups increases their vulnerability to sexual harassment. This is another important reason for seeking group identity balance wherever possible in workgroups. Where balance is not possible, it is important not only to discourage harassment but also to seek to appoint more than one woman to a work unit in which men predominate (Kanter, 1977b; Hemming, 1985).

Power Distribution

So far this chapter has focused on overall group demographics of organizations. In this section, attention will be given to the issue of the representation of diversity in the power structure of organizations. Some attention was given to this earlier in the discussion of power discrepancy as a source of intergroup conflict (Chapter Nine). Here I will first offer a perspective on how to assess power distribution in a way that is meaningful to organization development work on diversity, and then the importance and effects of intergroup power imbalances will be considered.

Power has frequently been defined as a measure of total influence that has both formal and informal components (Randolph & Blackburn, 1989). The primary formal source of power is authority, or the right to make decisions and to direct others. Informal sources of power include personal knowledge and personality. Since this chapter is addressing the integration of people of different group identities in the formal structure, we are primarily concerned with the authority structure of organizations. Four aspects of the formal authority structure are especially relevant: (1) analysis by organization levels, (2) interlevel gap analysis, (3) analysis of promotion potential, and (4) analysis of significant group decision-making bodies. Each of these will be discussed below.

Analysis by Organization Levels

Organizational authority structures are often hierarchical. Therefore one important thing to look at in assessing power distribution is the extent to which there is diversity throughout the management chain of command. For instance, one useful indicator is the percentage representation of the various culture groups in the senior management ranks of the organization. Such analyses often reveal a dismal picture of the level of structural integration. For example, here is a sample of data on the gender distribution of senior managers in the United States:

1. Nearly half of the 1,000 largest U.S. employers have no women on their boards of directors ("Women on Boards," 1992).
2. A study of the 4,000 highest-paid people at the 1,000 largest U.S. industrial and service-sector employers revealed that only 19 were women (Fierman, 1990).
3. A 1990 study of the directors of regional Federal Reserve Banks revealed that only 3 out of 72 (4 percent) were women (*Ann Arbor News*, Sept. 4, 1990).
4. Despite constituting nearly half the workforce and 25 to 35 percent of all managers, women represent only about 2 percent of senior managers (Morrison & von Glinow, 1990).

It should be noted that although the record of U.S. firms on integration of women into senior management is unequivocally poor, the record is even worse in many other nations of the world, including Japan and Germany (Antal & Kresbach-Gnath, 1987; Steinhoff & Tanaka, 1987).

Interlevel Gap Analysis

A second type of assessment of diversity in power distribution, which is related to the previous one, is what I call "interlevel gap analysis." Proportionate-group-size analyses at various hierarchical levels become more meaningful when the percentages are compared across levels. The interlevel gap refers to the difference between the percentage representation of a group in the overall workforce (or at the bottom of the organizational hierarchy) and its percentage representation at various higher levels of authority. As Tables 11.1, 11.2, and 11.3 illustrate, the gaps between minority and majority group representation are often quite substantial.

Table 11.1. Gender Analysis of Television, Radio, and Newspaper Industries.

	Percent female
Top management	6
General managers	8
Middle management: Advertising director Sales manager	16–18
Lower management: Local sales manager Managing editor Advertising manager	24–33
Nonmanagement: Advertising sales News reporting	36–55

Source: Adapted from Wall Street Journal, April 10, 1989.

Table 11.2. Race and Gender Analysis of General Motors, 1987.

	Percent White males
Managers and officers	77
Professionals	66
Sales workers	71
Office/clerical	16
Total workforce	60

Source: General Motors U.S. employment at December 31, 1987, EEO-I Statistics.

Table 11.3. Race Analysis of Xerox Corporation, 1987.

	Percent non-White
Managers	19
Professionals	20
Sales people	21
Total workforce	24

Source: Adapted from Solomon, 1989.

In Table 11.1, women make up 36 to 55 percent of the nonmanagement group but only 6 percent of the top management group. Table 11.2 makes a similar point from the perspective of the majority group. If we use the total workforce profile as a base, men are overrepresented in sales, management, and professional jobs by 6 to 17 percent while they are underrepresented by 44 percent in the low-level office and clerical job category. These examples illustrate a typical pattern of minority group/majority group distribution by levels: namely, that majority group members are overrepresented at the higher levels and underrepresented at the lower levels, while the reverse is true for minority-group members. Also a part of the pattern is that the size of the gap typically widens as we ascend the organizational hierarchy. It has been well documented in the literature that entry-advancement gaps of 30 percent or more for minority groups are not unusual in American firms (Cox, 1991). Nevertheless, Table 11.3 makes it clear that such huge gaps are not inevitable. The Xerox data illustrate a level of structural integration that is far above average in American industry. Not surprisingly, Xerox has been widely cited as a leader in organization development work related to structural integration.

Analysis of Promotion Potential

A third type of measurement of power distribution is cross-group comparisons of promotion potential. The expression of promotion potential takes a number of forms, including formal promotion potential ratings, participation in high potential career development programs, and assessments of promotion readiness (e.g., ready now, ready within one year). The inclusion of this factor in defining and measuring power distribution is important for several reasons. First, the pool of individuals with high potential is a major source of candidates for future leaders in organizations. Thus to a large extent the high-potential list defines the authority figures of the future. In addition, persons tagged as having high potential may have more influence than others at the same level in the organization. This is because senior managers view them as prospective peers while peers view them as prospective bosses, and thus both may be more receptive to their viewpoints than those of others who are not thought to have high potential.

Although diversity in high-potential pools and comparability across groups in promotion potential ratings is important in analysis of structural integration, relatively little published data exist on these measures. In our study of 125 Black and White public sector supervisors, Nkomo and I found no significant differences in ratings of readiness for promotion (Cox & Nkomo, 1986). However, in a more recent study of 828 Black and White managers in three large U.S. companies, Greenhaus, Parasuraman and Wormely (1990) found that Black managers had significantly lower prospects of promotion than White managers. In their study, the primary source of the lower promotability ratings appears to have been the lower performance ratings of Blacks. When performance ratings were controlled, the race effect was no longer significant. They nevertheless concluded that the Black managers were significantly more likely to be plateaued and noted the importance of examining performance evaluation processes for possible sources of unintentional bias.

In a study of the effects of age on promotability ratings of lower-level public sector managers, Nkomo and I found that older managers (forty and over) were rated significantly lower than younger managers on readiness-for-promotion ratings even when education, performance, and job tenure were held constant (Cox & Nkomo, 1992).

Finally, data that I recently reviewed at a medium-size U.S. research and development company indicated that among employees with high potential in the senior management succession pool, only 8 percent were women.

On balance, the limited available evidence suggests that group identities such as gender, race, and age do affect promotability assessment. More research is needed to clarify the impact of these and other group identities on the evaluation of promotion potential.

Analysis of Group Decision-Making Bodies

While it is true that Western organizations have historically emphasized the individual contributor, a significant number of decisions in organizations are made by groups. One obvious example is boards of directors, but there are numerous others. Steering committees, various task forces, and quality councils are among the decision bodies that require attention in a thorough analysis of organizational authority structures. For our purposes, the question of interest is the extent to which the diversity of the workforce is represented in such decision groups. Obviously, the presence of diversity in the groups that have the largest scope of authority are of greatest concern. This suggests that we begin with boards of directors. A recent study by Korn/Ferry International of the composition of boards of directors of 426 large American companies revealed a remarkable lack of diversity:

- Four out of ten companies responding had no women on their board.
- Seven out of ten companies had no non-White Americans on their board.
- Only 12 percent of the companies had a non-U.S. citizen on their board and only 6.7 percent had an American citizen with extensive international experience (Board of Directors, 1990; Korn/Ferry, 1990).

Perhaps the most disturbing of these results from a diversity viewpoint is the persistence of homogeneity of nationality on the boards, despite all of the recent discussion about globalization. In addition, although the Korn/Ferry study addressed the question of representation of at least one person of a certain type, the average board has thirteen members. There are therefore a large number of total board positions in the economy. Recent data indicate that 93 to 96 percent of the total board seats of American companies are held by White men (Fryxell & Lerner, 1989). Thus the degree of structural integration of persons from nonmajority culture groups in the decision bodies at the highest levels of business organization is miniscule.

Since participation on boards of directors is typically limited to high-ranking executives and business owners, increasing the levels of diversity in these decision groups is severely constrained by the limited number of persons in some culture groups who presently hold such positions. We may ask, however, if the quality of decision making might not be enhanced by broadening participation to include some lower-level managers. Moreover, to the extent that decisions are made by committees, there would seem to be a great opportunity to diversify the power structure of firms by making diversity a priority in appointments to other decision-making bodies, such as finance committees, management development committees, steering committees for various projects, quality councils, and so on. Unfortunately, organizations have often failed to capitalize on this opportunity because they have traditionally placed great emphasis on the organization level of prospective candidates for these decision-making bodies as well. Indeed, it is not uncommon for membership to be defined by position rather than individual traits. For instance, many of the most powerful committees are often defined as "all vice presidents" or "all department heads." When persons of lower levels are included, it is often on an ad hoc basis or as secretaries. Although there are logical reasons for favoring higher-level members of the organization in forming some of these committees, in my view a great improvement in diversifying the power structure of organizations could be made by raising the priority of diversity as a criterion in forming these groups. For example, a consulting client of mine recently formed a committee to hear and act on complaints of sexual and other forms of harassment. In its initial formation, level was the overriding criterion of selection. As a result, the company created a committee composed only of men.

This may be a somewhat extreme case, but in my experience— with the possible exception of diversity of function or department— achieving cultural diversity in the powerful committees of organizations has not been a high priority. This conclusion is supported by the Korn/Ferry study, which reports that although 65 percent of respondents said a director with international experience would be a valuable asset to the board, less than 10 percent actually had such a person on the board and less than 18 percent said that they were dissatisfied with the present composition of the board. This is a telling example of the lack of commitment to change that has plagued organization development related to diversity.

As organizations continue to decentralize and to increase the use of teams to make decisions formerly made by individuals, there is a great opportunity to increase levels of diversity in the power structure by raising the priority of diversity as a selection criterion in forming planning and decision-making groups.

In the previous sections, we addressed ways to define and measure power distribution as a component of structural integration. But the question arises as to why organizations should *want* to diversify power structures. Stated differently: What are the implications of power imbalances among different culture groups for the career experiences of members and for organizational effectiveness? This is the question addressed in the next section.

Consequences of Power Imbalances Among Culture Groups

One important implication of power imbalances among culture groups in organizations that was discussed in Chapter Nine is that such imbalances contribute to intergroup conflict. Thus, when workgroups are diverse and the power distribution is heavily skewed in favor of a certain group or groups, it will be more difficult for members of different culture groups to work harmoniously together and this may hamper organizational performance. Further, the need for better cooperation and smooth interpersonal relations among members of workgroups has been intensified by the recent emphasis on performing work in teams. When power in organizations is not systematically related to group identities such as gender, nationality, and racioethnicity, a major source of conflict is eliminated. Therefore, the reduction of intergroup conflict is a major reason for organizations to seek diversification in power structures.

Power Imbalances and the Performance Opportunity of Minorities

A second important, albeit more subtle, implication of power imbalances among culture groups in organizations is that such imbalances, especially when they persist over a long period of time, have the effect of reducing the motivation and the perceived opportunity among members of minority groups to participate and to excel to their fullest potential in diverse-group settings. One aspect of this is a role-modeling effect. This was illustrated to me in a recent interview with a White female manager in a large corporation when she responded to questions about how gender impacted her career experiences. She showed me a picture of the top two or three tiers of management in the company and asked me, "Do you see anyone here who looks like me?" What this woman was saying is that the absence of women at higher levels in the organization had a dampening effect on her motivation and her sense of opportunity to achieve to her full potential. I have heard similar comments from Europeans working in international corporations based in the United States, from Americans working for Canadian companies, and from Mexican Americans working in a U.S. manufacturing facility in which the labor force was 80 percent Hispanic while the management team was nearly all Anglo and where there had never been a Mexican American general manager at the plant.

Another aspect of this is what might be termed "differential perceived legitimacy." When workgroups are diverse but the power structure is heavily concentrated in one group, it is difficult for members of minority groups to be perceived by others, and even to perceive themselves, as leaders or potential leaders. This tendency is exacerbated by the fact that societies tend to develop status systems in which members of minority groups typically have low status (Ridgeway, 1991). Because of the predominance of one group in the power structure, it seems natural or more legitimate for majority group members to be leaders. By contrast, a member of a lower-status culture group never has a "natural" basis for authority and will have to struggle for legitimacy (Nilson, 1976; Wiley & Eskilson, 1982).

One research study supporting this conclusion is the work of Ross Webber (1974) on cross-cultural teams. In the study, 104 four-person teams of students were formed in which three members of each team were American White men and the fourth was either an American White woman (38 groups), an American Black man (10 groups), a European (or Canadian or Australian) Anglo man (10 groups), a European non-Anglo man (18 groups), a Japanese man (16 groups), or a Latin American (Mexican or South American) man (12 groups). No instructions on group structure were given. After students had worked together for 13 weeks and grades had been assigned (but not distributed), a series of questions were asked about team leadership, conformity behavior, and levels of participation in the groups.

The data indicated that 60 percent of European Anglo men and a third of American White men saw themselves as leaders in their groups. By contrast, only 5 percent of American White women, 16 percent of Latin American men, and none of the American Black males or Japanese men claimed that they were the task leaders in their groups. In addition, all persons rated as making the highest contributions were American White men, while American White women, non-Anglo European men, and Latin American men were two to three times more likely than American White men to be viewed by the American White men majority as contributing least to the group. Perhaps the most striking result, however, is that 100 percent of the American Black men and non-Anglo European men and two-thirds of the Latin American men were seen by at least one American White man member of their team as not conforming to the expectations of the group. By contrast only 17 percent of the American White men and none of the American White women were seen as nonconformists. In commenting on the results of the study, Webber wrote the following: "The American White male majority claimed task leadership for themselves or attributed it to other AWM's. They perceived all minorities as generally following and contributing relatively little. In turn, most minority members did not claim leadership. Those few that did strive for leadership were usually rejected" (p. 873).

Webber also states that the minority culture persons typically responded to rejection of their efforts to influence the work either by becoming passive, violating group norms, or withdrawing. Behaviors pertinent to the latter two categories included coming to meetings late and being unprepared.

Although this is a somewhat dated study and it utilized students rather than full-time workers in an employer setting, the data confirm my observations of a struggle for legitimacy, which is often reported by White women, non-White Americans, and non-Americans in predominantly White male American organizations. The following quotation, taken from my recent interviews with two

White female managers in a Fortune 1000 company, are illustrative: One stated: "I always feel pressure relating to how I present myself, constantly striving to establish professionalism. This creates a lot of stress. I can't let my guard down." The other manager observed: "It's hard to be a woman at _____ . You're not treated as a full player. The male managers often think women should mainly type. It's okay for them to do leg work on a project, but final decision making is taken over by a man. Sometimes I think men are not comfortable working with women as equals." It seems obvious that these employees were struggling to achieve a sense of personal efficacy and fullness of participation—a struggle that they felt was related to their identity as women in a male-dominated social system.

Several other writers have contributed to our understanding of the leadership legitimacy problem for minority group members. For example, Crocker and McGraw (1984) found that in ad hoc student groups, solo males were twice as likely as solo females to be chosen as leaders in groups composed predominantly of the opposite gender. It has also been shown that men in predominantly female occupations are favored over women for promotion and tend to be overrepresented among upper-level positions (Etzkowitz, 1971; Segal, 1962). This, of course, is in sharp contrast to the representation of women in the power structure of male-dominated occupations.

One final example of research relevant to differential perceived legitimacy is the work of Ramirez (1988, 1977) on social power and influence among Mexican Americans and Anglo Americans in predominantly Anglo organizational settings. Ramirez (1988) argues that when the power structure in a social system is systematically related to group identities such as race, members of racioethnic minority groups are perceived as being less legitimate sources of authority and this represents a subtle form of racism. He distinguishes between social systems in which culture groups have unequal social power and influence (USPI) and systems in which culture groups have equal social power and influence (ESPI). In USPI systems, intergroup relations tend to be characterized by the domination of majority group members and subordination of minority group members. By contrast, in ESPI systems intergroup relations between majority and minority group members will be more favorable and differential legitimacy for leadership will be minimized, because there is no empirical basis for linking racioethnicity to legitimacy of authority. Empirical studies on the USPI-ESPI model using Mexican American students indicate that those students who matriculated in ESPI school systems—e.g., where a substantial percentage of faculty and administrators were Mexican American—had more positive experiences than those students who matriculated in USPI schools. Among the specific differences were that ESPI students were less likely to say they had observed prejudice and discrimination, felt more confident about their own abilities, and were more likely to plan to attend college (Ramirez & Soriano, 1982).

For minorities in predominantly majority settings, the time and energy that is used to establish legitimacy could be more productively used to solve organizational problems. In addition, the withdrawal behaviors referred to earlier represent lost productivity and quality of work in organizations. Moreover, the reluctance or inability of members of out-groups to assume leadership positions represents a potential loss of leadership talent for organizations. For all of these reasons, persistent power imbalances among culture groups in a diverse organization pose hazards to organizational effectiveness.

Summary

The theory and research reviewed in this chapter illustrate that proportionate representation of various groups in an organization, and how power is distributed among identity groups, has significant implications for the experiences of organization members. On balance, those in the majority group are advantaged and those in minority groups are disadvantaged by the mere presence of imbalanced group types in organizations. Given the fact that many of these imbalances are embedded in the society itself, there is often no easy solution for these effects. However, this section has hopefully clarified the importance of seeking more balanced representation and power among culture groups in organizations. Even where it cannot be achieved, an understanding and appreciation of the effects of proportionate representation might enhance organizational efficacy with diverse workgroups.

Propositions for Discussion

Proposition 11.1:   Low-proportional representation of an identity group in the workforce of an organization will create obstacles to career success for members of this group.

Proposition 11.2:   Imbalances in the representation of various identity groups in the most powerful positions of organizations tend to create career obstacles for members of minority groups and to increase intergroup conflict related to biocultural identities of members.

Proposition 11.3:   Severe power imbalances among the various culture groups represented in an organization indirectly hinder organizational effectiveness.

12

Informal Integration

In the previous chapter we were concerned with the integration of persons of different group identities into the formal structure of the organization. In this chapter attention is turned to the informal organization. Previous theory and research has indicated that participation in informal groups in organizations plays an important part in the career success of individuals (Shaw, [1976] 1981; Burke, 1984; Gouldner, 1954; Blau, 1955). In one study, supervisors' level of personal acquaintance with subordinates was positively related to both performance ratings and actual sales productivity (Kingstrom & Mainstone, 1985). Research has also shown that persons who have low access to informal networks are less likely than those with high access to provide ideas on how to improve work quality or to believe that they can make a difference in how the organization is run (Pearlin, 1962). Thus access to informal networks has direct implications for the contributions of employees to total quality initiatives that depend heavily on employee involvement.

Theory and research from social psychology suggest that participation in informal groups is influenced by such factors as common language, perceived social similarity, and ethnocentrism (Brass, 1985). Since language, social similarity, and ethnocentrism are all closely related to culture identity, this chapter will consider how group identities such as racioethnicity, gender, and nationality may impact participation in informal groups.

The principal aspects of participation in informal groups are (1) access to social networks (informal communication networks and establishment of friendship ties), and (2) mentoring activity. Therefore these two topics will be addressed in depth in this chapter.

Impact of Diversity in Social Networks

Social networks are important vehicles for communication in organizations (Guetzkow, 1965) and for personal efficacy of organization members (Dalton, 1959; Lincoln, 1982). However, research has also shown that participation and centrality in such networks is heavily influenced by friendship ties (Lincoln & Miller, 1979). Further, structural properties of organizations often constrain the ability of women and nonmajority men to participate in informal networks (Ibarra, 1993). Paramount among these structural properties is the relative lack of availability of persons of similar group identities in positions of high influence. Thus, in social systems where members have historically been concentrated in one culture group, it may be difficult for members from other culture groups to join and fully utilize informal groups. For example, White women and non-Whites may have difficulty with informal integration in predominantly White male networks in the United States and Europe. The Maoris may have difficulty with participation in Pakeha networks in New Zealand, Japanese women may be excluded from informal networks of workers in Japan, and so on.

Numerous other writers have contributed to our conceptual understanding of how group identities affect informal integration in organizations (Thompson & Ditomaso, 1988; Kanter, 1977b; Viega, 1976; Henning & Jardim, 1976; Bartol, 1978). Nevertheless, there is very little actual data on the extent to which participation in informal groups is influenced by gender, racioethnicity, and nationality, and virtually none on effects of other group identities such as physical ability.

The empirical research that has been published on this issue offers somewhat inconsistent results as to whether and how group identities impact social network participation (Brass, 1985; Ibarra, 1992; Burke, 1984; Blau, 1962).

In perhaps the most relevant empirical study for our purposes, work and social network ties were studied for 314 employees of five different organizations in various industries by Lincoln & Miller, (1979). The authors found that race had a significant effect on social networking in three of the five organizations and that gender had a significant effect on social networking in two of the five organizations. Unfortunately, Lincoln and Miller do not specify the exact racial composition of the sample, but they make it clear that majority group members faired better by stating that "white males with high education in formal positions of authority have high probabilities of occupying the most central locations in the network space" (p. 193). Further, Lincoln and Miller add: "We are less sanguine about the implications for rational design of our findings that sex and race have strong effects on network ties . . . but since they tend to exclude women and non-whites from friendship networks, we might conclude that to the extent that friendship networks influence organizational process, reason gives way to prejudice" (p. 197).

On balance, the Lincoln and Miller study supports the notion that lower participation or less centrality in informal groups may hinder career success for women and non-Whites in predominantly White male organizations. However, the fact that significant race and gender effects were found in some of the organizations and not others suggests that these effects are not inevitable. More needs to be learned about the conditions under which these effects are more or less likely to occur.

Also, in my own recent research of diversity effects among three hundred male and female employees of a Fortune 500 company, I found that women were significantly less likely than men to say that they frequently participated in informal social activity with co-workers. Non-Whites (30 Asians, 20 Blacks, and 15 Hispanics) were not significantly less likely to report participation than Whites, but less than half of all respondents believed that White women (43 percent agreement), non-White men (48 percent agreement), or non-White women (36 percent agreement) had the same access to important informal communication networks as White men.

The fact that members of cultural minority groups may have a more difficult time integrating into informal networks is easily understandable in light of research on homogeneity and group cohesiveness. Sociocultural homogeneity tends to make relationships more predictable and to facilitate communications (Lincoln & Miller, 1979). Thus we would expect a preference for interacting with members of one's own culture group, especially in an informal context, to be prevalent in organizations. That this preference is true for minority group members as well as majority group members is easily demonstrated by the tendency for members of these groups to sit together at lunch and to form their own, culture-identity-based support groups. However, a point made earlier that bears repeating here is that because the power structure of most organizations is heavily skewed toward majority group members, the segregation of informal networks has vastly different career implications for minority group members than for majority group members.

Mentoring

Mentoring has been defined as a relationship between a younger adult (protégé) and an older, more experienced adult (mentor) in which the mentor provides support, guidance, and counseling to enhance the protégé's success at work and in other arenas of life (Kram, 1985). Kram has further refined the definition of mentoring by distinguishing between career support that focuses specifically on job-related goals and psychosocial support that emphasizes psychological and emotional well being (Kram, 1983, 1985). Thomas (1990) takes this distinction a step further by conceptualizing two separate types of "developmental" relationships. Those emphasizing the career support he calls sponsorship, while he reserves mentoring for relationships in which both career and psychosocial assistance are provided. In addition, the mentoring relationship is characterized by interdependence, long duration, and mutuality of interest.

Kram and Isabella (1985) have demonstrated that peers may serve as effective mentors, and thus the source of the support does not always have to be someone at a higher organization level. Nevertheless, mentors at higher levels have clear advantages in the type of career support they can provide. Accordingly, in this chapter, *mentoring* will refer to both career and psychosocial support by a person at a higher organization level. Further, the emphasis will be on the career functions of mentoring.

Value of Mentoring

Research has clearly established the importance of mentoring to the career success of individuals. For example, a survey of 1,200 top managers from the largest U.S. companies shows that two-thirds of them had established a relationship with a mentor, and that executives who had established such a relationship earned more than those who had not (Klauss, 1981). Likewise, empirical research on the early career experiences of MBA alumni shows that actual promotions and compensation as well as satisfaction with compensation and benefits are positively related to the levels of mentoring (Dreher & Ash, 1990; Whitely, Dougherty, & Dreher, 1991).

The fact that mentoring is important to career outcomes is not lost on employees. For example, in my recent survey (referred to previously) of three hundred mostly managerial and professional employees in a large U.S. company, I found that 94 percent rated mentoring as important or very important as a factor in promotion to senior positions.

Effect of Group Identity on Mentoring

Given the importance of mentoring to career success, it is prudent to examine the extent to which mentoring activity may be influenced by the group identities of organization members. Available theory and research suggest that group identities impact mentoring activity in several ways. First, using a logic similar to that applied above to informal communication networks, similarity of group identity may enhance attraction and friendship between people. Indeed, Kram (1980) argues that the most effective mentoring relationships evolve from mutual attraction and interpersonal chemistry, and Tsui and O'Reilly (1989) have demonstrated the importance of demographic similarity to personal attraction. In a study of 272 middle manager superior-subordinate dyads, Tsui and O'Reilly (1989) found that personal attraction was lower in dyads where the superior and subordinate were of different genders. They did not find this effect in mixed race dyads. However, since race differed in only 20 of the 253 dyads, it is questionable that an adequate test of the race difference hypothesis was possible.

Thus prospective mentors may be more prone to select protégés who are similar to them in gender, race, nationality, and so on. Since most mentoring in organizations occurs informally and most persons at higher organization levels are majority group

members, members of other groups may be disadvantaged in securing mentors or may have less effective mentors, particularly
regarding career support (Noe, 1988).

In addition to the implications of same-group preferences discussed above, special circumstances of cross-gender mentoring relationships in organizations may also disadvantage women. Four
such circumstances that have been identified by experts in the field
are: (1) less informal contact, (2) stereotypes, (3) anxiety-
ambivalence about intimacy and physical attraction, and (4) concerns about the public image of the relationship (Raggins, 1989;
Clawson & Kram, 1984; Noe, 1988; Burke & McKeen, 1990).

The likelihood that women may not have the same access as
men to informal communication networks of organizations was
discussed in the previous section of this chapter. Such networks
provide a valuable source of contacts and opportunities to establish
friendships that may lead to the creation of mentoring relationships. Therefore, to the extent that women participate less in such
networks, or are less likely to use them effectively to build mentoring relationships, their opportunities for mentoring may be lower.

Stereotypes may also hinder cross-gender mentoring relationships. For example, Fitt & Newton (1981) found that male mentors
were less likely to assume women were competent and as a result
deferred establishing relationships with female protégés until they
had proved themselves. A second example occurred in my recent
work in two divisions of a large organization in which several female interviewees reported that some men have a tendency to relate
to them as they would to their wives or daughters rather than as
professional colleagues.

Some research suggests that the majority of mentoring relationships involve daily contact between mentors and protégés
(Burke & McKeen, 1990). In cross-gender mentoring, this level of
contact can lead to anxiety by mentors and protégés about physical
attraction and the prospect of intimacy and romantic involvement
(Clawson & Kram, 1984). The anxiety arising from the notion that
frequent cross-gender contact is related to romantic attraction is not
a paranoia. Quinn (1977) found that ongoing work-related contact
was a factor in 77 percent of romantic relationships among people
on the job. Further, if romance does develop between colleagues in

a work relationship, it has a great potential to disrupt job performance by the participants and those around them (Quinn & Lees, 1984). Also there is evidence that both men and women experience more anxiety in cross-gender than in same-gender mentor relationships (Kram, 1985; Phillips-Jones, 1982).

Thus a greater need for individuals to manage physical attraction and the temptation to form romantic relationships is one of the consequences of the increasing numbers of women in the workforce. It is probably inevitable that some employees will respond to this by withdrawal behaviors such as avoiding the formation of cross-gender mentoring relationships.

A fourth and closely related factor hindering cross-gender mentoring is what Clawson and Kram (1984) refer to as "the public image factor." This is the concern that others may perceive a relationship as involving a romantic attachment even though it does not. The concern is exacerbated if, as is often the case, the mentor is a high-level male and the protégé is a lower-level female. Based on observations in my recent consulting experience, this public image factor is a serious concern for both prospective mentors and protégés in many organizations. For example, when I recently conducted a workshop for a large company at a well-known hotel, a senior human resource manager told me that he wanted to invite members of his staff to the hotel for an evening meeting to run parallel with the workshop. He decided against it because his staff members were women and he was concerned about how it would look to his colleagues. Among the worries of the male mentor is that he may be perceived as taking advantage of his more powerful position, while the female protégé worries that she will be perceived as "sleeping her way to the top." Married workers of both genders are concerned about being perceived as having an affair. Such concerns are not frivolous but should not be allowed to block important organizational opportunities such as mentoring. Managers may have to adjust the times and locations for meetings, but avoidance of off-site contact in my view goes too far.

Cross-Race Mentoring

The literature on cross-race mentoring is much more limited than that of gender. Some of what has been said about cross-gender mentoring may also be said for race. For example, stereotypes of non-Whites as less capable may make mentors less prone to select non-Whites as protégés, and the problems of low representation at higher organization levels and lower access to informal networks in predominantly White male organizations may affect non-Whites and White women similarly (Ibarra, 1993).

Conceptual work by Thomas offers additional ideas on how racioethnic identity may influence mentoring in organizations. For example, he argues that deeply ingrained racial taboos and the greater uncertainty about outcomes that is experienced in cross-race mentoring combine to make cross-race relationships less complete and more instrumental (limited to career functions) than same-race dyads (Thomas, 1989a). In addition, he suggests that the success of cross-race mentoring relationships is partly determined by whether or not the mentor and protégé are at complementary stages of racioethnic identity development (Thomas, 1989b). (For stage models of racioethnic identity development, see Chapter Four.)

In sum, there appear to be a variety of reasons for expecting diversity in workgroups to make mentoring considerably more complicated and problematic. However, most of what has been presented here so far is conceptual. In the next section, empirical data relevant to identity effects on mentoring will be reviewed.

Group Identity Effects on Mentoring: Empirical Research

Most of the empirical research on the impact of group identities on mentoring has focused on gender. For the most part, this research shows that women—at least those in managerial and professional positions—do not report less access to mentoring than men. Studies of MBA alumni from a cross section of organizations by Cox and Nkomo (1991) and by Dreher and Ash (1990) found no significant gender differences in reported access to mentoring assistance over the course of the career. Noe (1988) studied mentoring of 43 mentors and 139 protégés in a formal mentoring program in nine educational institutions. He found that female protégés were rated as using mentors more effectively than male protégés. Raggins and McFarlin (1990) and Thomas (1990) also found no significant gender differences reported in mentoring.

One way to interpret these results is that women simply work harder to overcome the barriers to mentoring alluded to previously. However, another perspective is that women are more likely than men to acknowledge the assistance of mentors. This interpretation would be consistent with the emphasis on independence by men versus connectedness by women that has been cited as a cultural difference between men and women (Tannen, 1990; Belenky et al., 1986).

A third interpretation is that mentoring is much more essential for women professionals than it is for men. Thus, even though it may be far more difficult for women to obtain mentoring, it may also be the case that those without it simply do not make it into management, and therefore the research—which for the most part uses existing managers as subjects—covers relatively few unmentored women. This interpretation is supported by data on the percentage of high-level male and female managers who report having mentors. According to a study of 76 top executive women by Morrison, White, and Van Velsor (1987), 100 percent of the women had received mentor help. This compares with a 55 percent mentoring rate in an earlier study of executive men and a 67 percent rate for executives overall from a study of 1,200 top executives of the nation's largest companies, most of whom would, of course, be male (Klauss, 1981). Burke and McKeen (1990) cite this comparison, concluding that Morrison et al.'s results "reinforce the importance of mentors to careers, but highlight them as a factor more critical to the success of women than men" (p. 318).

This third interpretation suggests that the scarcity of women in senior management ranks of organizations may be partly due to the fact that many do not have mentors and yet cannot gain entry into these positions without them. My own view is that all three of these interpretations are correct.

Empirical research by David Thomas (1990) offers some support for the position that mentoring is affected by racioethnic identities. In his study of developmental relationships among two hundred Black and White managers, Thomas's hypotheses asserted that racioethnic identity affects mentoring relationships in several ways:

- Blacks have more developmental relationships outside the organization.
- Blacks have more relationships with persons other than immediate superiors.
- Blacks utilize mentoring relationships at later career stages.
- Psychosocial support is higher in same-race dyads than in mixed-race dyads.

The hypotheses were based on factors mentioned previously such as lower participation of Blacks in informal networks, an absence of Blacks at higher levels, and greater closeness and intensity of relationships when both parties are of the same racioethnic identity group. His data provided support for all except the third hypothesis.

Nkomo and I (1991) studied levels of mentoring assistance reported by 729 Black and White MBAs, including more than 100 from each of the four race/gender groups in the sample. We found that Blacks reported significantly less mentoring assistance than Whites but there were no significant gender differences.

Unfortunately, nearly all of the empirical work on group identity effects of mentoring have addressed quantitative measures of mentor help more than the quality of the relationships. As noted by Thomas (1990), there is a strong need for examination of qualitative measures such as the comparative duration of the relationship, the variety in types of support provided, and meeting frequency.

Formal Mentoring Programs

Partly as a response to the possibility that mentoring may not be as accessible to nonmajority group members, some organizations have created formal mentoring programs. Organizations that have used them include Fannie Mae, Merrill Lynch, AT&T, Jewel Companies, and Federal Express. In some cases these programs are available to all employees and in others they are targeted for members of culture groups that have been found to be excluded or disadvantaged in normal, informal mentoring activity. In formal mentoring programs, organizations facilitate the matching of mentors and protégés. They do so in a variety of ways, ranging from hosting of social events at which prospective mentors and protégés can meet and pursue matches of mutual interest on their own to assigning mentors to specific protégés. It should be noted that some experts believe that assigned mentoring does not work well (Kram, 1985). My own recommendations are these:

- Do not use formal mentoring unless explicit data indicate a need for it. The same principle applies to targeted mentoring programs.
- Use assigned mentors only as a last resort: maximize voluntary matches first.
- If mentors are assigned, make them preliminary assignments with review after six months and the possibility of reassignment or termination of participation in the program.

In addition to the above, scholars who have written about mentoring and the experience of organizations with formal mentoring programs indicate several principles that should be followed to increase effectiveness:

- Select mentors carefully to ensure that they are genuinely committed and good at development.
- Involve protégés in creating matches.
- Provide organizational incentives for being a mentor.
- Provide training for both mentors and protégés.
- Establish some formal mechanism to monitor progress of the relationships and to evaluate their effectiveness (Phillips-Jones, 1983; Klauss, 1981).

Summary

This chapter has discussed ways in which group identities such as gender, racioethnicity, and nationality may influence participation in career-relevant informal activities of organizations. The limited empirical data on the issues raised have also been reviewed. In general, there are strong conceptual arguments and some empirical verification that barriers to full informal integration may hinder career success among members of cultural minority groups. Thus full contribution of all organization members may be enhanced by actions to facilitate equal access to, and effectiveness of, informal networks of organizations.

Propositions for Discussion

Proposition 12.1:   In the typical organization with skewed identity representation, mentoring will be (a) more available and (b) of higher quality for majority group members than for minority group members.

Proposition 12.2:   When informal networks are not well integrated, the segregation of these networks will be a significant source of disadvantage to minority group members in terms of their ability to achieve career success and to contribute to the organization's goals.

Proposition 12.3:   Both majority and minority group members may experience more anxiety and uncertainty in cross-group mentoring relationships than in same-group relationships.

Proposition 12.4:   Much of the segregation in informal networks is due to cultural ethnocentrism by members of all identity groups. However, the negative career impact of segregated networks will be greater for minority group members because of power imbalances in organizations.

13

Institutional Bias

When you talk about my experiences with racism, I have problems with that term because in a way, it glosses over the more subtle issues of how cultural groups interface with institutions which operate according to implicit cultural assumptions. Nobody has to personally discriminate, it's simply that if work has to be done a certain way, it's based on certain cultural assumptions of how the work gets done, how do you write up a proposal for example. There are certain procedures, certain cultural ways of putting together a proposal. . . . If you think in a Western linear fashion, you go a-b-c. This is the way I make an effective argument. When you're from another background, the arguments get made in a different way, following a different kind of logic. That's real subtle (Khoo, 1988, p. 88).

The above quotation taken from a colleague's interview of a third generation Chinese American is one of the best expressions I have run across to capture the meaning of institutional bias. The term *bias* simply means a preference for a particular thing, person, style, and so on, compared to other possible things, persons, or styles. In the context of intergroup dynamics, an unfavorable bias toward one group implies a favorable bias toward another. *Institutional bias* refers to the fact that preference patterns inherent in how we manage organizations often inadvertently create barriers to full participation by organization members from cultural backgrounds that differ from the traditional majority group. That this phenomenon exists is easily understood when one considers organizational histories. Most large organizations were created decades or even centuries ago, and have subsequently been managed at the top level, at least until very recently, by a fairly homogeneous group of people. These "founding fathers" naturally reflected their own cultural biases and value systems in establishing the rules, policies, and practices that have shaped the organizations. For the most part, their rules, policies, and practices remain intact today despite the enormous changes that have occurred in the workforce during this century. In addition, when the attitudes, beliefs, and behaviors of many of the founders and senior managers of today's organizations were shaped (1930s–1950s), intergroup relations based on racioethnic, gender, nationality, and other group identities were overtly less tolerant and inclusive than they are today. Institutional bias evolved as a natural consequence of such organizational histories. Commenting on the phenomenon of institutional bias in U.S. organizations, Loden and Rosener (1991) explain: "As a result of our colonial history, most American businesses and institutions have been shaped primarily by the values and experiences of Western European white men. These 'founding fathers' were responsible for institutionalizing many of the norms, expectations . . . that are the stuff of contemporary organization cultures. One major consequence of these historical events has been the continual undervaluing of others with core identities different from those of Western European, white, heterosexual, physically able-bodied men" (p. 28).

As I have emphasized throughout this book, cultural comparisons between identity groups are a mixture of similarity and difference. Certainly, there are many points of overlap in the cultural preference patterns of organization members. We are concerned here, however, with the possibility of bias that may occur because of differences in cultures.

Examples of Institutional Bias

Table 13.1 lists thirteen common practices and characteristics of Euro-Western organizations that potentially create unfavorable bias toward members of one or more culture identity groups. The balance of this chapter will provide a discussion and some examples of these practices. As the discussion unfolds, keep in mind that in

**Table 13.1. Common Organizational Practices
That Tend to Create Institutional Bias.**

1. The fifty-hour-plus workweek and scheduling of weekend and evening meetings
2. The emphasis on self-promotion behaviors in hiring and promotion interviews
3. The use of self-evaluations/statements of accomplishment in performance appraisal processes
4. A policy of maintaining separation of work and personal/family life
5. The tendency toward standardization of all types
6. The use of brainstorming as a common idea generation device
7. The use of verbal glibness and polished English in presentations as a significant criterion in promotion, job assignments, and performance appraisal
8. The tendency toward institutional support of monolingualism in work and educational institutions
9. An orientation in appraisal and reward systems favoring individualism over collective action and teamwork
10. Reliance on interviews (mostly using majority-group interviewers) and informal recommendations and referrals as prime tools in hiring and promotion processes
11. The use of a payback period as a criterion in promotion decisions and retraining
12. The tendency to define effective leadership in terms that reflect traits typical of the dominant group
13. Physical workplaces that assume a fully able-bodied workforce

most cases the practices discussed pose problems for all workers. The possession of a group identity that differs from the majority group, however, exacerbates the effect. When practices tend to impact differentially on workers from different cultural backgrounds, it indicates cultural bias in the people management systems of organizations.

The Fifty-Hour Workweek

Recently, during a focus group meeting for a financial services company, a number of professional and managerial women were commenting on how they experienced the organizational culture. One woman stated that she had just turned in a time report for 137 hours for the most recent two-week period. Another woman stated that she was manager in a unit in which all employees routinely worked more than 100 hours during a two-week period. Still another woman commented that meetings were sometimes scheduled to begin at 5:00 P.M. or 7:30 A.M. Based on my observations at other companies, the experience of these women is not unusual, a conclusion supported by a recent report of the International Labor Organization indicating that the typical workload in North America is between 48 and 49 hours a week (Briscoe, 1992).

Long hours and meetings scheduled before 8:00 A.M., after 4:00 P.M., or on weekends, especially on a continuous basis, present difficulties for all employees. However, such practices impact differentially on working mothers because they typically assume greater responsibility for care of children and family chores. For example, studies show that here in the United States, despite recent trends toward a greater role for husbands in home duties, women still do twice as much at home as men (Robinson, 1988). Nor is this bias limited to the United States. For instance, research indicates that 82 percent of all household chores in Havana, Cuba, are done by women, and the average time spent on household chores by Japanese men is fifteen minutes per day (Briscoe, 1992). In addition, there is evidence that the actual hours of employment worked by women is longer than for men in many parts of the world, including Western Europe, Asia, and Africa (Briscoe, 1992).

In addition to having greater time demands related to work and home responsibilities, the adverse emotional and psychological impact of long hours at work is greater for women than for men. Results from a recent survey of dual-career couples show that women are twice as likely as men to feel guilty about the effects on home and family life of working long hours and weekends (Simonetti, Nykodym, & Goralske, 1988).

Again, the point is not that the time expectations of jobs do not affect men, nor should the effects on men be minimized or overlooked, but that the impact on women is generally greater. This is the reason that such practices are relevant to the management of diversity in organizations. The expectation of long hours and meetings at odd hours inadvertently creates a systematic bias against the career success of women.

Self-Promotion and the Use of Self-Evaluations

Items 2 and 3 in Table 13.1 are closely related and therefore will be discussed together. A number of common business practices call for self-promoting behavior by employees. For example, in interviews candidates are often expected to sell themselves. This translates into describing themselves and their accomplishments in terms that are as flattering as possible and that emphasize personal achievement. Another example is that some organizations make use of self-appraisals as part of the formal performance assessment process. At one company where I recently did some work, the form on which these annual self-evaluations were done was informally referred to as the "brag sheet," signifying the general perception of the kind of behavior that was needed to effectively complete one. One person commented that "creative writing" was often used in completing the form.

The extent to which employees are comfortable, or even willing, to engage in this kind of self-promotional behavior varies considerably from person to person. Clearly many majority group members in a firm may be disadvantaged compared to bolder, more confident, or even more conceited colleagues, but there are also cultural differences that make this a diversity issue in organizations. Several of the relevant cultural differences are discussed in Chapter Seven of this book and so will only be mentioned briefly here. Practices emphasizing self-promotion may be particularly difficult for persons from Japanese and Chinese cultural backgrounds due to modesty norms, especially in interactions with superiors. For example, in a study that bears directly on the practice of self-appraisals, Farh, Dobbins, and Cheng (1991) compared self-ratings of performance to the ratings of supervisors in 900 superior-subordinate dyads in nine Chinese organizations. The authors hypothesized that cultural norms such as collectivism and modesty would cause the Chinese to refrain from exaggerating their achievements and possibly even to underrate their performance. They found that the Chinese workers did indeed consistently rate their performance lower than their supervisors rated it. The authors compared their findings to research on predominantly Anglo American samples (the gender and race of which were not specified) in which self-ratings were consistently higher than supervisory ratings. The authors conclude that Chinese employees "may evaluate themselves as less effective than equally performing U.S. employees and thus may be unfairly discriminated against in any administrative decisions which are based upon self-ratings" (p. 142).

Although this research was conducted with Chinese workers and not with Chinese Americans, evidence indicates that identification with root cultures persists even after many generations (see Chapter Four). There is no question that modesty norms and collectivism do operate to some degree in the cultural makeup of many Asian Americans. In addition, the research directly addresses the potential institutional bias in the human resource practices of multinational companies operating in Asia and for native-born Chinese employees of American companies. Another point to be noted is that decisions need not be based entirely on self-ratings for the bias to have a significant impact on an employee's career experiences.

Practices relying on self-promotional behavior are also likely to be especially troublesome for members of those American Indian tribes for whom silence and reserve are a sign of strength and are highly valued (Trimble, 1988). Finally, aggressive self-promoting behavior may be more acceptable from men than women. For example, as previously noted, Tannen's study (1990) of the source of communication differences between men and women suggests that men, more so than women, learn to use communication as a way to get attention from others. If this is true, then it may be easier for men to call attention to themselves and their accomplishments in a formal communiqué.

The Bureaucratic Model

Items 4 and 5 in Table 13.1 represent two aspects of the bureaucratic model of organizations as described by German sociologist Max Weber (1947). The fact that the principles of this model continue to be enormously influential in the shaping of organizations in the United States and other nations that were historically dominated by Western Europeans is widely acknowledged by experts on organizational design. Among them are Dick Daft and Richard Steers (1986), who write: "Each of Weber's bureaucratic dimensions exists in today's large organizations. These basic characteristics have become widely accepted as an appropriate way to organize" (pp. 224–225).

Despite its strong points and continued influence, the bureaucratic model is, in many respects, antithetical to the needs of culturally diverse workgroups (see Fernandez, 1991, and Jackson, 1992, for additional discussion of this point). The idea that work and family life should remain separate follows from the impersonality and the separation of person and job principles of the model. Because this compartmentalized approach to the work and family domains of life is well entrenched in U.S. companies, it is only in the past five or six years that a significant number of organizations have taken steps to support employees seeking to address work/family role conflict through such things as company-sponsored child care, liberalized leave policies, and flexible hours. As described earlier in our discussion of the fifty-hour workweek, the failure of organizations to respond to increased work/family conflict impacts differentially on women and men and thus becomes a form of institutionalized bias against female workers.

A second dimension of the bureaucratic model that is relevant to diversity in workgroups is the tendency toward standardization. Standardization is rooted in the bureaucratic principles of division of labor, impersonality, separation of job and jobholder, and emphasis on written rules and regulations (Randolph & Blackburn, 1989). The basic meaning of standardization is making things uniform and void of deviation from identified norms. Thus the term itself, in some respects, is the antithesis of diversity. On a practical level, standardization often translates into an inflexible system that responds unfavorably to anything beyond the ordinary. As such it can lead to a type of narrowness that impacts unfavorably on diversity of all types, including those based on group affiliations.

The following story is an example of how standardization creates problems in the context of diverse groups. In a recent workshop, a manager of diversity for a large U.S. firm told how until recently the company had standard retirement benefit policies around the world. In parts of South America, however, employees found the provision of a set amount per month for life very unattractive. Because of a history of political and economic instability, pensions were not valued unless they were given in the form of lump-sum payments at the time of retirement. Many would use these to invest in tangible assets such as land or in a business. Maintaining a uniform policy would not have served the needs of the diverse workforce of this multinational company well, so ultimately the policy was changed to accommodate the preference for different kinds of pensions.

Brainstorming, Verbal Fluency, and Monolingualism

Items 6 through 8 of Table 13.1 address a set of related issues that impact especially on Latino and Asian members of Euro-Western organizations. Brainstorming is a popular problem-solving and creativity technique used in interactive groups in which members, often extemporaneously, offer whatever ideas come to mind in a random, uncritical fashion. The objective is to surface as many relevant ideas as possible. Although this technique may be experienced as empowering and even fun by many workers, cultural traditions and language factors may make it more difficult to use effectively with members of some Asian and American Indian groups. This was alluded to briefly in Chapter Seven when speech anxiety and other communications differences and their effects were discussed. In discussing the tendency for many Asian Americans to be low-key in activities calling for high verbalization in predominantly Anglo settings, James Morishima (1981) makes the following point: "Rather than having cognitive deficiencies or a lack of linguistic facility, Asian Americans appear to be less verbal because of personality or situational variables. Shyness, speech anxiety, conformity to authority figures and reserve are frequently attributed to Asian/Pacific Americans" (p. 388).

Not only brainstorming but other common organizational practices related to verbal fluency may inadvertently disadvantage members of certain culture groups. This point was discussed at length in Chapter Seven and thus will only be touched upon here. In many organizations, a great deal of emphasis is placed on skill in oral presentations. Lasting impressions about the presenter's competence are often formed in these high-visibility activities. To the extent that such impressions are heavily influenced by the style (as opposed to the content) of the presentation, persons who are less verbal due to cultural traditions or second-language factors may be unfairly judged as less competent.

It should also be recognized that the use of one language itself creates an inevitable bias favoring native speakers of that language. In this regard I agree with Fernandez (1991) that actions which strengthen monolingualism work against the creation of multicultural organizations and that the dearth of bilingual education opportunities in the United States is inappropriate, given the diversity within the country and the increasing globalization of business.

This is not to say that the bias inherent in monolingualism is necessarily one that organizations should or can avoid entirely. However, it is important to acknowledge the disadvantage that some members of the organization may have because of it. The following are specific steps that native speakers can take to minimize the effects of the bias:

1. Allowing extra time for meetings in which the presenters are second-language speakers
2. Encouraging second-language members to present their own work rather than prepping a native speaker to present it
3. Focusing on the content of the presentation rather than on how it is presented and encouraging others to do the same. The latter may include challenging others to examine the reasons behind an unfavorable reaction to a presentation (substance versus style)
4. Requesting written material on the presentation so that the content can be reviewed
5. Honoring employee preferences, to the extent possible, regarding presenting ideas and proposals in writing rather than verbally
6. Encouraging second-language members to use both (or all) languages in any situation where they can be understood by everyone who is a party to the communiqué

The last two points require clarification. Recommendation 5 acknowledges that given enough time, most nonnative speakers will get whatever assistance is needed to communicate fully in the preferred language. In oral communication, however, the only opportunity for this is in awkward and sometimes embarrassing queries about how certain things should be said.

Recommendation 6 is a response to the controversy over whether languages other than the dominant language should be used in the workplace. Fernandez (1991) reports that nearly half of White males and American Indians react negatively to the use of languages by other workers that they do not understand. In my view, such attitudes have to be changed if diversity is to be valued and if multicultural organizations are to be created. Organizations can take a step toward this by making it official policy that *all* languages are acceptable as long as the person(s) to whom the communication is directed can understand the message.

Individualistic Reward Systems

Differences among culture groups related to individualism versus collectivism and some of their implications for practices of organizations were discussed in Chapter Seven. The research of Hofstede (1984) among others cited there establishes that individualism is a strong cultural theme in most Euro-Western organizations. It is manifested in such common practices as the use of sales contests, limiting bonus eligibility to the highest-performing individuals and to certain levels, payment by commissions, and ranking systems of promotion. What these techniques have in common is that rewards are based on workers standing out as individual achievers compared to their co-workers. While this approach is not necessarily wrong, it contains a certain bias that may disadvantage some workers because of their cultural heritage. For example, a well-known phrase expressing a Japanese perspective on this is "the nail that sticks out gets hammered down." Contrast the ideology expressed in this proverb to that conveyed by "the cream rises to the top" and "may the best man/woman win."

Biases Embedded in Selection Processes

Items 10 and 11 of Table 13.1 address selection and will be considered together in this section. Interviewing is the most widely used and most influential selection device of organizations (Arnold &

Feldman, 1986). Although interviews offer many benefits, two facts about them combine to create a strong potential for cultural-diversity-related bias: (1) the "similar to me" phenomenon and (2) the fact that interviewers, especially those making the final decisions, tend to be members of the dominant group.

The "Similar to Me" Phenomenon. Although most managers and professionals view themselves as objective, there is evidence to indicate that selection decisions are heavily influenced by the extent to which the decision maker views the job candidate as being like himself or herself. Arnold and Feldman (1986) cite examples of the "similar to me" phenomenon and summarize this way: "Of course, chemistry probably won't get an obvious bungler a good job, and where one candidate is clearly superior, it may not play a role at all. But in the common situation where three or four candidates all could handle the job, executives often lean to people who share their personal values, manner of dressing and even personal habits" (p. 439).

In a more systematic study of the "similar to me" phenomenon, Rand and Wexley (1975) designed an experiment in which 80 White male and 80 White female college students viewed a videotaped job interview in which Black and White interviewees responded to a set of twelve questions. The students were given biographical dossiers on each interviewee and were told to act as employment interviewers in viewing the tape. The dossiers and interviews were manipulated with the objective of making half of the interviewees biographically similar to the student raters and half of the interviewees biographically dissimilar to the student raters. After viewing the interviews, the students gave hiring recommendation scores for each of the interviewees. Results indicated that scores were significantly higher for the biographically similar candidates than for those who were dissimilar, and that biographical similarity accounted for 11 percent of the variance in the hiring recommendation scores. The authors concluded that "such 'similar to me' errors appear particularly distressing since often biographical items are unrelated to subsequent job success" (p. 541).

Interestingly, Rand and Wexley found that the race of the interviewee was not a factor in the operation of the "similar to me" phenomenon. It is important to note, however, that in the experiment they were able to eliminate any correlation between racioethnic identity and the background data. In actual job selections, however, no such standardization of backgrounds is possible. Therefore, to the extent that actual biographical background information is related to group identities such as race, the research suggests that the results of interracial interview dyads in organizational settings may indeed be influenced by racioethnic identity. This point is reinforced by the fact that the actual biographical information used by Rand and Wexley to create the similar/dissimilar dossiers was explicitly based on stereotypical differences between Blacks and Whites. All six items used to differentiate the interviewees were created by asking the students to identify White middle-class stereotypes of Blacks and of Whites. Thus the dissimilar condition was defined by using stereotypes of Blacks while the similar condition was defined as the White stereotype. For example, the description used for the biographically dissimilar person listed father's occupation as laborer, whereas the one for the biographically similar person listed it as office worker.

This research illustrates several important points. First, the fact that racioethnic stereotypes were used to define dissimilarity/similarity indicates that race was highly relevant to the hiring recommendations. Second, the fact that the students identified these particular stereotypes suggests that in a selection situation in which background data are not explicitly available, an interviewer might assume that the non-White candidate is less similar because of awareness of the stereotypes. For both reasons, the study supports the conclusion that group identities such as racioethnicity play a major role in the "similar to me" phenomenon.

The "similar to me" phenomenon would not necessarily produce institutional bias on the basis of culture identity if candidates of all group identities were equally likely to be demographically and culturally similar to recruiting decision makers. However, since the vast majority of selection decisions are made by majority group members, operation of the "similar to me" phenomenon does create a systematic bias against members of minority groups in organizations.

The Informal Network as a Selection Tool. Another form of institutionalized bias in selection processes occurs because of the importance of informal contacts, recommendations, and referrals as a source of information. As discussed in Chapter Twelve, it may be more difficult for women, non-White men, persons with disabilities, and others who are not majority group members to participate in informal communication and social networks. One way that organizations contribute directly to the problem of exclusion is by the types of company-sponsored social events that they select. For example, until recently Avon emphasized season's tickets to sporting events and referred to their annual management off-site meeting as "President's Golf Day." The change to a more diversified set of events occurred as a direct result of complaints by the first two female officers at the company (Jackson & Alvarez, 1992).

The importance of this issue as a possible barrier to career success has been widely acknowledged in previous research. For example, a recent survey of 245 CEOs and human resource professionals listed exclusion from the "old boy network" as the most widely cited career-related problem of female managers and professionals (Rosen, Miguel, & Pierce, 1989), and 1988 survey data compiled by Fernandez (1991) indicates that 87 percent of Blacks, 42 percent of other racioethnic minorities, and 36 percent of Whites believe that racioethnic minorities are excluded from informal work networks.

Loden and Rosner (1991) cite the case of the big eight accounting firms as an example of how this form of bias operates. They note that the ability to generate new business through social contacts is of particular importance in the public accounting industry, and that this disadvantages women, who have a difficult time breaking into the social circles that facilitate establishing such contacts.

The Use of Payback Period. Still another way that bias related to group identities enters selection decisions is through the use of the payback period as a criterion, especially in promotion decisions. In this context *payback period* refers to the expected number of years that an employee will work after a job change. Research and theory from the field of labor economics (often called human capital theory) posit that employers will be more likely to invest in training and promotions for employees who have longer payback periods (Rosenbaum, 1984). On the face of it this seems to make good business sense. The problem is that the use of payback periods in making decisions about training and promotion indirectly discriminates against older employees. Indeed, research conducted on entry-level management jobs shows that promotability is negatively related to age even for relatively young employees in their thirties and forties (Cox & Nkomo, 1992; Rosenbaum, 1984). In our study of 125 lower-level managers in a public sector firm, we found that even after controlling for education, performance, and job tenure, age had a negative effect on promotability ratings (Cox & Nkomo, 1992). Our findings were very consistent with those of other researchers, who have reported that first-level managers tend to be promoted to second level only until about age thirty-five and that promotion rates into middle management jobs drop off drastically after age forty.

While age effects are attributable to other factors such as age stereotypes, payback period is undoubtedly a part of the equation (Rosenbaum, 1984; Cox & Nkomo, 1992). To the extent that it is included in selection criteria in organizations, an indirect form of age bias will result.

Use of "Male" Traits in Defining Management and Leadership

Another subtle form of institutionalized bias is defining effective leadership or management traits in a way that is not identity-neutral. Sometimes, such as when traits like aggressiveness and ability to work independently are specified in performance rating forms, this form of bias is explicit in the criteria used. In other cases it occurs more informally through the images that supervisors hold about the ideal manager and the translation of such images into management actions such as performance ratings and rankings for promotion.

One example of this is the work of Gary Powell (1988) on gender bias in defining management behavior. His research methodology essentially involves comparing characteristics that subjects define as male and female traits to those used to define effective managers. The findings have consistently shown that both men and women define good management in ways that are decidedly biased toward traditional male traits. Based on his analysis of earlier research and his own data Powell concludes, "In summary despite the increase in female managers, and no matter what questionnaire or study design has been used . . . people have described men as more like good managers than women, and good managers as higher in stereotypically masculine traits than stereotypically feminine traits. Men and women at all career stages examined, including practicing managers . . . share the same biases about management" (p. 148).

Powell adds that images about what makes a good manager have essentially remained unchanged thus far despite the increased representation of women in managerial jobs. This is no doubt partly due to the fact that women continue to have very low representation in the more powerful higher-level management jobs where their impact on organizational culture would be more noticeable.

Physical Construction of Worksites

Institutional bias sometimes occurs because the physical facilities in many organizations were designed for fully able bodied workers. With the passage of the American Disabilities Act and the expectation of renewed efforts to gain access to the workplace for the estimated six million unemployed persons with disabilities, U.S. firms need to evaluate accessibility more fully than in the past. Not only must building entrances be barrier-free but such things as availability of audio and visual aids, equipment for the sight-impaired, desk heights, width of aisles, and location of elevators must be assessed. Attention to these things not only accommodates existing employees but says to prospective workers who have disabilities that they are welcome and valued.

Summary

Because most organizations were founded and managed in their formative years by culturally homogeneous leadership groups, biases unfavorable to members of other cultural backgrounds may have become ingrained in their culture and management practices. This chapter has discussed thirteen specific types of ingrained biases in institutions. Because such biases are inherent in standard practices, they are usually quite invisible to most members of an organization until an audit of the organizational culture is conducted and insight into cultural differences among various identity groups is provided. The formal conduct of such cultural audits is a major organization activity that will be discussed in Chapters Fourteen and Fifteen.

Propositions for Discussion

Proposition 12.1:   Organizations in which a particular culture group has been dominant since they were founded will tend to have biases ingrained in culture and management practices that create barriers to full participation and success for members from other cultural backgrounds.

Proposition 12.2:   Specific areas in which institutionalized cultural bias occurs in organizations include (a) norms about hours of work and expected meeting times, (b) performance appraisal processes, (c) job interviews, (d) policies and benefits related to work/family role balance, (e) policies and practices related to language and oral presentations, (f) stereotypical images of effective leadership behavior, and (g) the physical design of the workplace. (Note: this is not intended to be an exhaustive list.)

PART FIVE

MANAGING DIVERSITY: GUIDELINES FOR LEADERSHIP

In Part One, I argued that managing diversity is among the most important challenges facing leaders in the nineties. Parts Two through Four provide a text on how cultural diversity affects behavior in diverse workgroups. These segments are directed toward building individual effectiveness for working in and leading diverse workgroups. In this last section, the material is directed toward leaders who are charged with planning and executing organization change to create what I have called the multicultural organization model. Since organization development work on diversity has thus far been the subject of very little systematic theory and research, this segment of the book will not contain extensive references to the literature. Instead, my experience as a consultant and the experience other practicing managers and consultants will be used as a basis for the material presented here. The conceptual models presented in this section are based largely on my articles "The Multicultural Organization" (Cox, 1991) and "Managing Diversity: Implications for Organizational Competitiveness" (Cox, 1991).

14

A Model to Guide
Organization Change

Creating a Vision

Like other major organization changes, enhancing organizational capability to manage a diverse workforce should begin with creation of a vision that specifies, in broad terms, the objective of the change. As indicated previously, the objective of managing diversity work is to create organizations in which members of all sociocultural backgrounds can contribute and achieve their full potential. I will use the term multicultural to refer to organizations that achieve this objective. Organization change work can be facilitated by explicitly identifying the characteristics of multicultural organizations. Toward this end, the conceptual framework of organization-level factors introduced in Part Four along with the intergroup conflict factors from Part Three may be used here to form a typology of organizations in terms of climate for diversity.

Three organization types will be discussed: the monolithic organization, the plural organization, and the multicultural organization. The application of the six-factor conceptual framework to describe the three organization types appears in Table 14.1.

Monolithic Organization

The most important single fact about the monolithic organization is that it is not culturally integrated even in the formal structure. The organization is demographically as well as culturally homogeneous. In the United States and much of Western Europe, such organizations are characterized by substantial White male majorities in the overall employee population, with relatively few White

225

Table 14.1. Types of Organizations.

Dimension	Monolithic	Plural	Multicultural
1. Culture	Ignores or actively discourages diversity	Ignores or tolerates diversity	Values diversity
2. Acculturation process	Assimilation	Assimilation	Pluralism
3. Degree of structural integration	Minimal	Partial	Full
4. Degree of informal integration	Minimal	Limited	Full
5. Institutional cultural bias in HR systems	Ubiquitous	Prevalent	Minimized or eliminated
6. Intergroup conflict	Minimal due to identity homogeneity	Significant	Minimized by management attention

Source: Adapted from Cox, 1991. Used by permission.

women, racioethnic minorities, or foreign nationals in management jobs. In addition, these organizations feature extremely high levels of occupational segregation, concentrating women and racioethnic minority men in low-status jobs such as secretaries and maintenance. Thus the representation of persons from minority culture backgrounds is very limited in the overall work population as well as in the power structure of the organization.

To a large extent, the characteristics of the monolithic organization along the framework's other four dimensions follow from the relative absence of people from different cultural backgrounds. The effect of hiring decisions in the organization is to exclude persons who are demographically different from the majority, and the effects of cultural difference on organizational experiences are generally ignored. Persons from nonmajority backgrounds who do enter the organization must adopt the existing organizational norms, framed by the majority group as a matter of organizational survival. Finally, because the organization has been designed and managed almost exclusively by members of one culture group, bias unfavorable to persons of other cultural backgrounds is embedded in the practices and policies of the organization.

One positive note is that intergroup conflict and the other potential drawbacks of diversity are minimized in this type of organization by virtue of the relative homogeneity of the workforce.

It should be emphasized that the creation of the individual characteristics of monolithic organizations as specified in Table 14.1 is not always deliberate. Some have a tendency to occur as a natural consequence of the homogeneity of membership. Examples of monolithic organizations in the United States include many private educational institutions and many small businesses, especially those located in rural areas. Examples outside the United States include many Japanese companies.

Aside from the rather obvious downside implications of the monolithic model in terms of under utilization of human resources and social equality, the monolithic organization is not a realistic option for most large employers in the 1990s. To a significant degree, large U.S. organizations made a transition away from this model during the 1960s and 1970s. This transition was spurred by a number of societal forces, most notably the civil rights and feminist movements and the beginnings of changes in workforce demographics, especially in the incidence of career-oriented women. Many organizations responded to these forces by creating the plural organization.

Plural Organization

The plural organization differs from the monolithic organization in several important respects. In general, it has a more heterogeneous membership than the monolithic organization and takes steps to be more inclusive and accepting of persons from cultural backgrounds that differ from the dominant group. These steps include affirmative action programs; manager training on equal opportunity issues such as civil rights laws, the ADA, and sexual harassment; and audits of compensation systems to ensure the absence of discrimination against minority group members. As a result of these steps, the plural organization achieves a much higher level of structural integration and may have a lower incidence of institutionalized bias than the monolithic organization.

The plural organization represents a marked improvement over the monolithic organization in effective management of employees of different cultural backgrounds. Nevertheless, this type of organization is not multicultural. The problem of skewed representation across functions, organization levels, and workgroups—typical in the monolithic organization—is also present in the plural organization. For example, in many large U.S. organizations, racioethnic minorities now make up 20 percent or more of the total workforce. Examples include General Motors, Chrysler, Stroh Brewery, Philip Morris, Coca-Cola, and Anheuser-Busch. However, the representation of non-Whites in management in these same companies averages less than 12 percent (Cox, 1991). A similar picture exists in workgroups. For example, while more than 20 percent of the clerical and office staffs at General Motors are minorities, they represent only about 12 percent of technicians and 13 percent of sales workers. Thus the plural organization features only partial structural integration.

In addition, the plural organization continues the assimilation approach to acculturation that is characteristic of the monolithic organization. As a result, the plural organization tends to be diverse in terms of phenotype, but genuine cultural diversity in these organizations may actually be quite limited. The failure to address cultural aspects of integration is a major shortcoming of the plural organization form, and is a major point distinguishing it from the multicultural organization. Likewise, although the greater structural integration and the more tolerant culture of the plural organization improve opportunities for nonmajorities to participate in informal networks of the organization, their participation is still quite limited, as noted in Chapter Twelve. Finally, types of institutional bias, such as those discussed in Chapter Thirteen, continue to occur.

The plural organization form has been prevalent in the United States since the late 1960s and in my judgment represents the typical large firm today. These organizations emphasize an affirmative action approach to managing diversity. During the 1980s and continuing to the present, increased evidence of resentment toward affirmative action among White males has begun to surface. They argue that such policies, in effect, discriminate against White males and therefore perpetuate the practice of using group identities such as racioethnicity, nationality, or gender as a basis for making personnel decisions. In addition, they argue that it is not fair that contemporary Whites be disadvantaged to compensate for management errors made in the past. This will be discussed more extensively in Chapter Fifteen. As suggested in Chapter Nine, this backlash effect, coupled with the increased number of women and non-White men in the organization, often creates greater intergroup conflict in the plural organization than was present in the monolithic organization.

The Multicultural Organization

In discussing cultural integration aspects of mergers and acquisitions, Sales and Mirvis (1984) argue that an organization which simply contains many different culture groups is a plural organization. They consider an organization to be multicultural only if it values this diversity. An understanding of the distinction between tolerating diversity and valuing it follows from a recognition of the shortcomings of the plural organization as outlined previously. The multicultural organization has overcome these shortcomings. Referring again to Table 14.1, we see that the multicultural organization has the following characteristics:

1. A culture that fosters and values cultural difference
2. Pluralism as an acculturation process
3. Full structural integration
4. Full integration of the informal networks
5. An absence of institutionalized cultural bias in human resource management systems and practices
6. A minimum of intergroup conflict due to the proactive management of diversity

I submit that while few, if any, organizations have fully achieved these characteristics, they should be utilized to create a vision for organizational transitions to more effectively manage diverse workforces.

A Model to Guide Organization Change

It has been suggested here that multicultural organizations have specific characteristics that are different from most traditional organizations. It has also been suggested that organizations wishing to maximize the potential benefits of diversity and minimize potential drawbacks—e.g., in terms of workgroup cohesiveness, interpersonal conflict, turnover, and coherent action on major organizational goals—must transform monolithic and plural organizations into multicultural ones. A comprehensive organization development effort designed to improve organizational capability in managing cultural diversity, and to transform traditional organizations into multicultural ones, should contain the five key components shown in Figure 14.1. In the following section, each of the five components of the change model will be briefly discussed.

Leadership

Leadership refers to the need for champions of the cause of diversity who will take strong personal stands on the need for change, role-model the behaviors required for change, and assist with the work of moving the organization forward. As with any other major organization change effort, the support and genuine commitment of top management is especially crucial. This commitment must be reflected in several ways:

1. The commitment of resources to the effort
2. Inclusion of managing diversity as a component of the business strategy of the organization
3. A willingness to change (if necessary) corporatewide human resource management practices such as performance appraisal and compensation systems
4. A willingness to keep mental energy and financial support

Figure 14.1. Model for Planning Organization Change.

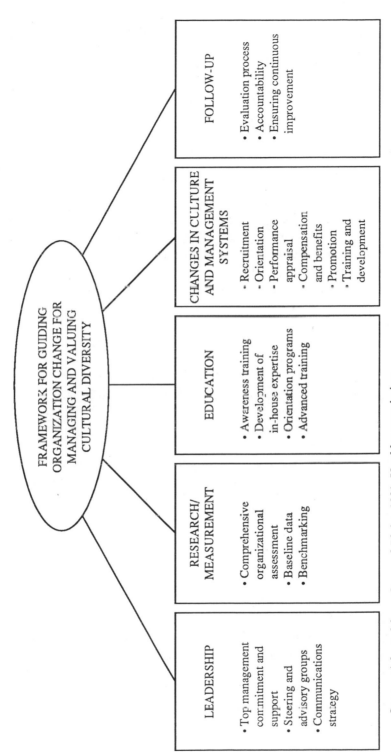

FRAMEWORK FOR GUIDING ORGANIZATION CHANGE FOR MANAGING AND VALUING CULTURAL DIVERSITY

LEADERSHIP

- Top management commitment and support
- Steering and advisory groups
- Communications strategy

RESEARCH/ MEASUREMENT

- Comprehensive organizational assessment
- Baseline data
- Benchmarking

EDUCATION

- Awareness training
- Development of in-house expertise
- Orientation programs
- Advanced training

CHANGES IN CULTURE AND MANAGEMENT SYSTEMS

- Recruitment
- Orientation
- Performance appraisal
- Compensation and benefits
- Promotion
- Training and development

FOLLOW-UP

- Evaluation process
- Accountability
- Ensuring continuous improvement

Source: Adapted from Cox and Blake, 1991. Used by permission.

focused on this objective for a period of years, rather than months or weeks

5.   Establishment of valuing diversity as a core value of the firm that receives the same priority as other core values such as safety, integrity, and total quality

Organizations that have taken a leadership role in managing diversity exemplify this commitment. For example, David Kearns (former chair of Xerox), John Houghton of Corning, Jim Preston of Avon, and Robert McAlister (former chair of U.S. West) are among the CEOs who have been highly visible supporters of managing diversity and of the valuing diversity philosophy. There is no question that the commitment at the top in these companies is a major reason that they are widely cited as benchmark companies in managing diversity work.

It should be emphasized that top management commitment alone is not sufficient. Also needed are champions at lower levels of the organization, especially key line managers. An example of this is the central role that William Hanson, vice president of logistics (formerly vice president of manufacturing) has played in the valuing diversity work at Digital Equipment Corporation.

Many organizations are addressing the leadership requirement in part by changes in organizational structure such as the appointment of full-time directors of diversity or diversity coordinators. More than half of the Fortune 500 now have a position of this type. At several companies, including General Electric, Corning, and Fannie Mae this is a high-level position that reports directly to the president. The job of these persons is to work with other members of the organization to plan and execute organization development work on diversity. Frequently their tasks include working closely with outside consultants, planning training activities, coordinating work across units so that learnings from one part of the organization are available in other sectors, and monitoring progress. In view of the magnitude and importance of the work, the creation of a full-time position does seem warranted in larger companies. There is the danger, however, that other members of the firm may rely too heavily on this person and not assume personal responsibility for organization change.

Another issue related to organizational structure is whether or not diversity change work should be housed with EEO work. In many companies, managers of diversity are former EEO officers and the two roles are combined. However, in an increasing number of companies these tasks are being separated. In some organizations, such as Fannie Mae, the manager of diversity is not even housed within the human resource function. One reason for this is that managers want to reinforce the message that managing diversity work is much broader than, and has fundamental differences with, the traditional EEO work. For example, unlike traditional EEO/ AA plans, managing diversity emphasizes (1) increasing knowledge of cultural differences, (2) analyzing human resource systems, and (3) recognizing a broader range of group identities, such as functional diversity and cross-national diversity.

A second way that organizations bring leadership to diversity work by changes in organizational design is through the formation of steering committees and advisory groups. These are normally composed of middle managers from a variety of task functions and are often headed by a senior manager. Although a full-time manager of diversity makes sense for larger companies, my advice is to use the manager of diversity in addition to, rather than as a substitute for, a broader involvement team such as a diversity task force. This is especially important in the early stages of the work. A major reason for this is that an interdepartmental team helps to gain commitment throughout the organization where the change in how people interrelate on a daily basis must take place.

Communications Strategy. An additional task of leadership is the development of an explicit strategy for communicating to the organization about the developmental work on diversity. This is needed for several reasons. First, the nature of the work itself deals with sensitive and sometimes emotional issues that are difficult to work on in organizations. How the work is presented to members of the organization therefore becomes more important. For example, it is important to help employees understand what is meant by managing diversity, how this is different from the affirmative action programs of the past, and to recognize that there are organizational performance implications for having and using cultural diversity well in the organization. A second reason is that many organizations have several other initiatives involving cultural change occurring at the same time. For example, cross-functional teams, total quality, employee involvement, and organizational career development are all major human resource initiatives in the United States at the present time. There is therefore a concern in many organizations that managing diversity will be viewed as the new "flavor of the month." One way to address this is to integrate the managing diversity work with one or more of the other initiatives. For example, at Exxon Research and Engineering Company, diversity is being managed as the "people side of the total quality process." An approach of planning organization development work on diversity as an integral part of the total quality process is being spearheaded by Terry Koonce, president, and Tom White, manager of human resources.

It is also clear that managing diversity is linked to cross-functional teams. One advantage of this kind of integrated approach is that it reinforces the fact that diversity dynamics are an integral part of everyday employee life and need to be considered in all activities involving people in organizations. A downside risk is that important aspects of the diversity work will be lost or watered down.

Another important aspect of the communication strategy is how, when, and to whom organizational data collected as part of the development process should be communicated. In this regard, it should be noted that even preliminary interviews to surface issues of diversity are a form of organizational intervention, which may create expectations of feedback among employees. My experience has been that organizational members will want to have some form of feedback on any diagnostic work that occurs, especially those who are personally involved in providing the data. Organizational leaders should therefore carefully think through what kind of feedback is to be provided.

Communication is also important to maintain momentum of the work as time goes on. This is particularly noticeable after awareness training has been completed. Some organizations have used company newsletters for this purpose. It is also a good idea to make updates on diversity initiatives a regular part of staff meetings. Bulletin boards are also useful for publication of special events such as diversity day celebrations or management achievement awards related to diversity.

Research/Measurement

The third key component is the collection of information about diversity-related issues. Many types of data are needed, including measures of the organizational culture, traditional equal-opportunity profile data, analysis of attitudes and perceptions of employees, and data that highlights differential career experiences of members from different cultural groups (e.g., whether promotion is influenced by age, gender, etc.).

Research has several important uses. First, it is often helpful in surfacing issues and concerns that may be useful to address in the education process. For example, data indicating differences of opinion about the value of diversity based on culture groups can be used as a launching point for mixed-culture discussion groups in training sessions. Second, research is needed to identify areas of organizational culture, management practices, and interpersonal relations where changes are needed and to provide clues as to how to make these changes. Third, research is a means of evaluating the change effort. Thus one aspect of the research program should be to obtain baseline data on key indicators of the diversity environment that can be updated periodically to assess progress. As with other key business strategies, when measurement is coordinated between organizations, some opportunity for external benchmarking is created. While external comparisons can be quite useful, the problems of noncomparability of data can be huge. It is therefore essential that attention be given to the selection of measures that can be standardized across organizations. An example might be turnover rates for specific classifications such as secretaries or engineers. Other examples include intergroup comparisons of perceptions about the quality of race and gender relations or of interdepartmental communications. Additional detail about measurement issues related to diversity are given in Chapter Fifteen.

Education

The most commonly utilized starting point for organization development work on managing diversity is some type of employee education program. Typically, the education program begins with a one to three-day workshop focusing on increasing awareness and sensitivity to diversity issues. It is highly desirable for this training to begin with the senior managers and then proceed throughout the rest of the organization. Ideally, all employees should be trained. Ortho Pharmaceuticals, Avon, and Citizens Insurance are just a few of the companies in which every employee has received awareness training as of this writing.

Most organizations have found it advantageous to have outside trainers assist with the workshops, at least for some initial period of time. However, for economic reasons as well as to build commitment, it is highly recommended that in-house expertise be developed for use in completing the training. I have found that an ideal approach is to create a culturally diverse team consisting of one or more outside consultants and internal trainers working together. Most experts on the subject matter are able to provide training designs and train-the-trainer workshops to help organizations launch their training efforts.

Hopefully this book has made clear that there is a considerable base of knowledge and expertise associated with understanding the effects of diversity in organizations. Therefore, as with any other activity involving specialized knowledge, it is vitally important to have subject-matter expertise as well as good facilitation skills in order to provide the highest quality education on this topic.

Awareness training for existing employees is only part of the education component of the model. Training must also be built into new-hire orientation programs so that coverage does not decline as employee turnover occurs. In addition, advanced training is essential. This training should focus more on building specific skills and helping individuals to understand their role in implementing the organization change process. For example, a planned format for advanced training prepared by the Information Technology Division of the University of Michigan covered the following topics:

1. Valuing diversity: tools for managing the differences (e.g., communication, interacting in a multicultural environment)
2. Developing managerial skills (e.g., matching people and jobs, rewarding performance, supporting lifestyles and life needs)
3. Recruiting for a diverse workforce
4. Culture by culture: learning from each other

There have been some attempts to formally assess the importance of awareness education as an influence on how people feel and think about diversity issues. These preliminary accounts indicate that even elementary education efforts do have a positive effect on perceptions and attitudes (Sonnenfeld & Ellis, 1992; Adler, 1986). Most experts agree that education is a crucial first step, however, it is important to recognize that it has limitations as an organization change tool and should not be used in isolation. It is also important to approach training as an ongoing education process rather than a one-shot seminar.

Culture and Management Systems Audit

The fourth component of the change model is a comprehensive assessment of the organizational culture and human resource management systems of the organization. The latter includes recruitment, training and development, performance appraisal, potential assessment and promotion, and compensation/benefits. This aspect of the work is sometimes referred to as a culture audit. The primary objectives of this assessment are (1) to uncover sources of subtle bias in the management practices and policies that may create barriers to performance or the recognition of performance for employees, (2) to identify ways in which the organizational culture may be inconsistent with the needs of a diverse workforce. Relating to the first objective, it is important to look beyond surface data in auditing management systems. For example, research that I have reviewed or conducted indicates that even when average performance ratings for majority and minority culture members are essentially the same, there may be subtle differences in such things as (1) the relative priority placed on individual performance criteria, (2) the distribution of the highest rating category, or (3) the relationship between performance ratings and promotion (Cox & Nkomo, 1986; Pazy, 1986). Thus the audit must be an in-depth analysis of these systems, and is often best done with the assistance of an external cultural diversity expert. Published examples of organizational assessment work on diversity include Thomas (1991), Fine, Johnson, and Ryan (1990), and Kossek and Zonia (1993). These examples vary in the scope of diversity issues addressed.

In further explanation of the second objective, consider a scenario in which an organizational culture places a high value on aggressiveness. Such a value might put individuals from certain identity groups of the organization at a disadvantage if the norms of their secondary/alternative culture discouraged this kind of behavior. As indicated in Chapter Seven, this is indeed the case for many Asians and for women in many countries of the world, including the United States. If for some reason the preservation of this value is viewed as central to organizational effectiveness, the solution may be to acknowledge that conforming to this norm places a greater burden on some members of the organization than on others, and that assistance to learn the behavior may be needed. However, this scenario more likely illustrates a situation in which the organizational values need to change so that other styles of accomplishing work are accepted and appreciated. A part of the culture audit is to identify the prevailing values and norms and then examine them critically in light of the diversity of the workforce.

It should be emphasized that the results of the audit must be translated into an action agenda for specific changes in the organizational culture and management systems. Before the assessment is undertaken, there should be a commitment from senior management to consider these changes seriously and to implement at least some of the recommendations that evolve from the audit. Finally, I believe these audits are properly viewed as relevant to all members of the organization. The overall objective is to identify and remove barriers to excellence. Barriers to the performance of all employees—and not just minority group members—are at issue.

Follow-Up

The final component of the model is follow-up. The two principal aspects of follow-up are to establish accountability for results and to create explicit mechanisms for evaluation of effectiveness. In addition, both accountability and evaluation should be governed by the philosophy of continuous improvement. This means that the goal is full participation of all members, and that adverse effects of group identity must be reduced to zero. I encourage organizations to think of this as analogous to the "zero defect" goal of total quality. Progress toward the multicultural organization ideal is acceptable only as an interim goal. The ultimate goal must be zero correlation of sociocultural identity with opportunity, motivation, and achievement as well as full capitalization on the potential benefits of a diverse workforce.

The follow-up component of diversity work requires that the change process be monitored and that the changes ultimately become institutionalized (i.e., part of the regular ongoing processes of the organization). Like other management efforts, work on diversity requires accountability and control. During the initial years of the organization development effort, strategic accountability rests with senior management, while operational accountability for overseeing the change process might be assigned to the diversity task force or a manager of diversity or both. Ultimately, accountability for preserving the changes must be established with every manager. In order to establish accountability, specific objectives related to diversity are needed, as well as changes in the performance appraisal and reward processes of the organization to reinforce the importance of meeting these objectives.

It is important that these objectives address a broader range of issues than the traditional workforce profile data monitored under affirmative action. Organizations need to assess managerial competency for leading diverse workgroups and build these assessments into both development efforts and performance evaluation ratings. U.S. West, Digital Equipment, and Corning are among the companies that have taken a lead in developing this kind of managerial accountability for diversity-related issues. U.S. West's Pluralism Performance Menu lists a set of quantitative and qualitative measures that are evaluated to assess performance on diversity-related aspects of management. Quantitative measures include a culture group profile of employees mentored and of persons moved for developmental purposes. Qualitative measures include activities to

support culture group–based resource groups and activities initiated by the manager for the purpose of promoting pluralism.

Accountability is further enhanced by providing incentives to
managers for performance on diversity-related goals. For example,
Security Pacific is among a number of companies that are giving
recognition awards to managers for excellence in managing diversity. These early efforts on accountability are encouraging; however,
there is a need for much additional work in this area to clarify
effective measures and methods.

***Evaluation: Measuring the Impact of Diversity and Its Manage-
ment in Organizations.*** While a major part of accountability is
monitoring and rewarding individual performance, there is also a
need for evaluation of organizational performance. It should be
emphasized that two distinct types of evaluation are needed. First,
we need to evaluate performance on the achievement of diversity-
related goals, and, second, we need to assess the impact of managing
diversity on other organizational performance indicators. For example, in order to measure progress toward creating the ideal organizational climate for diverse workgroups, we can measure such
things as levels of stereotyping and ethnocentrism. However, there
is also a need for additional measurement of the effect of diversity
climate on the economic performance of organizations. Establishing *direct* linkages of diversity dynamics such as enthnocentrism,
stereotyping, and minority group density with measures of organizational outcomes like profits is problematic for several reasons.
First and foremost is the fact that profits are influenced by so many
factors that it is difficult to isolate the specific causes of profit levels.
This fact is well understood by most managers with regard to organizational activities such as human resource initiatives and advertising. A second reason is that the linkages occur in a time-lag
fashion, so that changes in the causal factors may not be detectable
at the organizational outcome level for several years. A third factor
has to do with problems inherent in measuring and comparing the
variables across organizations. Since measures relating to diversity
are generally not well developed at this time, and since industries
(and even subindustries) vary widely in such things as profit mar-

gins, measurement validity for interorganizational analyses is difficult.

For all of these reasons, my message is to apply a stage model to evaluation. At stage 1 affective outcomes of individuals such as career satisfaction, job involvement, organizational commitment, and attitude changes should be evaluated. At stage 2 individual achievement measures such as intergroup differences in performance ratings, promotion rates, and compensation should be measured. At stage 3, organizational performance indicators such as work quality, turnover, productivity, and absenteeism should be addressed. Finally, market share and profitability should be examined as long-term measures of effectiveness.

Summary

Increased diversity presents challenges to business leaders who must maximize the opportunities that it presents while minimizing its costs. To accomplish this, organizations must be transformed from monolithic or plural organizations to a multicultural model. The multicultural organization is characterized by a culture that values diversity, pluralism acculturation, full integration of nonmajority members both formally and informally, an absence of bias in management systems, and a minimum of intergroup conflict. The organization that achieves these conditions will create an environment in which all members can contribute to their maximum potential. Toward this end, a model for organizational transformation has been outlined.

15

Tools for Organization Development and Change

In this final chapter, specific tools and techniques that have been successfully used by pioneering American organizations to begin the transformation from the monolithic or plural organization to the multicultural model will be discussed. Table 15.1 provides a list of tools that organizations have used to promote change toward a multicultural organization. The table is organized to illustrate my analysis of which tools are most helpful for each of the six dimensions listed in Table 14.1, in which the goals of change are specified.

Culture Change

The process of changing organizational cultures is a long-term and difficult process. There is inevitable resistance to alterations of fundamental ways of doing business, which in many companies have changed little in half a century. As difficult as it is, however, it is clear that excellence in managing diverse workgroups will require changes in culture for many organizations. Once the organization has the leadership commitment to change and a vision of what the goal of change is, there are three primary means by which organizational cultures are changed: (1) by selection processes, especially of managerial personnel, (2) by changes in management systems, especially of evaluation and reward systems, and (3) by ongoing education and communication activities. Points 2 and 3 are adequately explained elsewhere; however, a clarification of the first point may be needed. Very simply, I mean that cultures are changed by changing the type of people who work in the organization. People vary a great deal in their personal attitudes and value systems related to diversity issues. In the long run, behaviors will depend

Table 15.1. Tools for Organizational Transformation.

Model Dimension	Tools
I. Culture *Objective:* Create climate in which members of all identity groups excel	1. Hire or promote people who embrace the new values 2. Reinforce values in rewards and appraisal 3. Educate and communicate
II. Pluralism *Objectives:* Create a two-way socialization process Ensure influence of minority culture perspectives on core organization norms and values	1. Managing/valuing diversity (MVD) training 2. New-member orientation programs 3. Language training 4. Diversity in key committees 5. Explicit treatment of diversity in mission statements 6. Identity-based advisory groups 7. Create flexibility in norm systems
III. Structural integration *Objective:* No correlation between culture group identity and job status	1. Diversity in key committees 2. Education program 3. Affirmative action programs 4. Targeted career development programs
IV. Integration in informal networks *Objective:* Eliminate barriers to entry and participation	1. Mentoring programs 2. Company-sponsored social events 3. Support groups
V. Institutional Bias *Objective:* Eliminate bias ingrained in management systems	1. Culture audit 2. Survey feedback 3. Changes in manager performance evaluation and rewards 4. HR policy and benefits changes 5. Task forces
VI. Intergroup conflict *Objectives:* Minimize interpersonal conflict based on group identity Minimize backlash by dominant group members Promote intergroup understanding	1. Survey feedback 2. Conflict management training and conflict resolution techniques 3. MVD training 4. Core groups 5. EEO-related training

Source: Adapted from Cox, 1991. Used by permission.

greatly on what these attitudes and values are. By hiring and promoting people who are tolerant of differences and who embrace the
value-in-diversity philosophy on a personal level, organizations can
go a long way toward creating the multicultural organization. In
addition to the three primary methods of selection, rewards, and
education, virtually all of the other techniques mentioned in Table
15.1 will impact organizational culture to some degree.

Creating Pluralism

Table 15.1 identifies seven specific tools for changing organizational acculturation from a unilateral process to a reciprocal one in
which both minority culture and majority culture members are influential in creating the behavioral norms, values, and policies of
the organization. Examples of each tool are given below.

Training and Orientation Programs

The most widely used tool among leading organizations is managing or valuing cultural diversity training. Some guidance and examples of this tool were given in Chapter Fourteen, but several
additional points warrant mention. Many companies, including
AT&T, Exxon Research and Engineering, and Citizens Insurance
Company, have found that the use of line managers to facilitate
diversity training pays dividends in building organizational commitment to the effort. It is important to select a diverse group of
trainers, including a significant representation of White males—or
whatever the majority identity group is in the organization. It is
also important to select people who have developed insight into the
substance of the issues covered in Parts Two through Four of this
book. I have found that a good place to look for prospective facilitators is in the initial awareness workshops.

　　Another training issue is finding the right mix of intellectual
and emotion-based learning. A related issue is the extent to which
the personal experience of participants should be used as the vehicle
for learning versus that of videotapes or other indirect methods.
Three factors should guide these decisions: (1) the time available for
the training (don't plan on emotion and personal experience if time

is short), (2) knowledge of the intended audience (e.g., the likelihood of an explosion if personal testimonies are emphasized), and (3) the skill and experience of the facilitators (e.g., only highly skilled trainers should use a personal confrontation approach).

There are a variety of videotape packages available, of which perhaps the best known are Copeland-Griggs Productions's "Managing Diversity" series and BNA Communications's "Choices." These and other video tools are useful but should be used along with participant exercises and discussion and not as stand-alone training content.

As mentioned previously, some empirical data on the effectiveness of these training efforts is beginning to confirm their usefulness. In addition to the Sonnenfeld and Ellis research alluded to previously, a study of seventy-five Canadian consultants found that people exposed to even the most rudimentary form of training on cultural diversity are significantly more likely to recognize the impact of cultural diversity on work behavior and to identify the potential advantages of cultural heterogeneity in organizations (Adler, 1986). In addition, anecdotal evidence from managers of many companies indicates that valuing and managing diversity training represents a crucial first step for organization change efforts.

New member orientation programs are basic in the hiring processes of many organizations. Some companies are developing special orientations as part of their managing diversity initiatives. One example is Procter & Gamble's "On Boarding" program, which features special components for women and non-White hires and their managers.

Language training is especially important for companies hiring American Asians, Hispanics, and foreign nationals. However, in view of the globalization of business, knowledge of multiple languages should be viewed as a high-priority educational activity for all managerial and professional employees. To promote pluralism, it is helpful to offer second-language training to Anglos as well as the minority culture employees and to take other steps to communicate that languages other than English are valued. Leaders in this area include Esprit De Corp, Economy Color Card, and Pace Foods. For many years, the women's clothier Esprit De Corp. has offered courses in Italian and Japanese. At Economy Color Card, work rules are printed in both Spanish and English. Pace Foods, where 35 percent of employees are Hispanic, goes a step farther by printing company policies and also conducting staff meetings in Spanish and English. Motorola is a leader in the more traditional training for English as a second language, with classes conducted at company expense and on company time.

Ensuring Minority Group Input and Acceptance

The most direct and effective way to promote the influence of minority culture norms on organizational decision making is to achieve cultural diversity at all organization levels. For example, multinational companies would be wise to make participation of foreign nationals on their board of directors a high priority. However, an important supplemental method is through ensuring diversity on key committees. An example that was mentioned earlier is the insistence of USA Today president Nancy Woodhull on having gender, racioethnic, educational, and geographic diversity represented in all daily news meetings.

Another technique is explicitly mentioning the importance of diversity as a basis of competitive advantage and human resource quality in statements of mission and strategy. By doing this, organizations foster the mindset that increased diversity is an opportunity and not a problem. Examples of organizations that have done this are the University of Michigan, Exxon Research and Engineering, Buick Motor Division of General Motors, and the Careers Division of the National Academy of Management, which has fostered research addressing the impact of diversity on organizations by explicitly citing this as part of its mission.

Support/Advisory Groups

In many organizations, identity-based support groups such as women's networks have developed. In some cases the groups are of mixed identities, while in others they are homogeneous (e.g., Black managers associations). In addition to offering mutual support benefits for their members, these groups can be effectively used by organizational leaders as a means of broadening input for problem solving

and decision making in general, and especially for facilitating accomplishment of the organization's managing diversity strategy.
Organizations that have used such groups and found them to be
beneficial include Avon, Digital Equipment (where they are called
constituency groups), and U.S. West (where they are called resource
groups). By providing support groups direct access to the most senior executives of the company and giving them an advisory role,
the influence of minority group members on organizational culture
and policy can be accelerated. For example, U.S. West has a thirty-
three member Pluralism Council that advises senior management
on plans for improving the company's response to increased workforce diversity.

Finally, a more complex, but I believe potentially powerful,
tool for promoting change toward pluralism is the development of
flexible, highly tolerant climates that encourage diverse approaches
to problems among all employees. Such an environment is useful
to workers regardless of group identity but is especially beneficial
to people from nontraditional cultural backgrounds, because their
approaches to problems are more likely to be different due to past
norms. A company often cited for such a work environment is
Hewlett Packard. Among the operating norms of the company that
promote pluralism are (1) encouragement of informality and un-
structured work; (2) flexible work schedules and loose supervision;
(3) setting objectives in broad terms, with lots of individual employee discretion over how they are achieved; and (4) a policy that
researchers should spend at least 10 percent of company time ex-
ploring personal ideas. I would suggest that item 4 be extended to
all management and professional employees.

Creating Full Structural Integration

Despite the extensive effort that has been given to basic representa-
tional and glass-ceiling issues of diversity in the past twenty years,
these continue to be significant challenges for many organizations.
Affirmative action initiatives of various kinds continue to be paramount in addressing structural integration. Because of the centrality of structural integration to the overall managing diversity effort,

and because affirmative action has become increasingly controversial, this tool will be discussed at length here.

Affirmative Action

During the past twenty-five years, many American organizations have adopted affirmative action programs as an implementation tool for the goal of promoting equal opportunity. There is considerable evidence that these efforts have been highly effective in changing the proportional representation of women and of non-White men, especially in entry-level jobs and in lower-level management and professional jobs (Glasser, 1988; Glazer, 1988). However, despite its widespread use and effectiveness, affirmative action has increasingly come under attack and resistance in recent years (Lynch, 1991; Steele, 1990; Bunzel, 1990). In addition, many executives are somewhat confused about the role of affirmative action in the context of recent managing diversity initiatives. One important step toward unraveling some of this ambiguity is to clearly define terms.

What is Affirmative Action? There are at least three common beliefs about what affirmative action is that hinder its use. The first is that affirmative action requires the use of rigidly defined quotas for hiring specific numbers of minority group members. While quotas *may* be used in affirmative action programs, they are by no means a required feature and many contemporary programs do not use them. It is also important to distinguish between goals/timetables, which may be applied to any objective related to diversity, and quotas which generally refer to a "head-count" approach to equal opportunity.

The second belief is that affirmative action results in the selection of unqualified people and thus inevitably leads to a noticeable decline in the overall quality of human resources. While this result has occurred at times through misguided efforts, affirmative action was never intended to permit a lowering of minimum standards, and knowledgeable people on the subject stress that such actions actually undermine, rather than facilitate, equal opportunity.

The third, and perhaps most damaging, belief is that affirmative action is essentially reverse discrimination, so that opportunity for economic equality actually becomes lower for majority group members than for members of minority groups. This belief has roots in the celebrated *Bakke* case of 1978, in which a White applicant to medical school appealed the denial of admission on the grounds that he was discriminated against because he was White. The resulting Supreme Court decision upheld Bakke's claim in a narrowly construed opinion that left intact the legality of affirmative action in situations where a history of unequal opportunity could be shown.

To a significant extent, the potential for affirmative action to become a major source of intergroup conflict in organizations hinges on how reverse discrimination is defined and on beliefs about the status of equal opportunity in contemporary organizations. There seems to be little question that if selection decisions are viewed as isolated events, apart from the societal and organizational context in which they take place, affirmative action does give employment advantages to members of minority groups. From this perspective, reverse discrimination may be an appropriate evaluation of the situation. However, if the use of affirmative action in selection decisions is viewed in the context of overall employment opportunity and the history of opportunity (both within the organization and within the society), then characterizing it as reverse discrimination seems inaccurate. If people from certain targeted identity groups are disadvantaged in seeking to obtain the qualifications required for employment, and if there continues to be discrimination against them in the absence of affirmative action, then the use of affirmative action can be appropriately viewed as a balancing of overall employment-related opportunity to compete for a position (Dovidio, Mann, & Gaertner, 1989). It is tempting to think of the removal of affirmative action as eliminating identity group discrimination rather than as preserving discrimination in favor of the majority group. Thus it is possible to view affirmative action as a method to address the disadvantages that members of outgroups have due to a combination of ethnocentrism and unequal power distribution. To this extent, its use might be supported as a way to compensate for the existing discrimination. I sometimes get this point across in teaching about diversity by asking people if they can think of any time or circumstances in which their own identity may have been an advantage in seeking employment. A majority of people of all identities can answer yes to this. Then I ask what their answer would be if there were no such thing as affirmative action. With this scenario, most minority group members can no longer answer yes, pointing up the existing advantage for majority group members that affirmative action seeks to balance to some degree. This little exercise sometimes helps people to refocus on the reasons why affirmative action was created in the first place, and to address the difficult question of what might be an adequate substitute for it.

With these clarifications in mind, I will suggest that *affirmative action* in practice fundamentally means the explicit use of a person's group identity as a criterion in making selection decisions. Usually this means that among candidates who are qualified on other criteria, candidates of underrepresented groups are selected in preference to those from overrepresented groups. As the experience of Xerox in their balanced workforce plan has shown, this can include preferring White males for positions under some circumstances.

While this definition may be helpful in clarifying the type of behavior that affirmative action signifies, it may be useful to go beyond this and examine the motives for its use.

Motives for the Use of Affirmative Action. When viewed in the context of a valuing diversity philosophy, there are two distinctly different motives for the use of affirmative action. First, it addresses the equal opportunity goal, which is the traditional use of affirmative action. It is a tool for redressing past and present factors that tend to systematically advantage or disadvantage individuals based on group identities like gender and racioethnicity.

Second, the advent of the managing diversity perspective has given rise to an additional motive for the use of affirmative action, namely to enhance organizational performance through improvements in decision making, problem solving, marketing strategy, and creativity. Organizational leaders who believe there is direct positive value in diversity for the organization's economic mission may consider the use of affirmative action as a way to foster diverse perspectives for finding high-quality, creative solutions to organizational challenges.

The Future of Affirmative Action: A Proposed Reconfiguration. It has been argued here that the fundamental behavior of affirmative action—explicitly using a person's group identities in selection decisions—may derive from two types of organization goals. The advent of the value-in-diversity concept introduces a different way of viewing affirmative action, which organizations have only recently begun to consider. In view of the foregoing discussion, organizations might wish to approach affirmative action using the reconfiguration posed in Figure 15.1.

This reconfiguration suggests that the concept of equal opportunity be redefined to consider the total life history of a person as relevant in defining opportunity, rather than just the moment at hand. This broadening of the context for defining equal opportunity seems justified not only because educational and other opportunities to prepare for careers are influenced by group identities, but also because group identities often influence ratings of past achieve-

Figure 15.1. A Reconfiguration of Affirmative Action.

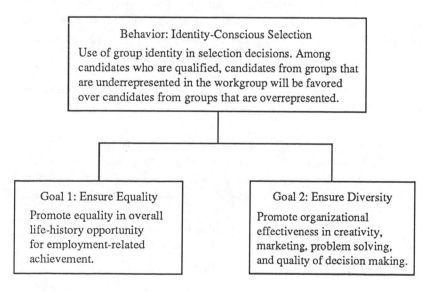

ment. For example, prejudice and discrimination may lead to an undervaluing of the work of nonmajorities. In view of this, one might question whether equal grade-point averages or job performance ratings for members of cultural minority groups, when achieved in majority-dominated systems, really represents equal ability and effort to perform. The reconfiguration of Figure 15.1 suggests that in order for overall employment-related opportunity to be equal, fairness must prevail in the opportunities to obtain the requisite qualifications for employment as well as in the competition for a current job vacancy. In this regard, organizations might use their considerable influence to promote change beyond their own boundaries. One example of this is the heavy investment of many organizations—including Sears, 3M, and Aetna Insurance—in partnership activities with educational and community groups to address the challenges of the undereducation of non-Whites in the United States.

A second implication of Figure 15.1 is that organizations seeking to exploit the potential benefits of diversity will be conscious of group identities such as gender, nationality, and racioethnicity as selection criteria in creating decision-making and problem-solving groups in the same way that the need for diverse departmental representation in such groups is being recognized. This perspective is implicit in the concept of valuing diversity that has been so widely advocated by managers and organizational consultants in recent years (Kleeb, 1989; Esty, 1988; Copeland, 1988; Cox & Blake, 1991).

The foregoing discussion suggests that organizations seeking to clarify the role of affirmative action efforts in a value-in-diversity environment should ask themselves a number of questions:

1. Do we believe that the history of discrimination in our society at large and/or in our own organization is such that certain gender, race, or other group identities have been disadvantaged and others advantaged in overall employment related opportunities?
2. Do we believe that diversity of racioethnic, gender, and other identities in the workforce brings net added value to the organization?

If the answer to question 1 or 2 is yes, then the organization must ask: do the benefits of the tool of affirmative action outweigh its costs? This question must, of course, be answered in light of the availability of alternative strategies for accomplishing the goals of ensuring equality and ensuring diversity. There is no question that affirmative action has a downside for both majority and minority group members. Majority group members may have to sacrifice some opportunities due to the current imbalance of opportunity. Members of minority groups must overcome the assumption by many that they were selected only because of their identity and not because of their talent. All employees must endure the unfortunate necessity of using a somewhat artificial tool to balance representation that ideally would occur naturally. If the notion of the value of diversity actually takes hold in organizations, it may enable both majority and minority group members to rationally view identity group consciousness as it is used in selection as simply a more comprehensive definition of legitimate criteria.

Other Tools to Promote Structural Integration

The objective of creating an organization in which there is no correlation between culture identity group and job status implies that minority group members are well represented at all levels, in all functions, and in all workgroups. Achievement of this goal requires that skill and education levels be evenly distributed. Educational statistics indicate that the most serious problems occur with Blacks and Hispanics (Wilson, 1987).

A number of organizations have become more actively involved in various kinds of educational programs. The Aetna Life Insurance Company is such a leader. It has initiated a program of jobs in exchange for customized education taught by community agencies and private schools in addition to its own in-house basic education programs. The company has created an Institute for Corporate Education with a full-time director. Other companies participating in various new education initiatives include PrimAmerica, Quaker Oats, Chase Manhattan Bank, Eastman Kodak, and Digital Equipment. In Minnesota, a project headed by Cray Research and General Mills allows businesses to create schools of their own design. I believe that business community involvement in joint efforts with educational institutions and community leaders to promote equal achievement in education is critical to the future competitiveness of U.S. business. Business leaders should insist that economic support be tied to substantive programs that are jointly planned and evaluated by corporate representatives and educators.

A number of companies—e.g., Mobil Oil, Exxon, IBM, U.S. West, and McDonald's—have initiated special career development efforts for minority personnel. IBM's long-standing Executive Resource System is designed to identify and develop minority talent for senior management positions. McDonald's Black Career Development Program provides career enhancement advice and fast-track career paths for minorities. Company officials have stated that the program potentially cuts a fifteen-year career path to regional manager by 50 percent. U.S West's Women of Color program has given high-potential non-White women special development attention. The program was initiated after internal data showed that non-White women had a far lower probability of reaching middle management than any other race/gender group in the company. In the first three years of the program, half of the participants received promotions. At Exxon Research and Engineering, high-potential women and non-White men are placed on targeted five-year development plans and their progress is monitored closely by supervisors.

Creating Integration in Informal Networks

One tool for facilitating the inclusion of non-majority-group members in the informal networks of organizations is company-initiated mentoring programs. This was discussed in Chapter Twelve. One issue that arises is whether or not such programs should target only nonmajority members instead of all employees. If resources permit, there are clear advantages to having the program include all employees, or all employees of certain job categories. However, if company-specific research shows that mentoring is less available to members of certain identity groups, the data can be used to justify and bolster support among majority group employees for targeted mentoring programs. Examples of companies that have established such targeted mentoring programs are Chemical Bank and General Foods.

A second technique for facilitating informal network integration is company-sponsored social events. In planning such events, multiculturalism is fostered by selecting both activities and locations with a sensitivity to the diversity of the workforce.

A third idea for promoting informal integration is to utilize identity-based support groups. As mentioned previously, there are many organizations in which members of minority groups have formed their own professional associations to promote information exchange and social support. There is little question that these groups have provided emotional and career support for members who traditionally have not been participants of in-group social networks. A somewhat controversial issue is whether these groups hinder the objective of informal network integration. Many believe that they tend to promote divisiveness and reduce incentives for nonmajorities to seek inclusion in informal activities with majority group members. Others deny these effects. I am not aware of any hard evidence on this point. There is a dilemma here in that full inclusion in the informal networks is at best a long-term process, and there is widespread skepticism among minorities as to its eventual achievement. Even if abolishing the minority group associations would eventually promote full integration, the absence of a support network of any kind in the interim could be a devastating loss to minority group members.

The existence of these groups presents the opportunity to use them to promote integration by arranging joint meetings between various groups and by creating groups with heterogeneous membership. There is no reason that mixed-identity support groups should not be formed. The experience of Digital Equipment is illustrative in this regard. The company found that in the initial stages of development of support groups, membership tended to be more exclusive, but over time, and with the urging of company management, many of the groups broadened their membership to include people of other group identities. This involved the elimination of boundaries around organization level as well as gender and other identities. Given the above, my overall conclusion with regard to these groups is that, when used properly, they are more helpful than harmful to the goal of informal integration, at least in the short term.

Eliminating Institutional Bias

Tools for addressing the problem of institutional bias include the culture audit, survey feedback, changes in performance appraisal and reward systems, changes in human resource policies and benefits, and the use of task forces. The culture audit was discussed in Chapter Fourteen. This is the organizational diagnostic tool that undergirds the other tools to be discussed in this section.

Survey Feedback

Survey feedback is a standard organization development tool through which survey data are collected and then presented to organization members as a means of building commitment for change and showing the needed directions for change. It may be used on both an organization and an individual level and both are recommended. Internal research on various aspects of employment experience organized by culture group can provide a powerful tool for change. One company that utilizes this tool is Time Inc., where an evaluation of the compensation of women and men in the same jobs is conducted annually to ensure comparable pay and equal treatment.

On an individual manager level, survey feedback may be used to identify development needs for more effectively managing diverse groups. By careful selection of both the survey items and the respondents, relevant measures for the management of diversity can be obtained. My experience suggests that this type of research-based approach is underutilized by organizations.

Revamping Reward and Appraisal Systems

An absolutely essential tool for addressing institutional bias is changes to ensure that the organization's performance appraisal and reward systems reinforce the goal of excellence in the management of diversity. Again, results of the culture and systems audits will provide the needed direction by showing what aspects of these processes may contain unintended barriers to members from certain culture groups. In many cases, the assessment will reveal changes that are needed to better manage workers regardless of group identities. However, to properly plan changes in this area that take into account the cultural diversity in the workforce, considerable expertise on diversity issues will be required.

Companies that have taken steps in this direction include Baxter Health Care, Exxon Research and Engineering, Coca-Cola, Corning, and U.S. West. Baxter and Coca-Cola tie compensation to manager performance on diversity management efforts. Both U.S. West and Exxon Research and Engineering have integrated managing diversity goals that go beyond identity headcounts into their performance appraisal processes. Again, there are two distinct goals in making changes to appraisal and reward systems. First, any bias in the process itself (as discussed in Chapter Twelve) must be eliminated, and, second, performance on managing diversity goals must be built in.

Benefits and Work Schedules

The elimination of institutional bias is also facilitated by changes in human resource policies and benefit plans that make it easier for employees to balance work and family role demands. Many companies have made such changes in areas like child care, work schedles, and parental leave. NationsBank, Arthur Anderson, Levi Strauss, Merck, and IBM are examples of companies that have gone farther than most. NationsBank's Select Time project allows even officers and professionals in the company to work part-time for several years and still be considered for advancement. Arthur Anderson has taken a similar step by allowing part-time accountants to stay on-track for partnership promotions. Levi Strauss and Merck are among the national leaders in comprehensive work-family programs covering everything from paternity leave to part-time work with preservation of benefits. IBM is a leader in a consortium of companies that have partnered to share the cost of improving child-care and elder-care support for their employees. This kind of organizational accommodation will make it easier to hire and retain both men and women in the 1990s as parents struggle to balance time demands at work and home. It is especially important for women, because they are more likely to be in single-parent situations.

Task Forces

A final tool for removing institutional bias is diversity task forces and special committees to monitor organizational policy and practices for evidence of cultural bias on an ongoing basis. An example of what I consider to be a well-designed task force committee is the one used by Philip Morris, which is composed of a diverse group of managers from various organization levels, including some senior managers. This composition combines the power of senior executives with the insight into needed changes that the minority representatives can provide. The Pluralism Council of U.S. West, referred to earlier in this chapter, is another outstanding example. Many companies have designated special committees to process sexual harassment complaints. The "hostile environment" form of sexual harassment is a classic example of institutionalized bias. My advice is that in addition to hearing complaints, these committees might also take proactive steps such as conducting periodic focus groups to discuss employee perceptions about progress and to get ideas for ways to further reduce the probability of harassment on an ongoing basis.

Intergroup Conflict

Experts on conflict management have noted that a certain amount of interpersonal conflict is inevitable and perhaps even healthy in organizations (Northcraft & Neale, 1990). However, conflict becomes destructive when it is excessive, not well managed, or rooted in struggles for power rather than the differentiation of ideas. In Chapter Nine I noted that intergroup conflict often increases in culturally diverse workgroups. This is due to many factors, including language barriers, culture clashes, and resentment by majority group members of what they may perceive as preferential treatment of minority group members.

Suggestions were offered in Chapter Nine for resolving conflict in diverse workgroups; therefore I will comment only briefly here. Available tools for organizations for reducing identity group–related conflict and promoting harmonious intergroup relations include survey feedback, conflict management training, diversity awareness training, core groups, and EEO-related training. The technique of survey feedback has already been discussed. One example of its use to address intergroup conflict is Procter & Gamble's use of data on the average time needed for new hires of various culture groups to become fully integrated into the organization. They found that join-up time varied by race and gender, with White males becoming acclimated most quickly and Black females taking the longest of any group. These data were useful to diffuse criticism of their On Boarding program referred to earlier.

Another example is Corning Glass Works's strategy of fighting White male resistance to change with data showing that White male promotion rates were indeed much higher than those of other groups. A similar strategy has been used by U.S. West, which used data indicating that promotion rates for White men were sixteen times higher than those of non-White women to launch their Women of Color program. The beauty of this tool is that it provides the double benefit of a knowledge base for planning change and leverage to win employee commitment to implement the needed changes.

As suggested in Chapter Nine, conflict management techniques may be applied to minimize intergroup conflict related to group identities. Experts can assist managers in learning and developing skill in applying alternative conflict management techniques such as mediation and superordinate goals. Managing conflict is one of several general management skills that is made more crucial, and yet more difficult, by the greater diversity of the workforces in the 1990s.

A number of organizations have used regularly scheduled group meetings of people from diverse cultural backgrounds (often called core groups) as a tool to change culture and improve intergroup relations. These groups typically meet on company time to explicitly examine attitudes, beliefs, and feelings about culture group differences and their effects on behavior at work. A leader in the use of this technique is Digital Equipment, where such groups have been the centerpiece of their valuing differences work for many years. At Digital, these small voluntary groups, composed of people from various organization levels, work toward four major objectives:

1. Stripping away stereotypes
2. Examining underlying assumptions about out-groups
3. Building significant relationships with people that individual group members regard as different
4. Raising levels of personal empowerment

Digital's experience suggests that a breakthrough for many organizations will be achieved by the simple mechanism of bringing discussion about group differences out in the open. Progress is made as people become more comfortable directly dealing with the issues. My own view is that this is one of the most powerful tools available for organization change work related to managing diversity.

There are a variety of training and development activities that are designed to increase knowledge of equal opportunity–related issues. Most plural organizations have used equal opportunity seminars for many years. These include sexual harassment workshops, training on civil rights legislation, and workshops on sexism and racism.

Some of this training is specifically designed to create attitude changes. For example, Northern Telecom has used a program designed specifically to help employees deal with racial prejudices. Eastman Kodak's training conference for its recruiters is designed to eliminate racism and sexism from the hiring process. This type of training often features exercises that expose stereotypes of various groups that are prevalent but rarely made explicit and may be subconscious. Many academics and consultants have also developed bias-reduction training. An example is the Race Relations Competence Workshop, a program developed by Clay Alderfer and Robert Tucker of Yale University. They have found that participants completing the workshop have more positive attitudes toward persons of other racioethnic groups.

Finally, the managing and valuing diversity training discussed previously is a major tool for avoiding or reducing identity-related conflict. This training must be handled skillfully in order to avoid polarization, which may make intergroup relations worsen rather than improve. Suggestions toward this end were offered earlier in Chapter Fourteen and in this chapter.

Summary

This chapter has discussed twenty tools and techniques being used by organizations to transform monolithic and plural organizations into multicultural organizations. Few companies have had comprehensive efforts in place long enough for meaningful evaluation of their success to be conducted. Fortunately, information sharing on these efforts among organizations has greatly accelerated in recent years. As the work evolves, the evaluation of the experiences of organizations utilizing these tools will enable us to refine organization development practices in this area.

Conclusion

One objective of this book was to illustrate that there is a substantial base of knowledge that can be used to inform the processes of teaching, research, and organization change on the topic of cultural diversity. One conclusion I draw from consideration of this base of knowledge is that the effects of cultural diversity on organizational behavior and performance are highly complex and very powerful. Thus the undertstanding of these effects should be a high priority for practitioners and scholars alike, and there is a great need for additional learning in this field. Hopefully the material contained here will facilitate this learning. At the same time, our knowledge of cultural diversity effects in organizations is still evolving, and we are presently in the early stages of its development. If employers and scholars can increase partnerships to expand the base of knowledge on diversity and its effects, we can do a better job of preparing for one of the greatest challenges of the twenty-first century.

References

Abrams, J. (1992, November 30). Study: Sexual harassment global. *Ann Arbor News*, p. A6.

Abrams, D., & Hogg, M. A. (1990). *Social identity theory*. New York: Springer-Verlag.

Adams, K. A., & Landers, A. D. (1978). Sex differences in dominance behavior. *Sex Roles, 4*(2), 215–223.

Adler, N. (1986). *International dimensions of organization behavior*. Boston: Kent Publishing.

Adorno, T. W., Frenkel-Brunswik, E., Levinson, D. J., & Sanford, R. N. (1950). *The authoritarian personality*. New York: HarperCollins.

Alderfer, C. P. (1982). Problems of changing White male's behavior and beliefs concerning race relations. In P. S. Goodman & Associates (Eds.), *Change in organizations* (pp. 122–165). San Francisco: Jossey-Bass.

Alderfer, C. P., Alderfer, C. J., Tucker, L., & Tucker, R. (1980). Diagnosing race relations in management. *Journal of Applied Behavioral Science, 16*, 135–166.

Alderfer, C. P., & Smith, K. K. (1982). Studying intergroup relations embedded in organizations. *Administrative Science Quarterly, 27*, 5–65.

Alderfer, C. P., & Thomas, D. (1988). The significance of race and ethnicity for understanding organizational behavior. In C. L. Cooper & I. Robertson (Eds.), *International review of industrial and organizational psychology* (pp. 1–41). London: Wiley.

Alderfer, C. P., Tucker, R. C., Morgan, D. R., & Drasgow, F. (1983). Black and White cognitions of changing race relations in management. *Journal of Occupational Behavior, 4*, 105–136.

Allport, G. W. (1954). *The nature of prejudice*. Reading, MA: Addison-Wesley.

Antal, A. B., & Kresbach-Gnath, C. (1987). Women in management: Unused resources in the Federal Republic of Germany. *International Studies of Management and Organization, 16*, 133–151.

Antonak, R. F. (1988). Methods to measure attitudes towards people who are disabled. In H. E. Yuker (Ed.), *Attitudes toward persons with disabilities* (pp. 109–102). New York: Springer.

Armstrong, M. J. (1987). Interethnic conflict in New Zealand. In J. Boucher, D. Landis, & K. A. Clark (Eds.), *Ethnic conflict*. Newbury Park, CA: Sage Publications.

Arnoff, C. (1974). Old age in prime time. *Journal of Communication, 24*, 86–87.

Arnold, H., & Feldman, D. (1986). *Organizational behavior*. New York: McGraw-Hill.

Asante, M. K., & Asante, K. W. (Eds.). (1985). *African culture*. Westport, CT: Greenwood Press.

Ashforth, B., & Mael, F. (1989). Social identity theory and the organization. *Academy of Management Review, 14*(1), 20–39.

Babaron, O. A., Good, P. R., Pharr, O. N., & Suskind, J. A. (1981). Cross-cultural issues in mental health: Minority perspectives. In J. A. Suskind, *Institutional racism & community competence*. Rockville, MD: Nimh.

Bailey, J. (1989, November). How to be different but equal. *Savvy Woman*, p. 47.

Bailyn, L. (1987). Experiencing technical work: A comparison of male and female engineers. *Human Relations, 40*, 299–312.

Bartol, K. M. (1978). The sex structuring of organizations: A search for possible causes. *Academy of Management Review, 3*, 805–815.

Bassin, M. (1988). Teamwork at General Foods: New and improved. *Personnel Journal, 67*, 62–70.

Bateman, T. S., & Zeithaml, C. (1990). *Management: Function and strategy*. Homewood, IL: Irwin.

Beehr, T. A., Tabor, T. D., & Walsh, J. T. (1980). Perceived mobility channels: Criteria for intraorganizational job mobility. *Organizational Behavior and Human Performance, 26*, 250–264.

Belenky, M. F., Clinchy, B. M., Goldberger, N. R., & Tarule, J. M. (1986). *Women's ways of knowing*. New York: Basic Books.

Bell, E. L. (1990). The bicultural life experience of career-oriented Black women. *Journal of Organizational Behavior, 11,* 459-477.

Bergmann, B. R., & Krause, W. R. (1968). Evaluating and forecasting progress in racial integration of employment. *Industrial and Labor Relations Review, 18,* 399-409.

Berry, J. W. (1980). Social and cultural change. In H. C. Triandis & R. W. Brislin (Eds.), *Handbook of cross-cultural psychology* (pp. 211-279). Boston: Allyn & Bacon.

Berry, J. W. (1983). Acculturation: A comparative analysis of alternative forms. In J. Samunda & S. L. Woods (Eds.), *Perspectives in immigrant and minority education* (pp. 66-77). Lanham, MD: University Press of America.

Berry, J. W. (1987). Acculturation and psychological adaptation: A conceptual view. In J. W. Berry & W. Annis, *Ethnic psychology: Research and practice with immigrants, refugees, native peoples, ethnic groups and sojourners* (pp. 41-50). Lisse, Netherlands: Swets & Zeitlinger; Berwin, PA: Swets North American.

Best, D. L. (1985). An overview of findings from children's studies of sex-trait stereotypes in 23 countries. In R. Rath, H. S. Asthana, D. Sinha, & J. B. P. Sinha (Eds.), *Diversity and unity in cross-cultural psychology* (pp. 261-271). Lisse, Netherlands: Swets & Zeitlinger.

Bielby, W., & Baron, J. N. (1986). Men and women at work: Sex segregation and statistical discrimination. *American Journal of Sociology, 91*(4), 759-799.

Bigoness, W. (1988). Sex differences in job attribute preferences. *Journal of Organizational Behavior, 9,* 139-147.

Bilimoria, D., & Cooperider, D. (1991, October). *The Romanian orphans program: Challenges and responses of the collaborative alliance.* Presented at the annual meeting of Research on Non-Profit Organizations and Voluntary Action, Chicago.

Blakeslee, S. (1989, February 1). Women, Blacks don't receive fair share of kidney transplants. *Ann Arbor News,* p. B4.

Blalock, H., Jr. (1967). *Toward a theory of minority-group relations.* New York: Wiley.

Blau, P. M. (1955). *The dynamics of bureaucracy.* Chicago: University of Chicago Press.

Blau, P. M. (1962). Patterns of choice in interpersonal relations. *American Sociological Review, 27,* 41-55.

Blau, P. M. (1977). A macrosociological theory of social structure. *American Journal of Sociology, 83,* 26–54.

Bobo, L. (1988). Group conflict, prejudice and the paradox of contemporary racial attitudes. In P. Katz & D. Taylor (Eds.), *Eliminating racism* (pp. 85–109). New York: Plenum Press.

Boddewyn, J. J. (1991). Controlling sex and decency in advertising around the world. *Journal of Advertising, 20*(4), 25.

Brass, D. J. (1985). Men's and women's networks: A study of interaction patterns and influence in an organization. *Academy of Management Journal, 28*(2), 327–343.

Brenner, O. C., & Tomkowicz, J. (1982). Job orientation of Black and White college graduates in business. *Personnel Psychology, 35,* 89–103.

Breton, R., Burnet, J., Hartmann, N., Isajiw, W., & Lennards, J. (1975). Research issues on Canadian cultures and ethnic groups: An analysis of a conference. *Canadian Review of Sociology and Anthropology, 12,* 81–94.

Brewer, M. B. (1979). In-group bias in the minimal intergroup situation: A cognitive-motivational analysis. *Psychological Bulletin, 86,* 307–324.

Brewer, M. B., & Miller, N. (1984). Beyond the contact hypothesis: Theoretical perspectives on desegregation. In N. Miller & M. B. Brewer (Eds.), *Groups in contact* (pp. 281–302). San Diego, CA: Academic Press.

Briscoe, D. (1982, September 7). Overworked, underpaid. *Ann Arbor News,* p. A5.

Broedling, L. A. (1975). Relationship of internal-external control to work motivation and performance in an expectancy model. *Journal of Applied Psychology, 60,* 65–70.

Broman, C. L., Neighbors, H. W., & Jackson, J. S. (1988). Racial group identification among Black adults. *Social Forces, 67,* 146–158.

Brown, D. (1970). *Bury my heart at Wounded Knee.* Troy, MO: Holt, Rinehart & Winston.

Buckley, J. E. (1971). Pay differences between men and women in the same job. *Monthly Labor Review, 101,* 17–22.

Budner, S. (1962). Intolerance of ambiguity as a personality variable. *Journal of Personality, 30,* 29–50.

Bull, R., & Rumsey, N. (1988). *The social psychology of facial appearance.* London: Springer-Verlag.

Bunzel, J. (1990, March/April). Exclusive Opportunities. *American Enterprise, 1,* 46–51.

Buono, A. F., & Kamm, J. B. (1983). Marginality and the organizational socialization of female managers. *Human Relations, 36*(12), 1125–1140.

Burke, R. J. (1984). Relationships in and around organizations: It's both who you know and what you know that counts. *Psychological Reports, 55,* 299–307.

Burke, R. J., & McKeen, C. A. (1990). Mentoring in organizations: Implications for women. *Journal of Business Ethics, 9,* 317–322.

Butler, J. S., & Holmes, M. D. (1984). Race, separatist ideology, and organizational commitment. *Social Science Quarterly, 65*(1), 138–149.

Campbell, A. (1971). *White attitudes toward Black people.* Ann Arbor: Institute for Social Research.

Campbell, D. T. (1965). Ethnocentric and other altruistic motives. In D. Levine (Ed.), *Nebraska symposium on motivation* (pp. 283–311). Lincoln: University of Nebraska Press.

Cannings, K. (1988). Managerial promotion: The effects of socialization, specialization and gender. *Industrial and Labor Relations Review, 42*(1), 77–88.

Cash, T. F., Gillen, B., & Burns, D. S. (1977). Sexism and "beautyism" in personnel consultant decision making. *Journal of Applied Psychology, 62,* 301–310.

Cash, T. F., & Kilcullen, R. N. (1985). The eye of the beholder: Susceptibility to sexism and beautyism in the evaluation of managerial applicants. *Journal of Applied Social Psychology, 15,* 591–605.

Chan, W. (1986). *Chu Hsi and neo-Confucionism.* Honolulu: University of Hawaii Press.

Chang, E. C., & Ritter, E. H. (1976). Ethnocentrism in Black college students. *Journal of Social Psychology, 100,* 89–98.

Chatman, J. (1989). Improving interactional organizational research: A model of person-organization fit. *Academy of Management Review, 14*(3), 333–349.

Chatman, J. (1991). Matching people and organizations: Selection and socialization in public accounting firms. *Administrative Science Quarterly, 36,* 459–484.

Chung, R. L. (1988a). People's Republic of China. In R. Nath (Ed.), *Comparative management: A regional view* (pp. 139–168). Cambridge, MA: Ballinger.

Chung, R. L. (1988b). Toward a conceptual paradigm of international business negotiations. *Advances in International Comparative Management, 3,* 203–219.

Clark, C. X. (1975). Race, life style, and rule flexibility: A field experiment in institutional behavior. *Organizational Behavior and Human Performance, 13,* 433–443.

Clawson, R., & Kram, K. (1984, May/June). Managing cross-gender mentoring. *Business Horizons,* pp. 22–32.

Clayton, S. D., & Tangri, S. S. (1989). The justice of affirmative action. In F. A. Blanchard & F. J. Crosby (Eds.), *Affirmative Action in Perspective* (pp. 177–192). New York: Springer-Verlag.

Cleveland, J. N., & Landy, F. J. (1983). The effects of person and job stereotypes on two personnel decisions. *Journal of Applied Psychology, 68,* 609–619.

Clifford, M., & Walster, E. (1973). The effect of physical attractiveness on teacher evaluation. *Society of Education, 46,* 248.

Cockrel, K. (1989, November 16). Housing discrimination against Hispanics found in Holland. *Ann Arbor News.*

Cohen, D. (1988, February). The Blackfeet discover capitalism. *Success,* pp. 56–59.

Cole, R. E., & Deskins, Jr., D. R. (1988). Racial factors in site location and employment patterns of Japanese auto firms in America. *California Management Review, 31,* 9–22.

Collins, S. M. (1989). The marginalization of Black executives. *Social Problems, 36*(4), 317–331.

Comadena, M. E. (1984). Brainstorming groups: Ambiguity tolerance, communication apprehension, task attraction, and individual productivity. *Small Group Behavior, 15*(2), 251–264.

Copeland, L. (1988, June). Valuing workplace diversity. *Personnel,* pp. 52–60.

Costo, R. (Ed.). (1970). *Textbooks and the American Indian.* San Francisco: Indian Historian Press.

Cote, J. A., & Tansuhaj, P. S. (1989). Culture bound assumptions in behavior intention models. *Advances in Consumer Research,* *16,* 105–109.

Cox, T. H. (1985). Production control at Carbide Products. In J. B. Miner, T. M. Singleton, & V. Luchsinger (Eds.), *The practice of management* (pp. C86–C93). Columbus, OH: Merrill.

Cox, T. H. (1991). The multicultural organization. *The Executive,* *5*(2), 34–47.

Cox, T. H., & Blake, S. (1991). Managing cultural diversity: Implications for organizational competitiveness. *The Executive,* *5*(3), 45–56.

Cox, T. H., & Finley-Nickelson, J. (1991). Models of acculturation for intraorganizational cultural diversity. *Canadian Journal of Administrative Sciences,* *8*(2), 90–100.

Cox, T. H., & Harquail, C. V. (1991). Career paths and career success in the early career stages of male and female MBAs. *Journal of Vocational Behavior,* *39,* 54–75.

Cox, T. H., Lobel, S., & McLeod, P. (1991). Effects of ethnic group cultural difference on cooperative versus competitive behavior in a group task. *Academy of Management Journal,* *34,* 827–847.

Cox, T. H., & Nkomo, S. M. (1986). Differential appraisal criteria based on race of the ratee. *Group and Organizational Studies,* *11,* 101–119.

Cox, T. H., & Nkomo, S. M. (1990). Invisible men and women: A status report on race as a variable in oganizational behavior & research. *Journal of Organizational Behavior,* *11,* 419–431.

Cox, T. H., & Nkomo, S. M. (1991). A race and gender group analysis of the early career experience of MBAs. *Work and Occupations,* *18*(4), 431–446.

Cox, T. H., & Nkomo, S. M. (1992). Candidate age as a factor in promotability ratings. *Public Personnel Management,* *21*(2), 197–210.

Cox, T. H., & Nkomo, S. M. (In press). Race and ethnicity. In R. Goliembewski (Ed.), *Handbook of organizational behavior.* New York: Marcel-Decker.

Crocker, J., & McGraw, K. M. (1984). What's good for the goose is not good for the gander: Solo status as an obstacle to occupational achievement for males and females. *American Behaviorial Scientist,* *27,* 357–369.

Crosby, F., Bormely, S., & Saxe, L. (1980). Recent unobtrusive studies of Black and White discrimination and prejudice: A literature review. *Psychological Bulletin, 87,* 546–563.

Cross, W. E., Jr. (1971). The Negro-to-Black conversion experience: Toward a psychology of Black liberation. *Black World, 20*(9), 13–27.

Crutsinger, M. (1990, September 4). White men dominate Federal Reserve: Study. *Ann Arbor News.*

Curnow, T. C. (1989). Vocational development of persons with disability. *Career Development Quarterly, 37,* 269–278.

Cusack, S. (1990, June). Who needs on-site child care? *Computerworld,* pp. 97–99.

Daft, R., & Steers, R. (1986). *Organizations: A micro/macro approach.* Glenview, IL: Scott-Foresman.

Dalton, M. (1959). *Men who manage.* New York: Wiley.

Darmon, R. (1990). Identifying sources of turnover cost. *Journal of Marketing, 54,* 46–56.

Davis, L. (1980). When the majority is the psychological minority. *Group Psychotherapy, Psychodrama and Sociometry, 33,* 179–184.

Davis, L. (1985). Group work practice with ethnic minorities of color. In M. Sundel et al. (Eds.), *Individual change through small groups* (pp. 324–343). New York: Free Press.

Davis, L., & Burnstein, E. (1981). Preference for racial composition of groups. *Journal of Psychology, 109,* 293–301.

De Anda, D. (1984). Bicultural socialization: Factors affecting the minority experience. *Social Work, 29,* 101–107.

Deaux, K., & Emswiller, T. (1974). Explanations of successful performance in sex-linked tasks: What is skill for the male is luck for the female. *Journal of Personality and Social Psychology, 29,* 80–85.

Delgado, M. (1981). Hispanic cultural values: Implications for groups. *Small Group Behavior, 12*(1), 69–80.

Denison, D. (1990). *Corporate culture and organizational effectiveness.* New York: Wiley

Deshpande, Hoyer, & Donthu, J. (1986). The study of ethnic affiliation: A study of the sociology of Hispanic consumption. *Journal of Consumer Research, 13,* 214–220.

Devanna, M. A. (1984). *Male/female careers—The first decade: A study of MBAs.* New York: Columbia University Graduate School of Business.

DeVos, G. A. (1980). Ethnic adaptation and minority status. *Journal of Cross-Cultural Psychology, 11*(1), 101–124.

de Vries, S. (1992). *Working in multi-ethnic groups: The performance and well being of minority and majority workers.* Amsterdam: Gouda Quint bu-Arnhem.

Dickens, F., & Dickens, J. B. (1982). *The Black manager: Making it in the corporate world.* New York: AMACOM.

Dietrick, E. J., & Dobbins, G. J. (1991). The influence of subordinate age on managerial actions: An attributional analysis. *Journal of Organization Behavior, 12,* 367–377.

Dovidio, J. F., Mann, J., & Gaertner, S. L. (1989). Resistance to affirmative action: The implications of aversive racism. In F. A. Blanchard & F. J. Crosby (Eds.), *Affirmative action in perspective* (pp. 83–102). New York: Springer-Verlag.

Downing, L. L., & Monaco, N. R. (1986). In group/out group bias as a function of differential contact and authoritarian personality. *Journal of Social Psychology, 126,* 445-452.

Dreher, G. F., & Ash, R. A. (1990). A comparative study of mentoring among men and women in managerial, professional and technical positions. *Journal of Applied Psychology, 75*(5), 1–8.

Dreyfuss, J. (1990, April 23). Get ready for the new workforce. *Fortune,* pp. 167–181.

Dutton, J. E., Dukerich, J. M., & Harquail, C. V. (1992). The organizational self: Linking organizational identity and image to individuals through the process of organizational identifying. Working paper, University of Michigan.

Eagly, A. H. (1983, September). Gender and social infuence: A social psychological analysis. *American Psychologist, 38*(9), 971-981.

Eagly, A. H., & Johnson, B. T. (1990). Gender and leadership style: A meta-analysis. *Psychological Bulletin, 108*(2), 233-256.

Eagly, A. H., Makhijani, M. G., & Klonsky, B. G. (1992). Gender and the evaluation of leaders: A meta-analysis. *Psychological Bulletin, 111*(1), 3–22.

Eden, D. (1984). Self-fulfilling prophecy as a management tool: Harnessing pygmalion. *Academy of Management Review, 9*(1), 64–73.

Eden, D. (1990). Industrialization as a self-fulfilling prophecy: The role of expectations in development. *International Journal of Psychology, 25,* 871–886.

Eden, D., & Shani, A. B. (1982). Pygmalion goes to boot camp: Expectancy, leadership and trainee performance. *Journal of Applied Psychology, 67,* 194–199.

Edfelt, R. (1986). A look at American managerial styles. *Business, 36*(1), 51–54.

Eisenberger, R., Fasolo, P., & Davis-LaMastro, V. (1990). Perceived organizational support and employee diligence, commitment, and innovation. *Journal of Applied Psychology, 75*(1), 51–59.

Eller, M. E. (1990). Sexual harassment: Prevention, not protection. *Cornell H.R.A. Quarterly, 3,* 84–89.

England, P. (1984). Wage appreciation and depreciation: A test of neoclassical economic explanations of occupational sex segregation. *Social Forces, 62,* 726–749.

Epstein, C. F. (1988). *Deceptive distinctions: Sex, gender and the social order.* New York: Yale University Press; New Haven and London: Russell Sage Foundation.

Esty, K. (1988). Diversity is good for business. *Executive Excellence, 5,* 5–6.

Etzkowitz, H. (1971). The male sister: Sexual separation of labor in society. *Journal of Marriage and the Family, 33,* 431–434.

Everett, M. (1990). Let an overweight person call on your best customers? *Sales and Marketing Journal, 142*(4), 66–70.

Farh, J. L., Dobbins, G. H., & Cheng, B. (1991). Cultural relativity in action: A comparison of self-ratings made by Chinese and U.S. workers. *Personnel Psychology, 44,* 129–147.

Farley, L. (1978). *Sexual shakedown: The sexual harassment of women on the job.* New York: McGraw-Hill.

Feinstein, S. (1989, October 10). Being the best on somebody's list does attract talent. *Wall Street Journal.*

Feldman, D. D. (1981). The multiple socialization of organization members. *Academy of Management Review, 6*(2), 309–318.

Fernandez, J. P. (1981). *Racism and sexism in corporate life: Changing values in American business.* Lexington, MA: Lexington Books.

Fernandez, J. P. (1991). *Managing a diverse workforce.* Lexington, MA: Lexington Books.

Fernandez-Barillas, H. J., & Morrison, T. L. (1984). Cultural affiliation and adjustment among male Mexican-American college students. *Psychological Reports, 55,* 855–860.

Festinger, L. (1957). A theory of cognitive dissonance. Stanford: Stanford University Press.

Fiedler, F. E. (1966). The effect of leadership and cultural heterogeneity on group performance: A test of the contingency model. *Journal of Experimental Social Psychology, 2,* 237–264.

Fierman, J. (1990, July 30). Why women still don't hit the top. *Fortune,* pp. 40–62.

Fine, M. G., Johnson, F. L., & Ryan, M. S. (1990). Cultural diversity in the workplace. *Public Personnel Management, 19*(3).

Firebaugh, G., & Davis, K. (1988). Trends in antiblack prejudice, 1972–1984: Region and cohort effects. *American Journal of Sociology, 94*(2), 251–272.

Fitt, L. W., & Newton, D. A. (1981). When the mentor is a man and the protégé is a woman. *Harvard Business Review, 59,* 56–60.

Fitz, B. E. (1985). Avoiding culture shock. *China Business Review, 12*(6), 24–26.

Foeman, A. K., & Pressley, G. (1987). Ethnic culture and corporate-culture: Using Black styles in organizations. *Communications Quarterly, 35,* 293–307.

Forsythe, S. M. (1990). Effect of applicant's clothing on interviewer's decision to hire. *Journal of Applied Social Psychology, 20*(19), 1579–1595.

Fottler, M. D., & Bain, T. (1980). Sex differences in occupational aspirations. *Academy of Management Journal, 23,* 144–149.

Fryxell, G. E., & Lerner, L. D. (1989). Contrasting corporate profiles: Women and minority representation in top management positions. *Journal of Business Ethics, 8,* 341–352.

Fullerton, H. N. (1987, September). Labor force projections: 1986–2000. *Monthly Labor Review,* pp. 19–29.

Gerbner, G., Gross, L., Elley, M., Jackson-Beeck, M., Jeffries-Fox, S., & Signorielli, N. (1977). TV violence profile #8. *Journal of Communication, 27,* 171–180.

Germans try to stem right wing attacks against foreigners. (1991, December 4). *Wall Street Journal.*

Ghali, S. B. (1977). Culture sensitivity and Puerto Rican clients. *Social Casework, 58,* 459–468.

Giles, M. W., & Evans, A. (1986). The power approach to intergroup hostility. *Journal of Conflict Resolution, 30*(3), 469–486.

Gilligan, C. (1982). *In a different voice: Psychological theory and women's development.* Cambridge: Harvard University Press.

Glasser, I. (1988). Affirmative action and the legacy of racial injustice. In P. A. Katz & D. A. Taylor (Eds.), *Eliminating racism* (pp. 341–358). New York: Plenum Press.

Glazer, N. (1988). The future of preferential affirmative action. In P. A. Katz & D. A. Taylor (Eds.), *Eliminating racism* (pp. 329–340). New York: Plenum Press.

Goff, S. J., Mount, M. K., & Jamison, R. L. (1990). Employer supported child care, work/family conflict, and absenteeism: A field study. *Personnel Psychology, 43,* 793–809.

Goffman, E. (1979). *Gender advertisements.* New York: Macmillan.

Goldstein, I., & White, C. (1985). Residential segregation and color stratification among Hispanics in Philadelphia: Comment on Massey and Mullan. *American Journal of Sociology, 91,* 391–395.

Gouldner, A. W. (1954). *Patterns of industrial bureaucracy.* New York: Free Press.

Graham, R. J. (1981, March). The role of perception of time in consumer behavior. *Journal of Consumer Research, 7,* 335–342.

Green, S. G., & Mitchell, T. R. (1979). Attributional processes of leaders in leader-member interactions. *Organizational Behavior and Human Performance, 23,* 429–458.

Greenhaus, J. H., & Parasuraman, S. (in press). Job performance attributions and career advancement prospects: An examination of gender and race effects. *Organizational Behavior and Human Decision Processes.*

Greenhaus, J. H., Parasuraman S., & Wormely, W. (1990). Effects of race on organizational experiences, job performance evaluations and career outcomes. *Academy of Management Journal, 33,* 64–86.

Greenwood, R., & Johnson, V. A. (1987). Employer perspectives on workers with disabilities. *Journal of Rehabilitation, 53,* 37–46.

Gregory, A. (1990). Are women different and why are women thought to be different? Theoretical and methodological perspectives. *Journal of Business Ethics, 9,* 257–266.

Guetzkow, H. (1965). Communication in organizations. In J. G.

March (Ed.), *Handbook of organizations* (pp. 534-572). Chicago: Rand McNally.

Gutek, B. A. (1985). *Sex and the workplace: The impact of sexual behavior and harrassment on women and men and organizations.* San Francisco: Jossey-Bass.

Gutek, B. A., & Cohen, A. G. (1987). Sex ratios, sex role spillover, and sex at work: A comparison of men's and women's experiences. *Human Relations, 40*(2), 97–115

Gutek, B. A., Cohen, A. G., & Konrad, A. M. (1990). Predicting social-sexual behavior at work: A contact hypothesis. *Academy of Management Journal, 33*(3), 560–577.

Hadjifortiou, N. (1983). *Women and harassment at work.* London: Pluto Press.

Hall, D. T. (1976). *Careers in organizations.* Pacific Palisades, CA: Goodyear.

Hall, E. T. (1976). *Beyond culture.* New York: Doubleday.

Hall, E. T. (1982). *The hidden dimension.* New York: Doubleday.

Hamilton, A., & Veglahn, P. A. (1992). Sexual harassment: The hostile work environment. *Cornell H.R.A. Quarterly, 33*, 88–92.

Harlow, D. (1973). Professional employees' preference for upward mobility. *Journal of Applied Psychology, 57*(2), 137–141.

Hazuda, H., Stern, M., & Haffner, S. M. (1988). Acculturation and assimilation among Mexican-Americans: Scales and population-based data. *Social Science Quarterly, 69*(3), 687–706.

Heilman, M. E., & Guzzo, R. A. (1978). The perceived cause of work success as a mediator of sex discrimination in organizations. *Organizational Behavior and Human Performance, 21*, 346–357.

Helgesen, S. (1990). *The female advantage: Women's ways of leadership.* New York: Doubleday.

Helms, J. E. (Ed.). (1990). *Black and White racial identity.* New York: Greenwood Press.

Helms, J. E., & Giorgis, T. W. (1980). A comparison of the locus of control and anxiety level of African, Black American and White American college students. *Journal of College Student Personnel, 21*(6), 503–509.

Helping pregnant workers pays off. (1987, December 2). *USA Today.*

Hemming, H. (1985). Women in a man's world: Sexual harassment. *Human Relations, 38*(1), 67–79.

Henning, M., & Jardim, A. (1976). *The managerial women.* New York: Pocket Books.

Hewstone, M., & Ward, C. (1985). Ethnocentrism and causal attribution in Southeast Asia. *Journal of Personality and Social Psychology, 48*(3), 614–623.

Hispanics harassed by FBI, agent says. (1988, November 4). *Ann Arbor News,* p. C2.

Hoffman, C., & Hurst, N. (1990). Gender stereotypes: Perception or rationalization? *Journal of Personality and Social Psychology, 58*(2), 197–208.

Hoffman, E. (1985). The effect of race ratio composition on the frequency of organizational communication. *Social Psychology Quarterly, 48*(1), 17–26.

Hoffman, L. R., & Maier, N. R. F. (1961). Quality and acceptance of problem solutions by members of homogeneous and heterogeneous groups. *Journal of Abnormal and Social Psychology, 62*(2), 401–407.

Hofstede, G. (1980, Summer). Motivation, leadership and organization: Do American theories apply abroad? *Organizational Dynamics, 9,* 43–62.

Hofstede, G. (1984). The cultural relativity of the quality of life concept. *Academy of Management Review, 9,* 389–398.

Horwitz, T., & Forman, C. (1990, August 14). Clashing cultures. *The Wall Street Journal,* A1.

House, B. (1988). Power and personality in complex organizations. In B. M. Staw & L. L. Cummings (Eds.), *Research in organizational behavior* (Vol. 10, pp. 305–358). Greenwich, CT: JAI Press.

Howe, K. R. (1977). *Race relations. Australia and New Zealand: A comparative survey, 1770's–1970's.* Wellington, New Zealand: Methuen.

Hymowitz, C. (1989, February 16). One firm's bid to keep Blacks; women. *Wall Street Journal,* p. B1.

Ibarra, H. (1992). Homophily and differential returns: Sex differences in network structure and access in an advertising firm. *Administrative Science Quarterly, 37*(3), 442–447.

Ibarra, H. (1993). Personal networks of women and minorities in management. *Academy of Management Review, 18*(1), 56–87.

Ijzendoorn, M. H. (1989). Moral judgement, authoritarianism, and ethnocentrism. *Journal of Social Psychology, 129*(1), 37–45.

Ilgen, D. R., & Youtz, M. A. (1986). Factors affecting the evaluation and development of minorities in organizations. In K. Bowland & G. Ferris (Eds.), *Research in personnel and human resource management: A research annual* (pp. 307–337). Greenwich, CT: JAI Press.

Jablin, F. M. (1987). Organizational entry, assimilation and exit. In F. Jablin, L. L. Putnam, K. H. Roberts, & L. W. Porter (Eds.), *Handbook of organizational communication: An interdisciplinary perspective* (pp. 679–740). Newbury Park, CA: Sage.

Jackson, S. E. (1991). Team composition in organizational settings: Issues in managing an increasingly diverse workforce. In S. Worchel, W. Wood, & J. A. Simpson (Eds.), *Group process and productivity* (pp. 138–173). Newbury Park, CA: Sage.

Jackson, S. E., & Associates (Eds.). (1992). *Diversity in the workplace.* New York: Guilford Press.

Jackson, S. E., & Alvarez, E. B. (1992). Working through diversity as a strategic imperative. In S. Jackson & Associates (Eds.), *Diversity in the workplace* (pp. 13–36). New York: Guilford Press.

Jackson, S. E., Brett, J. F., Sessa, V. I., Cooper, D. M., Julin, J. A., & Peyronnin, K. (1991). Some differences make a difference: Individual dissimilarity and group heterogenity as correlates of recruitment, promotions and turnover. *Journal of Applied Psychology, 75*(5), 675–689.

Jago, A., & Vroom, V. (1982). Sex difference in the incidence and evaluation of participative leader behavior. *Journal of Applied Psychology, 67*(6), 776–783.

Jamieson, D., & O'Mara, J. (1991). *Managing workforce 2000.* San Francisco: Jossey-Bass.

Janis, L. (1982). *Groupthink* (2nd ed.). Boston: Houghton Mifflin.

Jans, N. A. (1985). Organizational factors and work involvement. *Organizational Behavior and Human Decisions Processes, 35,* 382–396.

Jenkins, M. C., & Atkins, T. V. (1990). Perceptions of acceptable dress by corporate and noncorporate recruiters. *Journal of Human Behavior and Learning, 7*(1), 38–46.

Jenner, S. (1984). The British roots of business ideology. *Journal of General Management, 10*(1), 44–56.

Johnson, A. (1987, December). Women managers: Old stereotypes die hard. *Management Review, 76,* 31–43.

Johnson, C. (1988). Japanese-style management in America. *California Management Review, 30,* 34–45.

Johnson, S., & Johnson, D. W. (1972). The effects of other's actions, attitude similarity, and race on attraction towards others. *Human Relations, 25*(2), 121–130.

Johnston, W. (1991, March/April). Global work force 2000: The new world labor market. *Harvard Business Review, 69,* 115–127.

Jones, E. (1986). Black managers: The dream deferred. *Harvard Business Review, 64,* 84–93.

"Jury awarded $20.3 million to supervisor in lawsuit against Texaco." (1991, October 4). *Ann Arbor News.*

Jussim, L., Coleman, L., & Lerch, L. (1987). The nature of stereotypes: A comparison and integration of three theories. *Journal of Personality and Social Psychology, 52*(3), 536–546.

Juster, F. T. (1986). Gender and promotion. *Journal of Human Resources, 21*(3), 406–435.

Kagan, K., & Madsen, M. C. (1971). Cooperation and competition of Mexican, Mexican-American, and Anglo-American children of two ages under four instructional sets. *Developmental Psychology, 5*(1), 32–39.

Kagan, S. (1977). Social motives and behaviors of Mexican-Americans and Anglo children. In J. L. Martinez (Ed.), *Chicano psychology* (pp. 45–86). San Diego, CA: Academic Press.

Kallen, H. (1958, Winter). On americanizing the American Indian. *Social Research, 25,* 469–473.

Kanter, R. M. (1977a). Some effects of proportions on group life: Skewed sex ratios and responses to token women. *American Journal of Sociology, 82*(5), 965–990.

Kanter, R. M. (1977b). *Men and women of the corporation.* New York: Basic Books.

Kanter, R. M. (1983). *The change masters.* New York: Simon & Schuster.

Katz, I., Hass, R. G., & Bailey, J. (1988). Attitudinal ambivalence and behavior toward people with disabilities. In H. E. Yuker (Ed.), *Attitudes toward persons with disabilities.* New York: Springer.

Kauffman, N. (1987). Motivating the older worker. *SAM Advanced Management Journal, 52,* 43–48.

Key, W. B. (1976). *Media sexploitation.* Englewood Cliffs, NJ: Prentice-Hall.

Khoo, G. P. S. (1988). Asian Americans with power and authority in the corporate world: An exploratory investigation. Unpublished master's thesis. University of California, Santa Cruz.

Kim, J. S., & Campagna, A. F. (1981). Effects of flextime on employee attendance and performance: A field experiment. *Academy of Management Journal, 24,* 729-741.

Kingstrom, P. O., & Mainstone, L. E. (1985). An investigation of rater-ratee acquaintance and bias. *Academy of Management Journal, 28,* 641-653.

Kitano, H. (1976). *Japanese-Americans: The evolution of a subculture.* Englewood Cliffs, NJ: Prentice-Hall.

Klauss, R. (1981, July/August). Formalized mentor relationships for management and executive development programs in the federal government. *Public Administration Review, 41,* 489-496.

Kleeb, R. (1989, Summer). Mobil drills holes through the color barrier. *Business and Society Review, 64,* 55-57.

Kochman, T. (1981). *Black and White: Styles in conflict.* Chicago: University of Chicago Press.

Konrad, A. M., & Gutek, B. A. (1987). Theory and research on group composition: Applications to the status of women and ethnic minorities. In S. Oskamp & S. Spacapan (Eds.), *Interpersonal processes: The Claremont Symposium on Applied Social Psychology* (pp. 85-121). Newbury Park, CA: Sage.

Konrad, W. (1990, August 6). Welcome to the woman-friendly company. *Business Week,* pp. 48-55.

Kossek, E. E., & Zonia, S. C. (1993). Assessing diversity climate: A field study of reactions to employer efforts to promote diversity. *Journal of Organizational Behavior, 14,* 61-81.

Kram, K. (1980). *Mentoring processes at work: Developmental relationships in managerial careers.* Doctoral dissertation, Yale University.

Kram, K. (1983). Phases in the mentor relationship. *Academy of Management Journal, 26,* 608-625.

Kram, K. (1985). *Mentoring at work.* Glenview, IL: Scott, Foresman.

Kram K., & Isabella, L. (1985). Mentoring alternatives: The role of peer relationships in career development. *Academy of Management Journal, 28,* 110-132.

Lambert, W. (1977). The effects of bilingualism on the individual: Cognitive and sociocultural consequences. In P. A. Hurnbey (Ed.), *Bilingualism: Psychological, social, and educational implications* (pp. 15-27). San Diego, CA: Academic Press.

Landis, D., & Boucher, J. (1987). Themes and models of conflict. In J. Boucher, D. Landis, & K. A. Clark (Eds.), *Ethnic conflict: International perspectives* (pp. 18-32). Newbury Park, CA: Sage.

Lawler, E. E. (1973). *Motivation in work organizations*. Pacific Grove, CA: Brooks/Cole.

Lee, T. W., & Mowday, R. T. (1987). Voluntarily leaving an organization: An empirical investigation of Steers and Mowday's model of turnover. *Academy of Management Journal, 30*, 721-743.

Lester, R., & Caudill, D. (1987). The handicapped worker: Seven myths. *Training and Development Journal, 41*(8), 50-51.

Leung, K., & Bond, M. H. (1984). The impact of cultural collectivism on reward allocation. *Journal of Personality and Social Psychology, 47*(4), 793-804.

Levine, M. (1987). Making group collaboration work. *Production and Inventory Management, 28*, 31-33.

Lichtenberg, J. (1992). Racism in the head, racism in the world. *Report from the Institute for Philosophy and Public Policy, 12*(1), 3-5.

Lincoln, C. E. (1967). Color and group identity in the United States. *Daedelaus, 1*(2), 527-541.

Lincoln, J. R. (1982). Intra- (inter-) organizational networks. In S. B. Bacharach (Ed.), *Research in the sociology of organizations* (pp. 1-38). Greenwich, CT: JAI Press.

Lincoln, J. R., & Miller, J. (1979). Work and friendship ties in organizations: A comparative analysis of relational networks. *Administrative Science Quarterly, 24*, 181-199.

Linville, P. W., & Jones, E. E. (1980). Polarized appraisal of outgroup members. *Journal of Personality and Social Psychology, 42*, 193-211.

Lobel, S. A. (1988). Effects of personal versus impersonal rater instructions on relative favorability of thirteen ethnic group stereotypes. *Journal of Social Psychology, 128*(1), 29-39.

Loden, M., & Rosener, J. B. (1991). *Workforce America! Managing employee diversity as a vital resource.* Homewood, IL: Business One Irwin.

Lott, A. J., & Lott, B. E. (1965). Group cohesiveness as interpersonal attraction: A review of relationships with antecedent and consequent variables. *Psychological Bulletin, 64,* 259–309.

Louis, M. R. (1980). Surprise and sense-making: What newcomers experience in entering unfamiliar organizational settings. *Administrative Science Quarterly, 25,* 226–251.

Lynch, F. R. (1991). *Invisible victims: White males and the crisis of affirmative actions.* New York: Praeger.

Malekzadeh, A., & Nahavandi, A. (1990). Making mergers work by managing cultures. *Journal of Business Strategy, 11,* 55–57.

Mandell, B., & Kohler-Gray, S. (1990). Management development that values diversity. *Personnel, 67,* 41–47.

Marin, G., & Triandis, H. C. (1985). Allocentrism as an important characteristic of the behavior of Latin Americans and Hispanics. In R. Diaz-Guerrero (Ed.), *Cross-cultural and national studies in social psychology* (pp. 69–80). Amsterdam: North Holland.

Marmer-Solomon, C. (1989, August). The corporate response to workforce diversity. *Personnel Journal,* pp. 43–53.

Massey, D. S., & Denton, N. A. (1988). Suburbanization and segregation in U.S. metropolitan areas. *American Journal of Sociology, 94,* 592–626.

Massey, D. S., & Mullan, B. P. (1984). Processes of Hispanic and Black spatial assimilation. *American Journal of Sociology, 89*(4), 836–872.

Matsumoto, G., Meredith, G., & Masuda, M. (1970). Ethnic identification: Honolulu and Seattle Japanese-Americans. *Journal of Cross-Cultural Psychology, 1*(1), 63–76.

McCarthy, H. (1985). Models of productive partnership between business and rehabilitation. In H. McCarthy (Ed.), *Complete guide to employing persons with disabilities* (pp. 131–169). Albertson, NY: Human Resources Center.

McClintock, C. G., & Allison, S. T. (1989). Social value orientation and helping behavior. *Journal of Applied Social Psychology, 19*(4), 353–362.

McConahay, J. B. (1982). Self-interest versus racial attitudes as correlates of anti-busing attitudes in Louisville: Is it the buses or the Blacks? *Journal of Politics, 44,* 692–720.

McConahay, J. B. (1983). Modern racism and modern discrimination: The effects of race, racial attitudes, and context on simulated living decisions. *Personality and Social Psychology Bulletin, 9,* 551–558.

McFee, M. (1968). The 150% man, a product of Blackfeet acculturation. *American Anthropologist, 70,* 1096–1103.

McGrath, J. E. (1984). *Groups: Interaction and performance.* Englewood Cliffs, NJ: Prentice-Hall.

McGrath, J. E., & Rotchford, N. L. (1983). Time and behavior in organizations. *Research in Organizational Behavior, 5,* 57–101.

McGuire, W. J., McGuire, C. V., Child, P., & Fujioka, T. (1978). Salience of ethnicity in the spontaneous self-concept as a function of one's ethnic distinctiveness in the social environment. *Journal of Personality and Social Psychology, 36*(5), 511–520.

McIntosh, P. (1988). White privilege and male privilege: A personal account of coming to see correspondence through work in women's studies. Working Paper No. 189, Center for Research on Women, Wellesley, MA.

McLeod, P. L., Lobel, S. A., and Cox, T., Jr. (1993). *Cultural diversity and creativity in small groups: A test of the value-in-diversity hypothesis.* Unpublished working paper, the University of Michigan, Ann Arbor.

Meglino, B. M., Ravlin, E. C., & Adkins, C. L. (1989). A work values approach to corporate culture: A field test of the value congruence process and its relationship to individual outcomes. *Journal of Applied Psychology, 75*(3), 424–432.

Meisenheimer, J. R. (1990, August). Employee absences in 1989: A new look at data from the CPS. *Monthly Labor Review,* pp. 28–33.

Mercer, M. (1988). Turnover: Reducing the costs. *Personnel, 5,* 36–42.

Merit Systems Protection Board. (1981). *Sexual harassment in the federal workplace.* Washington, DC: Office of Merit Systems Review and Studies.

Merton, R. K. (1948). The self-fulfilling prophesy. *Antioch Review, 8,* 193–210.

Meyerson, D., & Lewis, D. S. (1992). *Cultural tolerance of ambiguity.* Working paper, the University of Michigan, Ann Arbor.

Millum, T. (1975). *Images of women: Advertising in women's magazines*. Totowa, NJ: Rowman & Littlefield.

Mischel, W. (1977). The interaction of person and situation. In D. Magnussen & N. S. Endler (Eds.), *Personality at the crossroads* (pp. 333–352). Hillsdale, NJ: Erlbaum.

Mitroff, I., & Kilman, R. (1984). *Corporate tragedies: Product tampering, sabotage and other catastrophes*. New York: Praeger.

Montgomery, G., & Orozco, S. (1984). Validation of a measure of acculturation for Mexican-Americans. *Hispanic Journal of Behavioral Sciences, 6*(1), 53–63.

Morgan, G. (1989). Endangered species: New ideas. *Business Month, 133*(4), 75–77.

Morgenson, G. (1991, June 24). Where can I buy some? *Forbes*, pp. 82–84.

Morishima, J. (1981). Special employment issues for Asian Americans. *Public Personnel Management Journal, 10*(4), 384–392.

Morrison, A. H., White, R. P., & VanVelsor, E. (1987). *Breaking the glass ceiling: Can women reach the top of America's largest corporations?* Reading, MA: Addison-Wesley.

Morrison, A. M., & von Glinow, M. A. (1990). Women and minorities in management. *American Psychologist, 45*(2), 200–208.

Nahavandi, A., & Malekzadeh, A. (1988). Acculturation in mergers and acquisitions. *Academy of Management Review, 13*(1), 79–90.

Nakanishi, D. T. (1988). Seeking convergence in race relations research: Japanese-Americans and the resurrection of the internment. In P. A. Katz & D. A. Taylor (Eds.), *Eliminating Racism* (pp. 159–180). New York: Plenum Press.

Nemeth, C. J. (1985). Dissent, group process, and creativity. *Advances in Group Processes, 2*, 57–75.

Nemeth, C. J. (1986). Differential contributions of majority and minority influence. *Psychological Review, 93*, 23–32.

Nemeth, C. J., & Wachter, J. (1983). Creative problem solving as a result of majority versus minority influence. *European Journal of Social Psychology, 13*, 45–55.

Nilson, L. B. (1976). The occupational and sex-related components of social standing. *Social Research, 60*, 328–336.

Nkomo, S. M. (1992). The emperor has no clothes: Rewriting race in organizations. *Academy of Management Review, 17*, 487–513.

Nkomo, S. M., & Cox, T. H. (1989). Gender differences in the upward mobility of black managers: Double whammy or double advantage? *Sex Roles, 21,* 825-839.

Nobles, W. (1972). African philosophy: Foundations for Black psychology. In R. L. Jones (Ed.), *Black psychology* (pp. 18-32). New York: HarperCollins.

Noe, R. A. (1988). An investigation of the determinants of successful assigned mentoring relationships. *Personnel Psychology, 41,* 457-479.

Northcraft, G., & Neale, M. (1990). *Organizational behavior: A management challenge.* Chicago: Dryden Press.

O'Guinn, T. C., Faber, R. J., Curias, N.J.J., and Schmitt, K. (1989). The cultivation of consumer norms. *Advances in Consumer Research, 16,* 779-785.

Olson, C. A., & Becker, B. E. (1983). Sex discrimination in the promotion process. *Industrial and Labor Relations Review, 36,* 624-641.

Olson, J. E., & Frieze, I. H. (1987). Income determinants for women in business. In A. H. Stromberg, L. Larwood, & B. A. Gutek (Eds.), *Women and work* (pp. 173-206). Newbury Park, CA: Sage.

O'Reilly, C. A., III, Chapman, J., & Caldwell, D. F. (1991). People and organization culture: A profile comparison approach to assessing person-organization fit. *Academy of Management Journal, 34*(3), 487-516.

Orpen, C., & Nkohande, J. (1977, May). Self-esteem. Interval control and expectancy beliefs of White and Black managers in South Africa. *Journal of Management Studies,* pp. 192-199.

Ott, E. M. (1989). Effects of the male-female ratio. *Psychology of Women Quarterly, 13,* 41-57.

Ouchi, M. G. (1980). Markets, bureaucracies and clans. *Administrative Science Quarterly, 25,* 129-141.

Padilla, A. M. (1980). *Acculturation: Theory, models, and some new findings.* Boulder, CO: Westview.

Pascale, R. (1985). The paradox of corporate culture: Reconciling ourselves to socialization. *California Management Review, 27*(2), 26-41.

Patterson, G. A. (1989, October 13). Mazda's two top American aides at plant in U.S. quit, are succeeded by Japanese. *Wall Street Journal.*

Pazy, A. (1986). The persistence of pro-male bias despite identical information regarding causes of success. *Organizational Behavior and Human Decision Processes, 38,* 366–377.

Pearlin, L. I. (1962). Alienation from work: A study of nursing personnel. *American Sociological Review, 27,* 314–326.

Pettigrew, T. F. (1982). Prejudice. In S. Thernstrom, A. Onou, & O. Handlin (Eds.), *Dimensions of ethnicity: Prejudice.* Cambridge: Belkap Press, Harvard University Press.

Pettigrew, T. F., & Martin, J. (1987). Shaping the organizational context for Black American inclusion. *Journal of Social Forces, 43,* 41–78.

Pfeffer J., & Davis-Blake, A. (1987). The effect of the proportion of women on salaries: The case of college administrators. *Administrative Science Quarterly, 32,* 1–24

Phillips-Jones, L. (1982). *Mentors and protégés.* New York: Arbor House.

Phillips-Jones, L. (1983). Establishing a formalized mentoring program. *Training and Development Journal, 37,* 38–42.

Phinney, J. S. (1989). Stages of ethnic identity development in minority group adolescents. *Journal of Early Adolescence, 9*(1-2), 34–49.

Ponterotto, J. G. (1988a). Racial consciousness development among White counselor trainees: A stage model. *Journal of Multicultural Counseling and Development, 16,* 146–156.

Ponterotto, J. G. (1988b). Racial/ethnic minority research in the *Journal of Counseling Psychology*: A content analysis and methodological critique. *Journal of Counseling Psychology, 35*(4), 410–418.

Powell, G. (1988). *Women and men in management.* Newbury Park, CA: Sage.

Powell, G. (1990). One more time: Do female and male managers differ? *Academy of Management Executive, 4,* 68–74.

Provencher, R. (1987). Interethnic conflict in the Malay Peninsula. In J. Boucher, D. Landis, & K. Clark (Eds.), *Ethnic conflict: International perspectives* (pp. 92-119). Newbury Park, CA: Sage.

Pucik, V., Hanada, M., & Fifield, G. (1989). *Management culture and the effectiveness of local executives in Japanese-owned U.S. corporations.* Tokyo: Egon Zehnder.

Pulley, B. (1992, December 21). Culture of racial bias at Shoney's underlies chairman's departure. *Wall Street Journal.*

Quinn, R. (1977). Coping with Cupid: The formation, impact and management of romantic relationships in organizations. *Administrative Science Quarterly, 22,* 30–45.

Quinn, R. (1988). *Beyond rational management.* San Francisco: Jossey-Bass.

Quinn R., & Lees, P. L. (1984). Attraction and harassment: Dynamics of sexual politics in the workplace. *Organizational Dynamics, 13,* 35–46.

Raggins, B. R. (1989). Barriers to mentoring: The female manager's dilemma. *Human Relations, 42*(1), 1–22.

Raggins, B. R., & McFarlin, D. B. (1990). Perceptions of mentor roles in cross-gender mentoring relationships. *Journal of Vocational Behavior, 37*(3), 321–339.

Ramirez, A. (1977). Chicano power and interracial group relations. In J. L. Martinez, Jr. (Ed.), *Chicano psychology.* San Diego, CA: Academic Press.

Ramirez, A. (1988). Racism toward Hispanics: The culturally monolithic society. In P. A. Katz & D. A. Taylor (Eds.), *Eliminating racism* (pp. 137–153). New York: Plenum Press.

Ramirez, A., & Soriano, F. (1982). Social power in educational systems: Its effects on Chicanos' attitudes toward the school experience. *Journal of Social Psychology, 118,* 113–119.

Rand, T. M., & Wexley, K. N. (1975). Demonstration of the effect "similar to me" in simulated employment interviews. *Psychological Reports, 36,* 535–544.

Randolph, W. A., & Blackburn, R. S. (1989). *Managing organizational behavior.* Homewood, IL: Richard D. Irwin.

Raudsepp, E. (1988). Put teamwork in work teams. *Chemical Engineering, 95*(10), 113–114.

Redding, S. G. (1982). Cultural effects on the marketing process in Southeast Asia. *Journal of Market Research Society, 24*(19), 98–114.

Reder, M. W. (1978). An analysis of a small closely observed labor market: Starting salaries for University of Chicago MBAs. *Journal of Business, 16,* 263–297.

Reid, P. T. (1988). Racism and sexism: Comparisons and conflicts.

In P. A. Katz & D. A. Taylor (Eds.), *Eliminating racism* (pp. 203–219). New York: Plenum Press.

Rice, A. K. (1969). *Learning in groups*. London: Tavistock.

Ridgeway, C. (1991). The social construction of status value: Gender and other nominal characteristics. *Social Forces, 70*(2), 367–386.

Robinson, J. P. (1988, December). Who's doing the housework? *American Demographics,* pp. 24–28.

Rosen, B., & Jerdee, T. H. (1976). The nature of job related age stereotypes. *Journal of Applied Psychology, 61,* 180–183.

Rosen, B., Miguel, M., & Pierce, E. (1989). Stemming the exodus of women managers. *Human Resource Management, 28,* 475–491.

Rosenbaum, R. (1984). *Career mobility in a corporate hierarchy.* Orlando: Academic Press.

Rosenbloom, D. H. (1973, January/February). A note on interminority group competition for federal positions. *Public Personnel Management,* pp. 43–48.

Rosener, J. B. (1990, November/December). Ways women lead. *Harvard Business Review,* pp. 119–125.

Rosenthal, R. (1974). *On the social psychology of the self-fulfulling prophecy: Further evidence for pygmalion effects and their mediating mechanisms.* New York: MSS Modular Publications, 53.

Rotter, J. B. (1966). Generalized expectancies for internal versus external control of reinforcement. *Psychological Monographs, 80,* 1–28.

Rotter, N. G., & O'Connell, A. N. (1982). The relationships among sex-role orientation, cognitive complexity and tolerance for ambiguity. *Sex Roles, 8,* 1209–1220.

Rummell, R. J. (1976). *Understanding conflict and war.* New York: Wiley.

Sales, A. L., & Mirvis, P. H. (1984). When cultures collide: Issues of acquisition. In J. R. Kimberly & R. E. Quinn (Eds.), *Managing organizational transition* (pp. 107–133). Homewood, IL: Irwin.

Sanday, P. G. (1981). *Female power and male dominance: On the origins of sexual inequality.* Cambridge: Cambridge University Press.

Sandroff, R. (1988). Sexual harassment in the Fortune 500. *Working Woman, 13*(12), 69–73.

Schein, E. H. (1968). Organizational socialization and the profession of management. *Industrial Management Review, 9,* 1–16.

Schein, E. H. (1971). The individual, the organization and the career: A conceptual scheme. *Journal of Applied Behavioral Science, 7,* 401–426.

Schein, J. D. (1975). The deaf scientist. *Journal of Rehabilitation of the Deaf, 9*(1), 17–21.

Schneider, B. (1987). The people make the place. *Personnel Psychology, 14,* 437–453.

Schwartz, F. (1989, January/February). Management women and the new facts of life. *Harvard Business Review,* 65–76.

Schweltzer, N. J., & Deely, J. (1982, March). Interviewing the disabled job applicant. *Personnel Journal,* pp. 205–209.

Sears, D. O. (1988). Symbolic racism. In P. A. Katz & D. A. Taylor (Eds.), *Eliminating racism* (pp. 53–84). New York: Plenum Press.

Sears, D. O., & Kinder, D. R. (1970). *The good life, "white racism," and the Los Angeles voter.* Paper delivered at the annual meeting of the Western Psychological Association, Los Angeles.

Sears, D. O., & Kinder, D. R. (1971). Racial tensions and voting in Los Angeles. In W. Z. Hirsch (Ed.), *Los Angeles: Viability and prospects of metropolitan leadership.* New York: Praeger.

Segal, B. E. (1962). Male nurses: A case study in status contradiction and prestige loss. *Social Forces, 41,* 31–38.

Shaffer, D. R. (1985). *Developmental psychology: Theory, research and applications.* Pacific Grove, CA: Brooks/Cole.

Shaffer, D., Hendrick, C., Regula, R., & Freconna, J. (1973). Interactive effects of ambiguity tolerance and task effort on dissonance reduction. *Journal of Personality, 41*(2), 224–233.

Shaw, E. A. (1977). Differential impact of negative stereotyping in employee selection. *Personnel Psychology, 25,* 333–338.

Shaw, M. E. ([1976] 1981). *Group dynamics: The psychology of small group behavior.* New York: McGraw-Hill.

Shephard, C. R. (1964). *Small groups.* San Francisco: Chandler Publishing.

Sherif, M. (1966). *Group conflict and cooperation.* London: Routledge & Kegan Paul.

Sherif, M., Harvey, O. J., White, B. J., Hood, W. R., & Sherif, C. W. (1961). *Intergroup conflict and cooperation: The robbers' cave experiment.* Norman, OK: University Book Exchange.

Shimp, T. A., & Sharma, S. (1987). Consumer ethnocentrism: Construction and validation of the CETSCALE. *Journal of Marketing Research, 24*(3), 280–289.

Siegel, A. L., & Ruh, R. A. (1973). Job involvement, participation in decision making, personal background and job behavior. *Organizational Behavior and Human Performance, 9,* 318–327.

Siegel, S., & Kaemmerer, W. (1978). Measuring the perceived support for innovation in organizations. *Journal of Applied Psychology, 63*(5), 553–562.

Siehl, C., & Martin, L. (1984). The role of symbolic management: How can managers effectively transmit organizational culture? In J. G. Hunt, D. M. Hosking, C. A. Schriesheim, & R. Stewart (Eds.), *Leaders and managers: International perspectives on managerial behavior and leadership* (pp. 227–269). Elmsford, NY: Pergamon Press.

Sigelman, L. (1982). American's attitudes toward other nations: An attempt at explanation. *International Journal of Comparative Sociology, 23,* 98–105.

Simon, H. A. (1991). *Elison* v. *Brady*: A "reasonable woman" standard for sexual harassment. *Employee Relations Law Journal, 17*(1), 71–80.

Simonetti, J. L., Nykodym, N., & Goralske, J. M. (1988, January). Family ties: A guide for HR managers. *Personnel,* pp. 37–41.

Smircich, L. (1983). Concepts of culture and organizational analysis. *Administration Science Quarterly, 28,* 339–359.

Solomon, C. M. (1989). The corporate response to work force diversity. *Personnel Journal, 43–53.*

Sonnenfeld, J. A., & Ellis, C. (1992). *Diverse approaches to managing diversity.* Paper presented at the National Academy of Management Meeting, Las Vegas.

Sonnenfeld, J. A., Peiperl, M. A., & Kotter, J. P. (1988). Strategic determinants of managerial labor markets: A career system view. *Human Resource Management, 27,* 369–388.

South, S. J., Bonjean, C. M., Markam, W. T., & Corder, J. (1982). Social structure and intergroup interaction: Men and women of the federal bureaucracy. *American Sociological Review, 47,* 587–599.

Spector, P. E. (1982). Behavior in organizations as a function of employee's locus of control. *Psychological Bulletin, 91,* 482–497.

Stace, S. (1987). Vocational rehabilitation for women with disabilities. *International Labour Review, 126*(3), 301–316.

Staff. (1992, January–February). 1992 Hispanic 100: The one hundred companies providing the most opportunities for Hispanics. *Hispanic*, pp. 49–76.

Stanbeck, M. H., & Pearce, W. B. (1981). Talking to "the man": Some communication strategies used by members of subordinate social groups. *Quarterly Journal of Speech, 67*, 21–30.

Stayman, D. M., & Deshpande, R. (1989). Situational ethnicity and consumer behavior. *Journal of Consumer Research, 16*, 361–371.

Steele, S. (1990, May 13). A negative vote on affirmative action. *New York Times Magazine*, p. 46.

Steiner, I. D. (1972). *Group process and productivity*. San Diego, CA: Academic Press.

Steinhoff, P., & Tanaka, K. (1987). Women managers in Japan. *International Studies of Management and Organization, 16*, 108–132.

Stone, E. F., Stone, D. L., & Dipboye, R. L. (in press). Stigmas in organizations: Race, handicaps, and physical unattractiveness. In K. Kelley (Ed.), *Issues, theory and research in industrial/organizational psychology*. Amsterdam: Elsevier Science.

Stringer, D. M., Remick, H., Salisbury, J., & Ginorio, A. B. (1990). The power and reasons behind sexual harassment: An employer's guide to solutions. *Public Personnel Management, 19*, 45–52.

Strober, M. H. (1982). The MBA: Same passport to success for women and men? In P. A. Wallace (Ed.), *Women in the workplace* (pp. 25–44). Boston: Auburn House.

Sue, S., & Kitano, H. (1973). Stereotypes as a measure of success. *Journal of Social Issues, 29*(2), 83–98.

Sue, S., Zane, N., & Sue, D. (1985). Where are the Asian American leaders and top executives? *Research Review, 9*, 13–15.

Szapocznik, J., & Kurtines, W. (1980). Acculturation, biculturalism and adjustment among Cuban Americans. In A. Padilla (Ed.), *Psychological dimensions on the acculturation process: Theories, models, and some new findings* (pp. 139–159). Boulder, CO: Westview.

Szapocznik, J., Santisteban, D., Kurtines, W., Perez-Vidal, A., & Herdis, O. (1988). Bicultural effectiveness training: A treatment intervention for enhancing intercultural adjustment in Cuban

American families. *Hispanic Journal of Behavioral Sciences,* 6(4), 317–344.

Szapocznik, J., Scopetta, M., & King, O. E. (1978). Theory and practice in matching treatment to the special characteristics and problems of Cuban immigrants. *Journal of Community Psychology,* 6, 112–122.

Szilagyi, A. D., & Sims, H. P. (1975). Leader structure and subordinate satisfaction for two hospital administrative levels: A path analysis approach. *Journal of Applied Psychology, 60,* 194–197.

Tajfel, H. (Ed.). (1978). *Differentiation between social groups: Studies in the social psychology of intergroup relations.* San Diego, CA: Academic Press.

Tangri, S. T., Burt, M. R., & Johnson, L. B. (1982). Sexual harassment at work: Three explanatory models. *Journal of Social Issues, 38,* 33–54.

Tannen, D. (1990). *You just don't understand: Women and men in conversation.* New York: William Morrow.

Taylor, D. M., & Jaggi, V. (1974). Ethnocentrism and causal attribution in a South Indian context. *Journal of Cross-Cultural Psychology, 5,* 162–171.

Taylor, S., Fiske, S., Etcoff, N., & Ruderman, A. (1978). Categorical and contextual bases of person memory and stereotyping. *Journal of Personality and Social Psychology, 36*(7), 778–793.

Terpstra, D. E. (1989). Who gets sexually harassed? *Personnel Administrator, 34,* 84–88.

Thomas, D. A. (1989a). Mentoring and irrationality: The role of racial taboos. *Human Resource Management, 28*(2), 279–290.

Thomas, D. A. (1989b). *Strategies for managing racial difference in work-centered developmental relationships.* Unpublished working paper, Wharton School of Business, University of Pennsylvania.

Thomas, D. A. (1990). The impact of race on managers' experiences of developmental relationships: An intraorganizational study. *Journal of Organizational Behavior, 11*(6), 479–492.

Thomas, R. R., Jr. (1990, March/April). From affirmative action to affirming diversity. *Harvard Business Review, 68*(2), 107–117.

Thomas, R. R., Jr. (1991). *Beyond race and gender: Unleashing the power of your total work force by managing diversity.* New York: AMACOM.

Thompson, D. E., & Ditomaso, N. (1988). *Ensuring minority success in corporate management*. New York: Plenum Press.

Toren, N., & Kraus, V. (1987). The effects of minority size on women's position in academia. *Social Forces, 65*(4), 1090–1100.

Touhey, J. C. (1974). Effects of additional women professionals on occupational prestige and desirability. *Journal of Personality and Social Psychology, 29*, 86–89.

Triandis, H. C. (1976). The future of pluralism revisited. *Journal of Social Issues, 32*, 179–208.

Triandis, H. C., Hall, E. R., & Ewen, R. B. (1965). Member heterogeneity and dyadic creativity. *Human Relations, 18*, 33–55.

Triandis, H. C., McCusker, C., & Hui, C. H. (1990). Multi-method probes of individualism-collectivism. *Journal of Personality and Social Psychology, 59*, 1006–1020.

Trimble, J. (1987). American Indians and interethnic conflict. In J. Boucher, D. Landis, & K. A. Clark (Eds.), *Ethnic conflict* (pp. 208–230). Newbury Park, CA: Sage.

Trimble, J. (1988). Stereotypical images, American Indians, and prejudice. In P. Katz & D. Taylor, *Eliminating racism* (pp. 181–201). New York: Plenum Press.

Trost, C. (1990, May 2). Women managers quit not for family but to advance their corporate climb. *Wall Street Journal*.

Trotman-Reid, P. (1988). Racism and sexism: Comparisons and conflicts. In P. Katz and D. Taylor, *Eliminating racism* (pp. 203–219). New York: Plenum Press.

Tse, D. K., Lee, K., Vertinsky, I., & Wehrung, D. A. (1988). Does culture matter? A cross-cultural study of executives' choice, decisiveness, and risk adjustment in international marketing. *Journal of Marketing, 52*, 81–95.

Tsui, A. S., & O'Reilly, C. A. III. (1989). Beyond simple demographic effects: The importance of relational demography in superior-subordinate dyads. *Academy of Management Journal, 32*(2), 402–423.

Twenty-five best places for Blacks to work. (1992, February). *Black Enterprise*, pp. 71–96.

U.S. corporations with biggest foreign revenues. (1992, July 20). *Forbes*, pp. 150, 298–300.

Van Maanen, J. (1975). Police socialization: A longitudinal examination of job attitudes in urban police departments. *Administrative Science Quarterly, 20,* 207–228.

Van Maanen, J., & Schein, E. H. (1979). Toward a theory of organizational socialization. In B. Staw & L. L. Cummings (Eds.), *Research in Organizational Behavior* (Vol. 1, pp. 209–264). Greenwich, CT: JAI Press.

Vroom, V. H. (1964). *Work and motivation.* New York: Wiley.

Webber, R. (1974). Majority and minority perceptions and behavior in cross-cultural teams. *Human Relations, 27,* 873–890.

Weber, M. (1947). *The theory of social and economic organization* (A. Henderson & T. Parson, Trans.). New York: Free Press.

Weigel, R. H., & Howes, P. W. (1985). Conceptions of racial prejudice: Symbolic racism reconsidered. *Journal of Social Issues, 41,* 117–138.

Weiner, Y. (1988). Forms of value systems: A focus of organizational effectiveness and cultural change and maintenance. *Academy of Management Review, 13,* 534–545.

Werther, W. B., & Davis, K. (1993). *Human resources and personnel management.* New York: McGraw-Hill.

Whitely, W., Dougherty, T. W., & Dreher, G. F. (1991). Relationship of career mentoring and socioeconomic origin to managers' and professionals' early career progress. *Academy of Management Journal, 34*(2), 331–351.

Wiley, M. G., & Eskilson, A. (1982). The interaction of sex and power base on perceptions of managerial effectiveness. *Academy of Management Journal, 25,* 671–677.

Wilson, W. J. (1987). *The truly disadvantaged: Inner city, the underclass and public policy.* Chicago: University of Chicago Press.

Winokur, L. A. (1992, October 26). Harassment of workers by "third parties" can lead into maze of legal, moral issues. *Wall Street Journal,* pp. B1, B3.

Women on boards. (1992, June 16). *Wall Street Journal.*

Wong-Reider, D. (1982). Mismatches in self-identity and the adaptation of Asian students to living in a North American city. In R. Rath, H. S. Asthana, D. Sinha, & J. B. P. Sinha (Eds.), *Diversity and unity in cross-cultural psychology* (pp. 128–146). Kanpur, India: Pragya Prakashan Publishers. (1st Indian edition, 1985)

Wong-Reider, D. (1983). *Whites and native Indians in a bicultural setting*. Paper presented at the twenty-ninth annual meeting of the Southwestern Psychological Association Meeting, San Antonio, TX.

Wong-Reider, D. (1984). Testing a model of emotional and coping responses to problems in adaptation. *International Journal of Intercultural Relations, 8,* 153–184.

Wong-Reider, D., & Quintana, D. (1987). Comparative acculturation of Southeast Asian and Hispanic immigrants and sojourners. *Journal of Cross-Cultural Psychology, 18*(3), 345–362.

Yale University Films. (1985). *A class divided* [Film]. New Haven, CT: Yale University.

Youngblood, S. A., & Chambers-Cook, K. (1984, February). Child-care assistance can improve employee attitudes and behavior. *Personnel Administrator,* pp. 93–95.

Yuker, H. E. (1988). *Attitudes toward persons with disabilities.* New York: Springer.

Zeitz, B., & Dusky, L. (1988). *Best companies for women.* New York: Simon & Schuster.

Ziller, R. C. (1973). Homogeneity and heterogeneity of group membership. In C. H. McClintock (Ed.), *Experimental social psychology* (pp. 385-411). New York: Holt, Rinehart & Winston.

Zurcher, L. A, Zurcher, S. L., & Meadow, A. (1965). Value orientation, role conflict, and alienation from work: A cross-cultural study. *American Sociological Review, 30,* 539-548.

Name Index

Subject Index

A

Accountability, for organizational change, 239–240

Acculturation, to organizational culture, 165–168, 226, 228

Aetna Insurance: Institute for Corporate Education of, 253; partnerships of, 252

Affirmative action: concepts of, 248–250; motives for, 250–251; reconfigured, 251–253; for structural integration, 248–253

African Americans. *See* Blacks and Whites

African National Congress, 155

Age Discrimination Act of 1967, 12

Airtime in meetings, 125–126

Ambiguity tolerance: organizational culture and, 168–169; prejudice and, 65–66

American Indians: counseling services and, 31; cultural differences and, 106, 114–115; culture identity group and, 54, 60; institutional bias and, 212, 214, 216; intergroup conflict and, 141; prejudice and, 70, 72

Americans with Disabilities Act of 1990, 5, 12, 221

Anheuser-Busch, minorities at, 228

Arabs, cultural differences and, 109, 110, 118

Arthur Anderson, part-time workers at, 257

Asian Americans: collectivism for, 114, 115; cooperation for, 115–116; communication for, 122–123, 125–126; culture fit for, 174; growth rate of, 4; institutional bias and, 211–212, 214; language training and, 245; locus of control for, 118; marketing and, 29; prejudice and, 70; in social networks, 197; stereotyping of, 93, 96; time and space for, 110

Assimilation, to organizational culture, 166, 168, 169

Assumed characteristics theory, stereotyping and, 93

AT&T: mentoring at, 204; training at, 244

Attractiveness, prejudice and, 67, 74–75

Attribution theory: ethnocentrism and, 133–134, 135; prejudice and, 82–84; stereotypes and, 96–97

Audit, of culture and management systems, 237–238

Australia: ethnocentrism in, 130; individualism in, 114

Authoritarian personality: ethnocentrism and, 133; prejudice and, 65

Avon Corporation: awareness training at, 236; institutional bias and, 219; leadership at, 232; marketing by, 30; minority support group at, 148, 247

Author and Contributor

Taylor Cox, Jr., is associate professor of organization behavior and human resource management at the School of Business, the University of Michigan. He is also president of his own consulting firm, Taylor Cox Associates, which specializes in human resource work with diverse workgroups. As a consultant, Cox's experience includes the design and delivery of training programs on workforce diversity, design and implementation of culture audits, and human resource management systems changes, as well as advice to individual managers on planning and executing comprehensive organizational change work for managing diverse workforces. Products and services have been provided to more than a dozen private companies, including several Fortune 500 firms.

As a faculty member at Michigan and formerly at Duke University, Cox has taught organization behavior, human resource management, and manufacturing strategy to hundreds of MBA and undergraduate students. In addition to his degree program teaching, he has taught extensively in executive education programs. At Michigan, he is faculty director of the Organization Career Development Program, and he also teaches in executive education programs for the Industrial and Labor Relations Center at Cornell University.

As a researcher and writer, Cox has authored more than twenty articles and cases on the subjects he teaches. His contribution to the scholarship in the field of workforce diversity includes publication of more than ten articles in the last three years. In addition, he has worked on numerous committees and task forces dedicated to discussion and planning on diversity issues. This includes volunteer work for the U.S. Department of Labor, the American Assembly of

Collegiate Schools of Business, the National Academy of Management, and the Center for Creative Leadership.

Cox hold B.S. and MBA degrees from Wayne State University and a Ph.D. in organization behavior and psychology from the University of Arizona. In addition to a teaching career that spans more than twenty years, he has nine years of full-time management experience, including six years with the AT&T system.

Cox is an active speaker on human resources management with diverse workgroups. Organizations that have recently used his services in this capacity include the Buick Motor Division of General Motors, the Conference Board, the Japanese American Human Resource Association, and the Cornell University Center for Human Resource Management.

Celia V. Harquail (coauthor of Chapter Ten) is a doctoral student in the Organization Behavior Department of the School of Business at the University of Michigan. She is coauthor of several articles, including one with Taylor Cox, Jr., who serves as her dissertation adviser. Harquail spent several years as a sales and manufacturing manager for a large consumer products company. She holds an A.B. degree from Bryn Mawr College and a certificate in women's studies from the University of Michigan.

Her research focuses on the effects of social identity, cultural fit, and organizational culture on employee involvement, and on organizational identification.